AND ROMANS

PUBLICATION OF THIS BOOK HAS BEEN AIDED BY THE
LOUIS A. ROBB FUND OF PRINCETON UNIVERSITY PRESS
THIS BOOK HAS BEEN COMPOSED IN LINOTYPE CALEDONIA

CLOTHBOUND EDITIONS OF PRINCETON UNIVERSITY PRESS
BOOKS ARE PRINTED ON ACID-FREE PAPER, AND BINDING
MATERIALS ARE CHOSEN FOR STRENGTH AND DURABILITY

PRINTED IN THE UNITED STATES OF AMERICA BY
PRINCETON UNIVERSITY PRESS,
PRINCETON, NEW JERSEY

THE DRAWING ON THE FRONTISPIECE IS FROM *De gentium migrationibus* (BASLE, 1557) BY WOLFGANG LAZIUS (1514-1565), COURT PHYSICIAN AND HISTORIOGRAPHER TO THE AUSTRIAN HAPSBURGS. THE TITLE OF THIS BOOK ESTABLISHED "MIGRATIONS OF PEOPLES" (IN GERMAN, *Völkerwanderung*) AS AN ALTERNATIVE TO "BARBARIAN INVASIONS." COPY FROM THE LIBRARY OF WILLIAM H. SCHEIDE.

BARBARIANS AND ROMANS, A.D. 418-584

BARBARIANS

A.D. 418-584

THE TECHNIQUES OF ACCOMMODATION

BY WALTER GOFFART

PRINCETON UNIVERSITY PRESS

TO ROBERTA

CONTENTS

vii

CONTENTS

ABBREVIATIONS

Full bibliographic information for each modern work is given at the first citation in the notes. Subsequent references cite only the author's last name and a short title. The Index to Modern Authors (pp. 259-265) lists all references to secondary literature.

Ammianus	Ammianus Marcellinus *Rerum gestarum libri.* Edited and translated by J. C. Rolfe. 3 vols. Loeb. London, 1956-1958.
BEHE	Bibliothèque de l'École des Hautes Études, sciences historiques et philologiques. Paris, 1869—.
Budé	Collection des universités de France publiée par l'Association Guillaume Budé.
CE	*Codex Eurici.* Edited by K. Zeumer, MGH *Leges,* vol. 1. Edited by A. d'Ors. *Estudios Visigoticos,* vol. 2, *El Codigo di Eurico.* Instituto Juridico Español. *Cuadernos* 12. Rome, 1960.
Chron.	Chronicle(s).
CJ	*Codex Justinianus.* Edited by P. Krueger. 11th ed. Berlin, 1954.
CSEL	*Corpus scriptorum ecclesiasticorum Latinorum.* Vienna, 1867—.
CTh	*Codex Theodosianus.* Edited by T. Mommsen and P. M. Meyer. 2 vols. 2d ed. Berlin, 1954.
Dig.	Justinian *Digesta.* Edited by T. Mommsen and P. Krueger. 16th ed. Berlin, 1954.

Ennodius	Ennodius of Pavia *Opera*. Edited by W. Hartel. *CSEL* 6. Vienna, 1872.
FIRA 2	*Fontes iuris Romani antejustiniani*, vol. 2: *Auctores*. Edited by J. Baviera and J. Furlani. Florence, 1968.
Gregory of Tours, *Historiae, In gloria confessorum, Virtutes s. Iuliani*	Gregory of Tours *Historiarum libri X*. Edited by B. Krusch and W. Levison. MGH *Script. rer. Merov.*, vol. 1. 2d ed.; *Miracula et opera minora*. Edited by W. Arndt and B. Krusch, MGH *Script. rer. Merov.*, vol. 1, pt. 2.
HA	*Scriptores historiae Augustae*. Edited by Ernest Hohl. Rev. ed. 2 vols. Leipzig, 1971.
JRS	*Journal of Roman Studies*. Oxford, 1910—.
LBurg	*Leges Burgundionum*. Edited by L. R. de Salis. MGH *Leges*, vol. 2, pt. 1; translated by K. F. Drew, *The Burgundian Code*. 1949 (repr. Philadelphia, 1972).
LBurgExtrav	*Leges Burgundionum extravagantes*, in *LBurg*.
LVisig	*Leges Visigothorum*. Edited by K. Zeumer, MGH *Leges*, vol. 1.
LRB	*Lex Romana Burgundionum*, in *FIRA* 2, pp. 714-750.
Loeb	Loeb Classical Library.
MGH	Monumenta Germaniae historica.
AA	*Auctores antiquissimi.*
Capitularia	*Legum sectio II: Capitularia.*
Concilia	*Legum sectio III: Concilia.*

Formulae	*Legum sectio V: Formulae.*
Leges	*Legum sectio I: Leges nationum Germanicarum.*
Script. rer. Lang.	*Scriptores rerum Langobardicarum et Italicarum saec. IX-XI.*
Script. rer. Merov.	*Scriptores rerum Merovingicarum.*
Neues Archiv	*Neues Archiv der Gesellschaft für ältere deutsche Geschichtskunde,* Hanover, 1876-1936.
NMajor	*Leges novellae Majoriani, in CTh.*
Novel.	Justinian *Novellae.* Edited by R. Schoell and W. Kroll. 6th ed. Berlin, 1954.
NRHD	*Nouvelle revue historique de droit français et étranger.* Paris, 1855—.
NTheod II	*Leges novellae Theodosii II, in CTh.*
NValent III	*Leges novellae Valentiniani III, in CTh.*
PDipl	Gaetano Marini. *I papiri diplomatici.* Rome, 1805.
PItal	J. O. Tjäder. *Die nichtliterarische lateinische Papyri Italiens aus der Zeit 445-600.* Vol. 1. Lund, 1955.
Procopius *Bell. Pers., Bell. Vandal., Bell. Goth., Anecdota*	*Procopius.* Edited and translated by H. B. Dewing. Loeb. Vol. I (Persian War), vol. 2 (Vandalic War), vols. 3-5 (Gothic War), vol. 6 (Anecdota). London, 1953-1954.
PW	A. Pauly, G. Wissowa, and W. Kroll. *Real-Encyclopädie der klassischen Altertumswissenschaft.* Stuttgart, 1893—.

Sidonius *Carmina, Epistolae*	*Sidoine Apollinaire.* Edited and translated by André Loyen. Budé. Vol. 1 (Poèmes), vols. 2-3 (Lettres). Paris, 1960-1970.
Variae	Cassiodorus *Variae epistolae.* Edited by A. J. Fridh. *Corpus Christianorum.* Series Latina, 96. Turnhout, 1973. Edited by T. Mommsen, MGH, *AA*, vol. 12.
ZRG, Germ.	*Zeitschrift der Savigny-Stiftung für Rechtsgeschichte.* Germanistische Abteilung. Weimar, 1863—.

When no edition is specified for a source cited in the text, see under the author's name in the *Oxford Classical Dictionary.* Edited by N. G. L. Hammond and H. H. Scullard. 2d. ed. Oxford, 1970.

PREFACE

In 1844, Ernst Theodor Gaupp published a work entitled "The Germanic Settlements and Land-Divisions in the Provinces of the West Roman Empire." His main argument was that the Roman practice of compulsorily quartering soldiers on the civilian population played a vital part in the settlement of Burgundians and Goths in the western provinces during the fifth century. Gaupp's findings soon became standard historical doctrine and have remained so ever since. They sharply modified the idea that the barbarians had been conquerors of Gaul and Italy. The Germanic establishments in these lands seemed, on the contrary, to have been carried out in cooperation with the Roman authorities and in conformity with existing laws.

I only belatedly realized that Gaupp would be my model. What I began with, intending to write no more than an article, was the scattering of sources documenting the allotments to barbarians in Gaul and Italy. I wished to reconsider them in the light of what I had learned about late Roman tax law (and published in *"Caput" and Colonate*, 1974). I was also interested in what these sources might tell about the passage from Roman taxation to the seigneurial forms of the early Middle Ages, another problem that I had already been concerned with ("Three Notes," 1972). The footsteps I expected to be following were those of Ferdinand Lot, a guide and companion in almost all my studies, who in the same year published a monograph on the tax practices of the later empire and a long article on barbarian allotments. As the pages accumulated, however, it became apparent that I was exceeding Lot's scope. Where he had built on Gaupp, endorsing the latter's interpretation of Roman rules, I found it impossible to continue believing that the billeting of soldiers set a precedent for the award to barbarians of lands or revenues. The Goths and Burgundians had surely not acquired their properties by conquest, but there was more to say than had yet been said about the techniques that were applied to make room for them in the Western Empire. Much to Gaupp's credit, close to 150 years had elapsed before his book was found to need rewriting.

My introductory chapter, whose concern is with the barbarian invasions in general, descends from a lecture given at the Regional Seminar of the Centre for Medieval Studies, Toronto, in November 1972, as well as from a much altered second version, delivered at the American Historical Association meeting in Chicago in December 1974. I should like to express my thanks to the wise and learned participants at those sessions—J. M. Wallace-Hadrill (All Souls College, Oxford), Jeremy Adams (Southern Methodist), Thomas Bisson (California at Berkeley), and F. M. Clover (Wisconsin at Madison). Their severe criticism helped me very much in developing the third version, offered here, whose enduring flaws are mine alone.

Much of the research that has found its way into this book was carried out during my sabbatical leave of 1973-1974, when I held a fellowship from the American Council of Learned Societies and enjoyed the incomparable facilities of the Dumbarton Oaks Center for Byzantine Studies, Washington, D.C., as a visiting fellow. I am deeply grateful to both these institutions for their generous support of my work. It is also a pleasant duty to acknowledge the assistance I have repeatedly received from the University of Toronto, in one case, from funds supplied by the Canada Council. I feel fortunate indeed to serve a university that considerately subsidizes the minor, but potentially vexing, costs of research, such as the typing of a manuscript and the extravagant charges one must pay for photocopied extracts from periodicals no longer circulating between libraries.

Perhaps because my work straddles late antiquity and the early Middle Ages, I have tended to engage in dialogues with the dead more frequently than with living historians. One exception, thankfully acknowledged, is the thoughtful reading of my manuscript by Professor Robert S. Lopez of Yale University; I derived great profit from his comments in giving this book its final form. Mrs. Linda Wilding, Mrs. Eva Hollander, and Ms. Rea Wilmshurst are the typists whose combined efforts bridged the gap between my drafts and the typesetter; I thank them all for the care and helpfulness they showed in carrying out this task. I am also happy to record the contribution of my friend Elizabeth Brown (Brooklyn College, C.U.N.Y.): whatever felicity my title has is due to her ingenuity interacting with my wife's. To the latter, the dedication of this book attempts to express my feelings at the close of a trying period in both our lives.

Toronto, August 1979   W. G.

BARBARIANS AND ROMANS, A.D. 418-584

I

****

THE BARBARIANS IN LATE ANTIQUITY
AND HOW THEY WERE ACCOMMODATED
IN THE WEST

THIS study is concerned with an ostensibly peaceful and
smooth process: how the paraphernalia of Roman government, both military and civil, was used and adapted when,
in the fifth century, several barbarian peoples were accorded an establishment on provincial soil. The details of
these arrangements are worth investigating because they
tell us something about the prolongation of sophisticated
state institutions into the early Middle Ages and about the
conditions of property ownership in the earliest barbarian
kingdoms. Although one may doubt that the transfer of rule
from Roman to barbarian hands took place without violence
and disruption, there is no disputing the survival of a body
of evidence that documents a lawful adaptation of Roman
governmental practices to the novel requirements of Goths
and Burgundians. Almost all the evidence is concerned, not
with the moment of transition, but with the status quo many
decades after barbarian rule had begun; despite the passage of time and the crystallization of alien regimes, the
documented situation continues to betray its descent from
Roman public law. We are able to reconstruct how the barbarians fitted into the society of certain Western Roman
provinces, as well as to establish what had become of the
once pervasive mechanisms of taxation under new management.

The barbarian invasions form the background to the circumstances that the chapters to come will study. But how

3

are we to imagine these invasions? Many modern narratives are available, telling approximately the same story. None of them prepares us adequately for the undramatic adjustments between barbarians and Romans that we shall meet. The invasions, as currently presented, are an awesome spectacle, running parallel with Roman history itself for many centuries before the barbarians made permanent inroads into the empire. "It is essential . . . ," we are told, "to bear constantly in mind that the phenomenon we are observing is a migration of peoples, not merely an invasion of 'barbarians.' "[1] According to this traditional schema, the Germanic peoples had been in motion since the third or first century B.C., engaging in periodic mass migrations that pressed northern tribes down upon earlier emigrants to the south with such increasingly disruptive force that the Roman frontier, which had impeded the migrants' progress for several centuries, was torn down around A.D. 400. The moving Germanic masses then surged forward and halted in imperial territory.[2] Yet this final step turns out to be re-

[1] Joseph Vogt, *The Decline of Rome*, trans. Janet Sondheimer (London, 1967), p. 183.

[2] A vocabulary of floods, waves, and other vivid images suggestive of forces of nature has long been standard in accounts of the invasions. See, e.g., Lucien Musset, *Les Invasions*, vol. 1, *Les vagues germaniques*, Nouvelle Clio 12 (Paris, 1965), pp. 50-74. Musset is now available in a translation by E. and C. James (University Park, Penna., 1975), which I have not used. For a representative passage in which this imagery takes on a life of its own, see Geoffrey Barraclough, *The Medieval Papacy* (London, 1968), p. 28: "Fifteen years after Leo [the Great]'s death [461], the barbarian flood, whose beginnings he had seen, engulfed the West." This seems to refer to aliens pouring in, but the West was not invaded by anyone between 461 and 476. As explained by Ludwig Schmidt, "Die Ursachen der Völkerwanderung," *Neue Jahrbücher für das klassische Altertum, Geschichte und deutsche Literatur* 11 (1903): 340, the migrations can be thought to begin long before the Christian era (cf. below, at n. 44) or only with the Hunnic attack on the Goths in the 370s, which, even according to contemporaries like Ammianus Marcellinus (*Rer. gest.* 31. 2ff.), set in motion a chain of disasters. Dating from the Huns: Hans-Joachim Diesner, *Die Völkerwanderung* (Leipzig, 1976), pp.

4

markably modest: those involved in it were a mere handful of peoples, each group numbering at the most in the low tens of thousands, and many of them—not all—were accommodated within the Roman provinces without dispossessing or overturning indigenous society. In other words, the barbarians whom we actually find coming to grips with the Roman Empire in the fourth to sixth centuries, and leading the earliest successor kingdoms of the West, are remarkably deficient in numbers, cohesion, assertiveness, and skills— altogether a disappointment when juxtaposed with the long and massive migrations that are thought to characterize their past.[3]

The dimensions of this problem are better grasped by considering specific instances. The chapters to come will be concerned with the time when the Visigoths, Burgundians, and Ostrogoths obtained stable establishments on Roman soil. If the backdrop to each of these events were to be sketched, where should the story begin? Two very distinct courses are available to us, depending on the quality of evidence and the scale of conjecture and combination we are willing to tolerate. Those very strict in the selection and handling of sources will refuse to go farther afield than to the lands bordering the Roman Empire in the fourth century A.D. Those, however, who welcome a wider range of documentation and liberally resort to hypothesis and speculation will find it possible and even desirable to reach as

---

70-72, 86. The two beginning points are often treated as complementary; e.g., Pierre Courcelle, *Histoire littéraire des grandes invasions germaniques*, 3d ed. (Paris, 1964), pp. 14-20.

[3] Numbers: Schmidt, "Ursachen," p. 347, agreeing with Hans Delbrück, *Geschichte der Kriegskunst*, 3d ed. (Berlin, 1921), vol. 3, pp. 300-314. Cohesion: the many instances of barbarians fighting for Rome against their fellow tribesmen (Frankish generals in the fourth century; Sarus the Goth in the times of Alaric; the circumstances of the dissolution of the Vandal and Ostrogothic kingdoms; repeated Lombard defections to the Byzantines; etc.). Assertiveness: below, n. 54. Skills: E. A. Thompson, "Early Germanic Warfare," *Past and Present* 14 (1958): 2-29.

far out in space as Scandinavia and as far back in time as before the Christian era. This major difference of approach to the period of the barbarian invasions deserves to be spelled out and elaborated because little is said about it outside the German academic scene.[4]

If one takes a conservative course, the chain of events that ended in 418 with the settlement in Roman Aquitaine of the Visigoths led by Wallia should be traced back no earlier than the rebellion of Alaric in 395. The Goths whom Alaric led were then based in the Balkans, within the territories governed by the emperor of East Rome. It would not be amiss, however, to indicate the more remote background to the uprising. Earlier in the fourth century, the Goths had lived north and east of the Danube frontier of the Roman Empire (we would say in Rumania and south Russia), in lands that they had occupied for as long as anyone could remember. (By identifying them directly with the Scythians who had anciently inhabited these lands, Roman observers expressed the belief that the Goths were a new name, not a new population.) Direct neighbors of the empire, they were a normal part of the barbarian landscape, neither relentless enemies nor trustworthy friends. From the last third of the fourth century, the course of Gothic history was highly discontinuous; every major step taken by the (Visi)goths away from Rumania and south Russia

---

[4] A selective, but profound, account of the vagaries of recent German *Altertumskunde* is given by Rolf Hachmann, *Die Goten und Skandinavien*, Quellen und Forschungen zur Sprach- und Kulturgeschichte der germanischen Völker N.F. 34 (Berlin, 1970), pp. 145-220; cf. the review of T. M. Andersson in *Speculum* 46 (1971): 373-375. Equally revealing is the defense of traditional methods and tales by Ernst Schwarz, *Germanische Stammeskunde zwischen den Wissenschaften* (Constance-Stuttgart, 1967), pp. 7-53, and *Zur germanischen Stammeskunde. Aufsätze zum neuen Forschungsstand*, Wege der Forschung 249 (Darmstadt, 1972), pp. vii-xxx, 287-308 (the latter specifically against Hachmann). Malcolm Todd, *The Northern Barbarians, 100 B.C.-A.D. 300* (London, 1975), pp. 19-29, 55, and *passim*, provides an up-to-date summary of these difficulties from the archaeological standpoint.

implied a break in cohesion, the start of a new sequence of events whose relations to the immediate past seem tenuous and disconnected: an internal crisis in the 370s exacerbated by the apparently irresistible onset of the Huns; a partial and disorganized, though peaceful, migration onto Roman territory (376); an uprising marked by a great victory (378) but also entailing severe losses before the acquisition of a regulated status in the empire (382); and two major campaigns to the West as Roman auxiliaries with great loss of life (388, 394). Only after these incidents does one come to Alaric's rebellion of 395, which itself initiated two decades of campaigning punctuated by defeats as well as successes. No smooth line of historical narrative can connect the Goths in south Russia to the heterogeneous peoples led by Alaric and his successors in Italy, Spain, and Gaul during the first two decades of the fifth century. However Gothic in name, their following was no lineal prolongation of the nation that Athanaric had ruled in the 370s; it is more evocative of the great company of successive condottieri than of a phenomenon of popular migration.[5]

[5] Ludwig Schmidt, *Geschichte der deutschen Stämme bis zum Ausgang der Völkerwanderung. Die Ostgermanen*, 2d ed. (Munich, 1941), pp. 195-249 (to the Hunnic attack), 400-426 (to the establishment of the kingdom of Toulouse); Musset, *Vagues germaniques*, pp. 83-86; Ernst Stein, *Histoire du Bas-Empire*, vol. 1, trans. J. R. Palanque (Brussels, 1959), pp. 207, 216-217; André Piganiol, *L'Empire chrétien (325-395)* (Paris, 1947), pp. 211-214, 222-223, 247-248, 251-255, 260-261, 266-268. Bloodshed in the suppression of Maximus: Jerome *Epistolae* 60. 15, without specific reference to Goths. On the identification of recent peoples with older ones (Goths as Scythians), see the valuable, but unsympathetic, comments of J. Otto Maenchen-Helfen, *The World of the Huns*, ed. Max Knight (Berkeley, 1973), pp. 5-9. (The name Visigoth, which we associate with Alaric's people, is not attested until the sixth century.) Fustel de Coulanges, *L'invasion germanique et la fin de l'Empire*, 3d ed. (Paris, 1911), pp. 430-431, stressed discontinuity; Musset, *Vagues germaniques*, pp. 84-85, states that, after twenty-five years in the Balkans and eleven in Italy, the Visigothic people "n'est toujours qu'une armée errante"; to the contrary, Schmidt, *Ostgermanen*, p. 426 (chiefly on the basis of Isidore of Seville!). Socrates *Historia ecclesiastica* 4. 8

The exclusion from the preceding account of any earlier past for the Goths than their residence alongside the Roman frontier is not meant to depreciate them by comparison with peoples who have longer histories or to preclude the possibility that they had an ancient culture, identity, or past. The point is simply that a strictly controlled historical narrative presupposes a certain minimum of evidence, rather than a string of hypotheses and combinations; much as one might wish to write the ancient history of the Goths, the documentary basis for doing so is lacking. Tales of the early Goths were eventually told; the main ones that have reached us were set down in sixth-century Constantinople, and, not surprisingly, they have nothing in common with our standards of credible history. We can repeat these stories in their proper chronological and cultural context as testifying to a highly civilized desire to reconstruct the *origo gentis*. But, since such tales lay in the future, their contents would be out of place in a background to the Goths in fifth-century Aquitaine.[6] What is at stake in all this is not one's sympathy or antipathy toward barbarians, Germans, or Goths but, rather, a conception of how history in the modern manner may legitimately be assembled and written.

Equally conservative accounts may be given of the Burgundians and Ostrogoths. The Burgundians whom we shall be concerned with were the survivors of two devastating defeats, one by Roman troops, the other by Huns. The disasters of 435 and 436 wiped out a Burgundian kingdom in

conveys the Constantinopolitan idea that, after doing much damage, the Goths in the Balkans were wiped out.

[6] The work containing these tales of the early Goths is, of course, Jordanes *De origine actibusque Getarum* (commonly *Getica*), ed. Theodore Mommsen, MGH AA, vol. 5, about which more below. Although Jordanes wrote in Latin, he was a proper Byzantine, as made obvious by his chronicle of Roman history (*Romana*, ed. Mommsen, MGH AA, vol. 5). On origin stories, Elias Bickerman, "Origines gentium," *Classical Philology* 47 (1952): 65-81. Ammianus 15. 9, on the Gallo-Romans, clearly illustrates how such an account departs from our standards and expectations.

the Roman province of Germania II that had lasted a little over two decades and may have been about to expand its space.[7] The Burgundians in Germania II had not arrived from far away. In the second half of the fourth century, a Roman historian situates them at some distance east of the Rhine, settled to the north of the Alamanni and cooperating with the Roman army against this common enemy. The same author tells us that the Burgundians knew themselves to be descended from Romans, and another, a little later, specifies that the generals of Augustus had established them in camps as advance guards in the interior of Germany. Whatever these stories are worth, they imply that the fourth-century Burgundians were thoroughly rooted to the districts they inhabited.[8] Their roots were not so deep, however, that they stood their ground in the tumult of the early fifth century. How much did the Burgundians of the late 430s remember even of a homeland east of the Rhine? It was a severely chastened and diminished remnant that the West Roman government relocated southward from the Rhineland in 443, to a district where, in the century to come, the Burgundians never grew into a great or dangerous people.[9]

The Ostrogoths had an even more abbreviated past. For close to eight decades after the 370s, they had lived as sub-

[7] Schmidt, *Ostgermanen*, pp. 136-137; Musset, *Vagues germaniques*, pp. 111-112; K. F. Stroheker, *Germanentum und Spätantike* (Zurich-Stuttgart, 1965), pp. 257-258. Hydatius *Chron.* 108, 110, ed. Alain Tranoy, Sources chrétiennes 218-219 (Paris, 1974), vol. 1, p. 134, vol. 2, pp. 72-73 (commentary).

[8] Ammianus 28. 5. 9-11; Orosius *Historia adversus paganos* 7. 32. 12. Eduard Norden, *Alt-Germanien. Völker- und Namengeschichtliche Untersuchungen* (Leipzig, 1934), pp. 62-64, explained the Roman inspiration of these stories. Such inventions would have been worthless, however, if an alternative origin legend had been firmly entrenched among the Burgundians of the time.

[9] Schmidt, *Ostgermanen*, pp. 191-194; Musset, *Vagues germaniques*, pp. 112-115; Alfred Coville, *Recherches sur l'histoire de Lyon du Ve au IXe siècle (450-800)* (Paris, 1928), pp. 153-158, studied the evidence on Burgundian numbers; cf. Schmidt, *Ostgermanen*, p. 168.

9

jects of the Huns, eventually under the overlordship of Attila. When Attila's empire disintegrated (454) and the Gepids emerged as the direct heirs to the Hunnic position, the Goths led by Valamer sought the patronage of the East Roman emperor and obtained lands in the abandoned frontier province of Pannonia. The subsequent history of these Goths is comparatively well known, as might be expected of a tribe living continuously within the territory of the old empire. After Valamer died, his younger brother led a part of his people westward to eventual absorption by the Goths of Toulouse. The remainder came under the rule of Valamer's nephew Theodoric, who long served the emperor Zeno but then found it advantageous to move his followers against Odoacer, the "tyrant" of Italy (488). The Ostrogothic settlement that will later interest us occurred after Theodoric's people succeeded in wresting Italy from Odoacer's control.[10]

In part, these short Gothic and Burgundian backgrounds embody an admission of ignorance. The past of these tribes may have contained much more that was relevant to what they would become in the Roman provinces, but we simply are not informed. Deficient sources, however, are not the main justification for excluding references to earlier centuries. We have no reason to think that the distant past weighed more heavily upon barbarians than it did upon literate Romans. Fourth-century events in the empire took place with notable unconcern for historical precedent; the most ambitious histories written in the fifth century looked back only to Constantine.[11] Modern authors do not find it

[10] Jordanes *Getica* 268-296, offers an intelligible consecutive account; cf. Musset, pp. 92-93.

[11] The Chronicles of Eusebius and Jerome, as well as the *Breviaria* of Eutropius and Festus, suggest how much Roman history the fourth century was able to dispense with. Constantine as beginning: the church histories of Philostorgius, Socrates, Sozomen, and Theodoret (before 450); the Roman law gathered into the Code of Theodosius II (published 438); introductory chapters to the lost History of Malchus of Philadelphia (late 5th) and the last book of the lost

10

indispensable to evoke Augustus, Trajan, or Gallienus as relevant to the battle of Adrianople and its aftermath, and neither does an account of the growth of the Roman Empire obligatorily accompany one of its decline. According to students of the oral traditions surviving in twentieth-century Africa, the memory of a tribe reaches to the districts inhabited prior to the last migration but not any further back.[12] If this finding is valid for all nonliterate peoples, our information about the Goths and Burgundians, which stems from Roman writings, is considerably fuller than what was available to them from their own resources. The memory of the Visigoths in Aquitaine after 418 could have reached only to their Balkan homes before 395; that of the Burgundians in eastern Gaul after 443, to the Rhenish kingdom before 436; and that of the Ostrogoths in Italy, to their settlements in Pannonia and the Balkans between 454 and 488. Forgetfulness—the interruption and loss of oral memories—is probably an inevitable accompaniment of migrations.[13] For all these reasons, the fourth century may be

---

Chronicle of Hesychius of Miletus (ca. 518). For Malchus and Hesychius, see Wm. Christ, Wm. Schmid, and Otto Stählin, *Geschichte der griechischen Litteratur*, 6th ed., pt. 2, 2d half (Munich, 1924), pp. 1036, 1039.

[12] Yves Person, "Chronology and Oral Tradition" (1962), trans. Susan Sherwin, in Martin Klein and G. Wesley Johnson, eds., *Perspectives on the African Past* (Boston, 1972), p. 8: "A visual element . . . is almost always necessary to sustain [the] memory [of oral traditions]. Everything earlier fades within a man's lifetime." See also Ruth Finnegan, "A Note on Oral Tradition and Historical Evidence," *History and Theory* 9 (1970): 195-201, including important observations on the rarity of epics and other historical narratives in Africa, the unreliability of their transmission, and the special distortion of migration stories (pp. 196-198).

[13] Historical forgetfulness seems common in literate societies; e.g., the famous line of Ammianus about *antiquitatum ignari* (31. 5. 11). For a notable illustration, see Evagrius *Hist. ecclesiastica* 3. 41 (ca. 593): one proof of the superiority of Christian to pagan times was that the Roman emperors since Constantine had been more secure on their thrones than their pagan predecessors. The argument could work only

thought to afford an adequate perspective for barbarian enterprises from 395 onward. But this is by no means the more widely held view of the matter.

The longer perspective on the barbarian past can be expressed in generalizations as well as in the narrower form of individual tribal histories. To begin with generalization, one hears that ". . . the pressure of the northern peoples upon settled German tribes . . . continued until the [Roman] frontier was permanently breached. . . ."[14] A popular expansion of this thought involves the idea of a prolonged contest between Germans and the Mediterranean world that lasted from the expedition of the Cimbri and Teutones ca. 102 B.C. until the fall of the Western Empire. In this version, it seems to be presupposed that the northerners had a set goal that they kept moving toward—such as "the old objective of the wandering Indo-Germanic peoples"— and that, for a long time, the Romans stood in the way of their attaining it.[15] Even without reference to a goal, a connection is assumed to have existed between all the barbarian tribes speaking Germanic dialects, and the acts of any of them are held to be significant for all. Thus, after the disaster of Varus in A.D. 9, "free Germany became for the Roman Empire a lasting danger that one sought to avert by securing the frontier. . . . The recruitment of Germans into the Roman army only temporarily filled gaps and could not prevent it from happening that, from the beginning of

if all the overthrown western emperors from Constantine II to Romulus Augustulus were forgotten, as they obviously were.

[14] Edward Peters, *Europe: The World of the Middle Ages* (Englewood Cliffs, N.J., 1977), p. 43 (this textbook is chosen only for its recent date; many others might supply similar quotations).

[15] Hermann Aubin in *Neue Propyläen-Weltgeschichte*, ed. Willy Andrea, vol. 2 (Berlin, 1940), p. 78. Here as elsewhere I have translated the quotation. Aubin's narrative (pp. 52-78) is a notably colorful portrayal of the *Völkerwanderung*. For persistent ideas of a goal, or of the unavoidable attractions of the Mediterranean sun, Diesner, *Völkerwanderung*, p. 70.

the fifth century, Germanic tribes strove to erect states of their own on the soil of the Roman Empire."[16]

Such lines hint at a dangerous anachronism. United Germany is a phenomenon whose past extends no earlier than the ninth century; even though Tacitus wrote about Germania (ca. A.D. 98), he never imagined that the peoples whom he described formed anything more sophisticated than disunited tribes;[17] yet the talk in our books about Germans confronting and striving against the Roman Empire often implies that a single coherent entity lay beyond the Roman border and that it had united ambitions and aspirations vis-à-vis the empire. For this reason, a recent author who assembled Roman observations of the barbarian invasions was chided by a reviewer for providing only a "partial" picture, and future historians were invited to "try to build up a comprehensive picture of the German invasions from both sides."[18] By the terms of such reasoning, the Roman state looked outward toward a coherent "other side," rather too reminiscent of the Germany to come.

In narrative, migratory movements are what impart community to this "other side." The history assigned to every tribe consists primarily of a travel diary; Lucien Musset writes:

[16] Schwarz, *Zur germ. Stammesk.*, p. xviii. Stories of the same kind are familiar outside Germany; e.g., Daniel D. McGarry, *Medieval History and Civilization* (New York, 1976), pp. 69-70.

[17] Heinz Löwe in Bruno Gebhardt, *Handbuch der deutschen Geschichte*, 8th ed. (Stuttgart, 1954), p. 79, envisaged a caesura between the Germanic peoples, including the east Germans of the invasion period, and the beginnings of the German (*deutsche*) people in the ninth century—quite a novel organization of material by comparison with the 7th ed. of Gebhardt's *Handbuch* in 1930. Tacitus *Germania* 33 is the *locus classicus* on disunity; the sketch of 210 years of war between Rome and the Germans (*Germania* 37), which lies behind such modern narratives as cited above nn. 15-16, derives its unity from being written from the Roman standpoint. On the questionable continuity of tribes, see below, n. 30.

[18] Gerald Bonner, review of Courcelle, *Hist. litt.*, in *JRS* 56 (1966): 247.

13

The Burgundians . . . appear in the first century [A.D.] in the Baltic region as an element of the *Vindili* group; then they plunge into the interior, on the middle Vistula. But their language and traditions no doubt allow them to be derived from Scandinavia. Their east German dialèct was close to Gothic, and their traditions, gathered at a late date, lead to "the island called *Scandinavia*." In fact, several Scandinavian lands bear names analogous to theirs: the land of Borgund, on the Sognefjord in Norway, and especially the Baltic island of Bornholm (*Borgundarholm* in the thirteenth century).

From their Polish habitat, the Burgundians began in the course of the third century to slide toward the West. After 260, they are alongside the Alamanni. . . .[19]

The account may end here, for the sequel, related above, takes up the story from the point when the Burgundians were neighbors to the Alamanni. The longer background is highlighted by verbs of action. Emerging from Scandinavia, plunging to the middle Vistula, then sliding west, the Burgundians expressed the kind of *Wanderlust* that, by anticipation, explains their future advances to Roman soil.

The Goths play an extraordinarily important part in the extended scheme of barbarian history. A recent summary of their movements reads:

The best known of these migrating peoples were the Goths, who settled upon the banks of the Vistula at the beginning of the first century, and in Poland somewhat later. The Goths had come originally from the Baltic region. Further migrations from that region had begun

[19] Musset, *Vagues germaniques*, p. 111. Cf. Norden, *Alt-Germanien*, pp. 17-23, where the succession of (highly disparate) evidence is clearly visible. Norden, a classicist by training, was particularly impressed by the affirmation of Germanists that the Burgundians were east Germanic and therefore totally alien from their neighbors, the Alamanni (pp. 18 n. 1, 20-21). It would have been useful to add that nothing in the written sources tends to confirm this idea.

to press upon them, and in turn they began to migrate south and east. To the south, they encountered the Vandals and Burgundians, the periphery of the "neighborhood" settled tightly around the Roman frontier. The Goths continued to move south and east toward the Ukraine, but their movements and the pressures of the Gepid people following them disturbed the territorial settlements of other peoples and precipitated the progressive mass movements of still other tribes into territories ever closer to the Roman frontier.[20]

One pattern visible here is a chronological sequence: Vandals and Burgundians first, then Goths, finally Gepids. The Goths provided the push that, in our previous quotation, precipitated the westward "slide" of the Burgundians; in turn, the onset of the Gepids forced the Goths southeastward. The latter movement so disturbed the frontier peoples of the Roman Empire, one learns elsewhere, that they launched a great attack across the border; the then emperor, Marcus Aurelius, took years to subdue these attackers and to reestablish the northern frontier. According to modern historians of the empire, the reign of Marcus was the turning point from moderate to difficult imperial defense, and the Gothic movement indirectly occasioned this crucial change.[21] The chronological sequence in which the Goths are thought to have been involved turns easily into a pattern of causation influenced by ideas of panic rippling

[20] Peters, *Europe*, p. 42; cf. Musset, *Vagues germanique*, pp. 80-82.

[21] Gothic movement indirectly causing the attack on the empire: Schmidt, "Ursachen," p. 341; Aubin in *Propyläen-Weltgeschichte*, vol. 2, pp. 56-57; Musset, *Vagues germaniques*, p. 52. For a more reticent account, George Kossack in Fergus Millar, *The Roman Empire and Its Neighbours* (London, 1967), pp. 317-318. The turning point coinciding with Marcus Aurelius, typically, M. I. Finley, "Manpower and the Fall of Rome," in C. M. Cipolla, ed., *The Economic Decline of Empires* (London, 1970), p. 86. Todd, *Northern Barbarians*, p. 210, endorses this common opinion without stating whether there is any archaeological evidence substantiating it.

through a mob.[22] The Goths are also prominent because they were the subject of the earliest "barbarian history." This narrative locates their primitive home in Scandinavia and explicitly tells of migrations that took them to Scythia —south Russia northeast of the lower Danube; that it also dates these migrations to the second millennium B.C. is rarely taken to detract from their authenticity.[23]

This Gothic history was written at Constantinople in the middle of the sixth century, after the Goths had traveled very far indeed from where they had still lived in the 370s. Since its author completely disagrees with modern historians over the time when early migrations in eastern Europe took place, there is hardly any basis for charting the movements of east Germans (Vandals, Burgundians, Goths, and so forth) before the third century A.D., let alone for expressing them as a simple dramatic narrative.[24] Contemporary Roman observers were unaware that tides and waves of human beings were menacingly lapping at the barbarians residing just beyond the imperial borders. Their ignorance of such phenomena is so notorious that modern commentators sometimes point to it with annoyance: ". . . Claudian's contemporaries [ca. A.D. 400] did not understand why it was that fresh barbarian hordes kept battering at the frontiers

[22] Ferdinand Lot, *Les invasions germaniques* (Paris, 1935), p. 322: the foremost tribes "were driven forward by the pressure exerted by the tribes advancing behind them," with the result that any people invading the Roman world was itself "pressed forward in the manner of a man who, drawn into the surge of a maddened crowd, is thrown upon a neighbor and exerts upon it a pressure all the more irresistible for being involuntary."

[23] Jordanes *Getica* 9, 16-29. For arbitrary modern emendations of his dating, e.g., Kossack as above, n. 21, p. 318: the Goths "who, according to their migration myth, had landed in the Vistula estuary around the time of Jesus' birth, coming from Scandinavia." Mommsen's annotation sets out Jordanes's own choice of date.

[24] For an example whose special value is to spell out the limits of our knowledge, Christian Courtois, *Les Vandales et l'Afrique* (Paris, 1955), pp. 11-32.

of the empire. . . ."[25] The idea of migratory pressure is also somewhat strange in view of the well-documented events known to us. The onset of the Huns in the 370s did impel some Goths to abandon their lands and seek admission into the Roman Empire, but hardly another movement of the invasion period fits into this pattern of one people being pressed onward by another. (Even here, it is improbable that the Huns attacked because they needed or coveted the lands of the Goths for themselves.) The Vandals were not driven to North Africa nor the Saxons to Britain nor the Ostrogoths to Italy; no one has ever shown that the descent of Radagaisus upon Italy in 405, or the great Rhine crossing of 406/7, was carried out by tribesmen forced out of their lands by strangers whom they could not resist.[26] Since the Slavs subsequently filled the lands that the east Germans abandoned, it seems obvious that the fourth and fifth-century movements into the Roman Empire could not have been occasioned by a continual pressure of Germanic immigration from the north, least of all if that immigration occurred far in the past. The image of a crowded *barbaricum*, full of people being driven frantic by newcomers continually shoving in upon them, is entertaining but, at least to a conservative historian, is not borne out by the facts.

The examples cited of the Burgundians and Goths are

[25] Alan Cameron, *Claudian: Poetry and Propaganda at the Court of Honorius* (Oxford, 1970), p. 74.

[26] According to E. A. Thompson, *A History of Attila and the Huns* (Oxford, 1948), p. 28, "it is agreed" that the Huns impelled the crossing of 406 (citing Gibbon); similarly, Diesner, *Völkerwanderung*, pp. 126-127. For explicit counterarguments, Schmidt, "Ursachen," pp. 349-350 and Maenchen-Helfen, *World of the Huns*, pp. 60-61 (Radagaisus), 71-72. For a Roman text on pressure, see *Historia Augusta* (hereafter *HA*), *Marcus Aurelius* 14. 1: "Victualis et Marcomannis cuncta turbantibus, aliis etiam gentibus, quae pulsae a superioribus barbaris fugerant, nisi reciperentur, bellum inferentibus"; but when these lines were written, the Huns had already bumped the Goths.

also noteworthy for the manner in which the track of each tribe has been traced by modern scholarship. First, there is the composite and conjectural nature of the tale. In Musset's version, the Burgundians are said to be traceable to Scandinavia because "their traditions," gathered in an eighth-century hagiography, say so; because "their east German dialect"—unattested except for personal and place names presumed Burgundian by modern philologists—"was close to Gothic"; and because certain toponyms in Scandinavia, first attested in the late Middle Ages, have affinities to the Burgundian name. The Burgundians are also said to have lived near the Baltic or in Poland because the tribal name occurs in a list of Germanic tribes in Pliny's *Natural History*. The location of these tribes has occasioned much modern discussion. What is any of this worth? The contemporary information about what the Burgundians thought of their origins in the fourth century has been cited above: they were neither Scandinavian nor Polish nor otherwise exotic. The very late hagiography enshrines a literary borrowing from Frankish history, not a tribal memory or "saga."[27] Even if there were credible remnants of Burgundian dialect, its affinity to Gothic would be irrelevant to a history of migration.[28] As for Scandinavian toponyms, the

[27] The seventh-century Frankish chronicler whom we call Fredegar (3. 65, in MGH *Script. rer. Merov.*, vol. 2) tells a story of Lombard origins akin to that of the *Origo gentis Langobardorum* (in MGH *Script. rer. Lang.*); in writing about the early Burgundians, the eighth-century *Passio s. Sigismundi* (in MGH *Script. rer. Merov.*, vol. 2) plagiarized Fredegar. All this is learned work, not the pious collection of "popular traditions." Besides, the *Passio* is rightly said to be "durchaus fränkisch orientierte": Erich Zöllner, *Die politische Stellung der Völker im Frankenreich*, Veröffentlichungen des Instituts für österreichische Geschichtsforschung, ed. L. Santifaller, 13 (Vienna, 1950), p. 112.

[28] Similarly Diesner, *Völkerwanderung*, p. 130, drew ethnographic inferences from the Burgundians' long retention of nasalization. Yet Burgundian is extinct: Musset, *Vagues germaniques*, p. 48. On the surviving evidence for it, Schmidt, *Ostgermanen*, p. 191; Schwarz, *Zur germ. Stammesk.*, p. 301; and, especially, Hachmann, *Goten,*

precise value of such delicate data would first have to be ascertained; a name like Borgundarholm is surely explicable by other assumptions than that a nation called the Burgundians once lived there or passed by.[29] Much the same problem is raised by the mention in Pliny: what's in a tribal name? In Pliny at least, the name Burgundian—*Burgodiones* to be precise—antedates the fourth century. But a recognizable people bearing that name, a people whom we may meaningfully connect with fifth-century events, does not occur until long after Pliny and, then, far from the Baltic.[30] It is pointless to deny early Burgundian migrations;

---

p. 148, on its inadequacy. The writing of history out of linguistic evidence is basic to recent accounts of the migrations: Ernst Wahle in Bruno Gebhardt, *Handbuch*, 9th ed. (Stuttgart, 1970), vol. 1, pp. 41-43; to Schmidt, "Ursachen," p. 340, Germanic history began with the departure from the "indo-germanische Urheimat." For further illustration, Felix Dahn, "Die Ursachen der Völkerwanderung," in E. von Wietersheim, *Geschichte der Völkerwanderung*, 2d ed. (Leipzig, 1888), vol. 1, pp. 3-10. Such endeavors have very doubtful standing in a strictly linguistic perspective; see Calvert Watkins, "Language and Its History," in *Language as a Human Problem*, ed. Morton Bloomfield and Einar Haugen (New York, 1974), pp. 85-97.

[29] Cf. the cautious treatment of comparable data about the Vandals by Courtois, *Vandales*, pp. 15-17 (endless disagreements since, after all, there is no way to prove any hypothesis; besides "nothing allows us to establish the antiquity of these toponyms"). Similarly, Schmidt, *Ostgermanen*, pp. 551-552, on toponyms abusively associated with the Heruli. On the devastating weakness of such proof, Hachmann, *Goten*, pp. 150-153, 156-163; see also ibid., p. 34 n. 75, for interesting evidence on the change of historians' attitudes toward these toponyms between 1878 and 1939.

[30] Again, cf. Courtois, *Vandales*, pp. 21-28, with the great merit of opening with an exposition of the evidence; also, timely comments on the nature of peoples and tribes (pp. 26-27). The continuity of *Stämme* is one of the most tender points in Germanic *Altertumskunde*; note the confidence of Schmidt, *Ostgermanen*, p. 85; Schwarz, *Germ. Stammesk.*, opens by mentioning the fundamental criticism by Franz Steinbach in 1926 (p. 7), but goes on, in the traditional way, to treat each tribe as a fixed entity from prehistory onward. Further about this, Gerold Walser, review in *Historia* 7 (1958): 122-124. Ancient "tribal traditions" could hardly be passed along to very late writers

the questionable practice is to combine appallingly tenuous evidence in order to affirm them. What possible gain to our knowledge of the barbarians is there in doing so?

Much ink has flowed over the history of the Goths before they reached the south Russian districts where they were in contact with the Roman Empire. A question of surpassing concern to students of Jordanes, the Byzantinized Goth who wrote the first Gothic history, is the credibility of his early chapters, most of all, the assertion of Scandinavian origins.[31] Only one answer seems tolerable. For taking a different approach, the author of a recent, moderately critical book on the subject was stiffly rebuked by a leading spokesman for Germanic tribal studies (*Stammeskunde*):

> Hachmann gives himself great trouble . . . to establish how Germanists, historians, and prehistorians developed a "Scandinavia-topos"—Scandinavia as homeland of the Germanic tribes. . . . [But] one must not pursue secondary sources when primary ones are available. The report of Jordanes on the journey of the Goths over the Baltic is known and easy to consult in the *Getica*. The issue is only: does one believe it or not? is significance to

---

like Jordanes and Paul the Deacon unless the tribes were continuous entities; hence the recent stress upon an enduring *Traditionskern* (Schwarz, *Zur germ. Stammesk.*, p. viii), against which see the apt criticism of František Graus in *Historica* 7 (1963): 188-191.

[31] At a time when, for example, it generally goes unnoticed that Jordanes and Procopius lived at the same time and place, whole books fasten on the few chapters about Gothic origins: Curt Weibull, *Die Auswanderung der Goten aus Schweden* (Götenborg, 1958), healthily negative; Josef Svennung, *Jordanes und Scandia. Kritisch-exegetische Studien* (Stockholm, 1967)—more by Svennung on the same subject listed by Hachmann, *Goten*, p. 529; Norbert Wagner, *Getica. Untersuchungen zum Leben des Jordanes und zur frühen Geschichte der Goten*, Quellen und Forschungen zur Sprach- und Kulturgeschichte der germanischen Völker N.F. 22 (Berlin, 1967); Hachmann, *Goten*, pp. 15-143; Gilbert Dagron, "Discours utopique et récit des origines, 1: Une lecture de Cassiodore-Jordanès," *Annales: Économies, sociétés, civilisations* 26 (1971): 290-305.

be attributed to the three ships? how wide does one make the Swedish district of origin? are one large emigration or many small ones to be assumed?[32]

The orthodoxy called for here is of religious intensity. Jordanes himself was more relaxed. The verisimilitude he attributed to the migration tales is best measured by his dating them from 1490 to 1324 B.C.; for over a millennium and a half before the advent of the Huns, the Goths he wrote about occupied the lands where the Huns would find them. Modern scholars who make Jordanes's legend their own not only emend its date drastically but also look hard for linguistic, ethnographic, and archaeological elaborations, fitting together bits and pieces of the same type as were met in the Burgundian case. We hear, for instance, that "the true history of the Goths"—true, that is, as distinct from legendary "but not inadmissible"—"begins with Pliny, who, toward A.D. 75, cited the *Gutones*, and Tacitus, who, towards 98, knows the *Gothones*."[33] Prodigies of ingenuity are performed in creating arguments that sometimes are wholly circular.[34] By normal standards of source analysis,

[32] Schwarz, *Zur germ. Stammesk.*, pp. 299-300.

[33] Musset, *Vagues germaniques*, pp. 81, 80. "Not inadmissible" legends remind one of the verdict of the second Dreyfus trial: guilty of high treason but with "extenuating circumstances." Equally strange, the conclusion of Courtois, *Vandales*, p. 18: after immense effort, German erudition has only piled up hypotheses from which no certitudes may be extracted; but once this is said, "il ne me semble pas qu'il soit interdit à l'historien d'imaginer. . . ." Does the "true history" of tribes listed by Pliny and Tacitus begin even if the names never occur again?

[34] It would be invidious to cite examples. Some idea of the problem is suggested by Herwig Wolfram, "Athanaric the Visigoth: Monarchy or Judgeship. A Study in Comparative History," *Journal of Medieval History* 1 (1975): 261: although conceding that the premises of the proposed comparison are dubious and that a chronological leap of 350 years is involved, he concludes, nevertheless, that "a functional comparison . . . seems justified and may well be methodologically heuristic." For a valuable characterization of such writings, E. G. Stanley, *The Search for Anglo-Saxon Paganism* (Cambridge, 1975),

the early Gothic migrations in Jordanes are about as historical as the tales of Genesis and Exodus; to champion their simple equivalence to history is a task for religious fundamentalists.

The wellspring of such piety is not difficult to discern. A whole program, the collective endeavor of generations since the sixteenth century, appears to be at stake:

> As regards history in the narrow sense, it is to be said that a great intellectual impetus was needed to roll away the enormous burden of biblical-classical convention in historical conceptualization and to find an independent point of departure for German history outside the *orbis universus*. Yet German historical research set about this liberation from [the time of] Beatus Rhenanus and Wimpfeling onward and has achieved it.[35]

Another commentator is less confident but stresses the importance of somehow providing nonliterate Germania, not just with a past, but with a history:

> . . . the reports of the Roman writers must be regarded as one-sided and, since written sources are lacking, one must utilize other [sources] and thus endeavor to fill the gaps of ancient reports. To a historian of antiquity this may seem dangerous and unacceptable, since he knows only his sources from which he himself attempts to take as much believable matter as possible. But did only that happen which entered the Roman field of vision? Is it not

---

p. 122: "In [the last 150 years] the unknown (as I think, the unknowable unknown) was so firmly used to explain the known that scholars felt no doubt in their methods or results."

[35] Hermann Aubin, "Zur Frage der historischen Kontinuität im Allgemein," in Aubin, *Vom Altertum zum Mittelalter* (Munich, 1949), p. 70. Can history begin independently of the classical-biblical mainstream of historical technique? For example, will there now or eventually be African history that begins independently of European history? Aubin's statement has the value of forcing us to choose whether to endorse such a notion or not.

self-evident that right in the centuries around Christ's birth much went on within the Germanic world?

Greek and Latin authors . . . portrayed relations to the Germans from their own standpoint. Consequently it is the responsibility of Germanic *Stammeskunde* to liberate itself as much as possible from the one-sidedness of these sources. Understandably, this is not easy.[36]

It follows from this view that the scholars of today continue to have weighty obligations. The conviction that a great deal happened in the "Germanic world" should inspire them to portray from miscellaneous gleanings what no early narrator ever depicted. Moreover, they ought to rectify the one-sidedness of whatever narratives there are. Something very odd happens, however, when the bias of ancient authors in talking about early Germans is actually detected:

It is of course necessary to test the character of these important sources, to investigate the intentions of ancient authors, to discover their methods of work, to study how their conception of historical truth differs from that of today, to make out their relationship to their sources. But is one justified in considering only this standpoint? Should they not be trusted to have also acquired information from elsewhere or to have made use of personal information? . . . It would be wrong to think about [Caesar's] literary sources and his political intentions and to overlook his personal experiences with the Germans. The same questions will arise with Tacitus and Cassiodorus [-Jordanes].[37]

[36] Schwarz, *Germ. Stammesk.*, pp. 24, 7. The first part of the quotation is in criticism of Gerold Walser, *Caesar und die Germanen* (*Historia*, Einzelschriften, H. 1) (Wiesbaden, 1956).

[37] Schwarz, *Germ. Stammesk.*, p. 8, cf. *Zur germ. Stammesk.*, pp. xiv-xv. To show that an author could have obtained accurate information gets us little closer to proving that he did; obviously any ancient author stood nearer to the early Germans than we do even if he never wrote about them. Though paradoxical, the attitude ex-

In other words, criticism cannot be carried to such a point that it impugns the data that reconstructed "Germanic history" depends upon. At one moment, the Mediterranean observers may be qualified as one-sided and, at another, as sincerely committed to trustworthy and disinterested reporting about the early Germans.

This chapter was begun with the observation that general histories of the barbarian invasions are too theatrical to jibe with the known incidents of Roman-barbarian encounter in the fourth to sixth centuries such as those that are to be studied in the pages to come. It was also pointed out that two rather different historical backgrounds—short or long—could be given to such fifth-century peoples as the Goths and Burgundians. What ought now to be apparent is that the long background assigned to these peoples is intimately related to general histories of the barbarian invasions; it is, in effect, a large fragment of the other. Great efforts have been applied in the recent past to creating an "early German history" from which medieval and modern Germany would seem to derive, and very few positive steps have been taken, least of all by those writing in English or French, to counteract this enterprise.[38] The problem has been eloquently defined:

---

pressed by Schwarz has a distinguished precedent: as Weibull, *Auswanderung*, p. 15, pointed out, the scholar who brilliantly established the bookish character of Tacitus's information (Eduard Norden, *Die germanische Urgeschichte in Tacitus Germania* [Leipzig-Berlin, 1920]) did not think his findings limited the value of the *Germania* as a source on the early Germans.

[38] The outstanding French exception is Fustel de Coulanges, *Invasion germanique*. The heirs to this approach were Alfons Dopsch (in part) and Henri Pirenne (who circumvented the invasions); in France itself, notable medievalists like Lot, Marc Bloch, and Louis Halphen tended to take their barbarian history from Germany rather than from Fustel, whose promising aperçus were left undeveloped.

In beginning a new history of Germany, Josef Fleckenstein omits the usual account of the *Völkerwanderung* and opens instead with a chapter of apparently timeless historical sociology ("Die sozialen

24

. . . the concept "Germanic" is completely vague and stems from a purely learned construct of [the modern science of Germanic philology]. Whoever collates the sources of the individual Germanic areas—regardless of whether these sources are charters, chronicles, inscriptions, works of art, archaeological finds, etc.—is invariably struck by the great variety and differences that prevent one from yet speaking of a "Germanity" (*Germanentum*) at this time. . . . The notion of a united "Germanity," which was lovingly nurtured by historiography in conjunction with the Romantic [movement], still haunts historical writing, even though the postulates of this construct have long been shattered. . . . The specter of "Germanity" persists, unfortunately, in haunting the heads of individual scholars and political demagogues— those places outside which it has never existed.[39]

An affirmation is implicit in these lines of criticism, namely, that, if the anachronistic and untenable concept of *Germanentum* is to be rooted out, the history we write should explicitly reflect the diversity and disunity of the peoples that the Roman Empire faced across its borders.[40] This im-

---

Grundlagen"): *Grundlagen und Beginn der deutschen Geschichte*, Joachim Lenscher, ed., *Deutsche Geschichte*, vol. 1 (Göttingen, 1974), pp. 17-32. Although the exposition is of high quality, an opening chapter of this kind seems nevertheless to replace the traditional Exodus with something only slightly less mythical—a sort of Germanic garden of Eden. The questionable postulate expressed by Aubin (n. 35), "an independent point of departure for German history outside the *orbis universus*," continues to be affirmed.

[39] František Graus, *Volk, Herrscher und Heiliger im Reich der Merowinger* (Prague, 1965), pp. 23-24. Cf. Stanley, *Search*, p. 91: ". . . Grimm and those who followed him [regarded] Germanic antiquity as a common civilization of those who spoke the Germanic languages, and a civilization to which they clung tenaciously through the centuries."

[40] Perhaps the most valuable portrayal of this diversity is afforded by the early fourth-century *Laterculus Veronensis*, whose catalogue of "gentes barbarae quae pullulaverunt sub imperatoribus" not only

plies, more precisely, a reevaluation and de-emphasis of the phenomenon of migration.

A major rhetorical point in defense of "early German history" in the traditional manner is the question "Were there really no Germanic wanderings?" with the inevitable reply, ". . . the fact of such movements of peoples is established."[41] The flaw in such contentions is that, as social anthropologists remind us, movements of peoples are not specific to any period of time or to any ethnic group: "Of migrations there is no end, for man is always on the move."[42] What matters is not whether demonstrable migra-

---

reminds us of the many non-Germanic peoples along the frontier (e.g., Scoti, Sarmatae, Persae, Mauri), but also reflects official recognition of the presence of barbarians within the borders (Isauri in Asia Minor, Cantabri in Spain). Text in Alexander Riese, *Geographi Latini minores* (Heilbronn, 1878), pp. 128-129. The unique copy of the *Laterculus* is appended to the Christian influenced B version of the *Cosmographia* of Julius Honorius in an early seventh-century codex (Riese, *Geographi*, pp. xxxii-xxxiii, xxxvii). As argued by T. D. Barnes, "The Unity of the Verona List," *Zeitschrift für Papyrologie und Epigraphik* 16 (1975): 275-278, one internal contradiction in the list of provinces suggests that the document may not be homogeneous, but it remains to be shown whether its date differs markedly from that arrived at by A. H. M. Jones, "The Date and Value of the Verona List," *JRS* 44 (1954), 21-29. Cf. Stein, *Bas-Empire*, vol. 1, pp. 437-438 n. 22.

[41] Schwarz, *Germ. Stammesk.*, p. 24; *Zur germ. Stammesk.*, pp. xvi-xvii. For the indispensability of migrations as the integrative element in narratives of early German history, Schmidt, "Ursachen," p. 340.

[42] A. M. Hocart, quoted by Rodney Needham, introduction to A. M. Hocart, *Kings and Councillors*, ed. R. Needham (Chicago, 1970), pp. lv-lvi; further, the paraphrase of S. Ratzel on p. lxxiii: " 'Restless movement' is the characteristic of man . . . it can lead only to confusion to seek points of origin and routes of migration." Historians of the Middle Ages have too casually invoked migrations as a basis for periodization. E.g., Marc Bloch, *Feudal Society*, trans. L. A. Manyon (Chicago, 1961), p. 56, "Till [the eleventh century] . . . these great movements of peoples have in truth formed the main fabric of history in the West as in the rest of the world. Thenceforward the West would almost alone be free of them." Yet Europe has hardly been freer of "great movements" after that time than it was

tions exist—as, of course, they do—but what function they are called on to play in modern narratives. As must be apparent simply from the items that have been reviewed thus far, migrations have served as the factual underpinnings for the theory of early Germanic unity; if retraced with orthodox piety, they even lead back to prehistoric Scandinavia as the common motherland, the single womb that poured its progeny upon an expectant Europe.[43] By fastening upon and giving greatest prominence to the migrations that are common to many periods and peoples, historians have called into being a thematic entity that begins at latest with the Cimbri and Teutones wandering southward a century before Christ and closes with the Lombards invading Italy in A.D. 568. This is the famous "age of the migrations of peoples, by which is to be understood not only the period after the Hunnic invasion in A.D. 375 but already the period

---

before; it exported 80,000,000 people in the nineteenth century alone. Cf. Musset, *Vagues germaniques*, p. 43: the stability of west European population is normally taken for granted, as is that of the Roman Empire, with the period of the "great invasions" as a parenthesis of troubles between two eras of normality; "Il serait plus sage d'adopter une attitude inverse." Musset appears to identify stable government with stable population. They do not, in fact, necessarily coincide. The relative prevalence or absence of migrations seems as tenuous a basis for periodization as the prevalence or absence of wars. It is also doubtful that migrations, or any other feature of the "longue durée" for that matter, may correctly be said to constitute (in Bloch's words) "the main fabric of history."

[43] Diesner, *Völkerwanderung*, p. 87, because written in East Germany, suggests that this idea is no less acceptable to "socialist" than to "bourgeois" historians. Montesquieu's version of the same thought (ultimately derived from Jordanes) is quoted by Marc Bloch, "Sur les grandes invasions. Quelques positions de problèmes," in Bloch, *Mélanges historiques* (Paris, 1963), vol. 1, pp. 91-103, in a valuable historiographical survey. In addition to the derivation of individual peoples from Scandinavia by Jordanes, Fredegar, the *Passio Sigismundi*, etc., certain early ninth-century authors already expressed the thought that the Northmen were the common ancestors of all Germans: Zöllner, *Politische Stellung*, pp. 46-47, 52. It remained for modern authors to implement such an idea in historical narrative.

from the first century B.C. onward."[44] The mental landscape can only with great difficulty be cleared of such heavily beaten tracks, but, until it is, there can be no hope of improving our understanding of how, in late antiquity, several barbarian peoples came to establish kingdoms in western provinces of the Roman Empire.

One word more about migrations, even at the risk of belaboring the point. Spectacular incidents like the invasions of the Cimbri and Teutones, the attack of the Marcomanni and their confederates in the late second century A.D., and even the Rhine crossing of the Vandals, Sueves, and others in 406/7 are those that we most long to grasp from the standpoint of the invaders. The Greco-Roman accounts that we have are not so much one-sided as inadequate, raising more questions than they answer. That is regrettable but beyond remedy. Neither archaeology nor the other disciplines of prehistory have the resources needed to satisfy our curiosity.

What archaeology does confirm is that the Germanic peoples practiced settled modes of life, not nomadism of even a limited kind: "The overriding impression conveyed by the excavated sites is of stable and enduring communities, some occupying the same sites for many decades or even centuries, others shifting their dwellings without moving far beyond their original confines. . . . It is clear . . . that the early German economy . . . was probably essentially similar to peasant agriculture within the Western Roman provinces."[45] Moreover, archaeologists have now abandoned

[44] Schwarz, Zur germ. Stammesk., p. viii. Cf. n. 2 above. On the other hand, Rolf Hachmann, The Germanic Peoples, trans. James Hogarth (London, 1971), pp. 69-71, drew attention to a marked discontinuity between late B.C. and early A.D. in the archaeological evidence.

[45] Todd, Northern Barbarians, pp. 116-117, 131, explicitly correcting an historian of antiquity (M. I. Finley). Marc Bloch, "Une mise au point: les invasions," in Bloch, Mélanges historiques, vol. 1, pp. 116-118, gave a subtle and highly developed description of supposed Germanic nomadism, which he connected directly to the

the correspondence between, on the one hand, the cultural provinces inferred from material remains and, on the other hand, the approximate localization of tribes indicated by Greco-Roman writings. For the better part of this century, these two categories of information were believed to correspond.[46] As long as they were, a partnership of rare intensity could exist between archaeology, toponymy, and history; the dynamic syntheses of "early German history" that have been touched on in the preceding pages were all affected by the certitudes that seemed possible when cultural provinces were thought to coincide with (as well as to circumscribe) tribal territories. This postulate can no longer be entertained. Once it is accepted that Greco-Roman ethnography is not directly mirrored in the material remains of Germania, unwritten evidence loses most of its voice; it can be called on only in minor ways to amplify the testimony of literate observers. Any historical narrative of ours will be based almost exclusively on these observers and will consequently be bound to address itself, not to the Germanic tribesmen as they knew themselves or as archaeologists can know them, but merely to the neighbors of the Roman Empire—a collection of peoples who need have had

Völkerwanderung. Also, Robert Folz and others, *De l'Antiquité au monde médiéval,* Peuples et civilisations, vol. 5, 2d ed. (Paris, 1972), p. 36. Confirming Todd, Johannes Haller and Heinrich Dannenbauer, *Der Eintritt der Germanen in die Geschichte,* 4th ed., Sammlung Goschen 1117 (Berlin, 1970), pp. 20-21: the notion that the Germans were half-nomads is a major error.

The fact of stability has nothing in common with the allegation of a Germanic agriculture more progressive than that of the Roman Empire set out by William H. McNeill, *The Shape of European History* (New York, 1974), pp. 65-68. McNeill's contention, although presented as if it embodied a learned consensus, has no parallel in the literature known to me. It is patently incorrect. Cf. the long abandoned belief that the Germans' attaining the "stage" of settled agriculture created population pressure, which was thus the initial cause of their migrations: Dahn, "Ursachen der Völkerwanderung," pp. 5-6, 8-9.

[46] Todd, *Northern Barbarians,* pp. 20-21, 55. For a different perspective, Schwarz, *Zur germ. Stammesk.,* pp. x-xiii, 301-303.

no more in common than the Mediterranean perspective in which they were seen. The chronology and unifying theme of such a narrative derives necessarily from Roman history.

It was Rome that, by its expansion and high standards of security for the provinces, set a conspicuous frontier between itself and the varied aliens beyond. The fate of that border—hardly less of a burden for the empire to maintain than for the barbarians to endure—may well be the dynamic focus of the story. The emphasis on Rome ought not to be confused with the problematic idea of a "continuity" from Roman into medieval history.[47] On the contrary, the theme of Roman security gives prominence to the disruptive activities of Alamans, Franks, Goths, Vandals, and others in late antiquity and hardly denies their capacity for turning the course of events in novel directions. The only denial applies to the conspicuous fallacies earlier defined: that a coherent "other," or Germanic, side faced the empire and that this side had an inborn disposition—the accumulated steam of continual migrations—to break into Roman space. The Greco-Roman observers who will be relied on were well aware of the variety and disunity of the peoples facing them (even if all were called barbarians), and they had no illusions about migratory tides. A study based principally on their reports will be imperfect and, to some extent, one-sided, but all sources have shortcomings: our conviction that the barbarians had thoughts does not authorize us to imagine what they were. It is enough that the authentic experience of some contemporary observers should be reflected, rather than modern reconstructions, however well intentioned. Further clarity will result from recognizing

[47] Graus, *Volk, Herrscher,* pp. 19-21, 24. Graus's criticism, which stresses contemporary Roman statements suggestive of discontinuity, may make too little allowance for what Ammianus talked of when he said "falluntur malorum recentium stupore confixi" (31. 5. 11)— transitory misfortunes puffed up into unprecedented calamities by observers lacking historical perspective, a common enough phenomenon in our own experience.

that all writings emanate from the literate Mediterranean even when authored by a Goth, an Anglo-Saxon, or a Frank.[48] It was as converts to the religion of the empire that certain barbarians stopped being mere nuisances and threats to the imperial borders and became instead peoples with a past and, perhaps, even a future. The empire was as unifying a center for their emergence into history as it was for the expansion of Christianity.[49]

The essential point for the chapters to come is that the Goths and Burgundians in the provinces of the empire, as well as the Romans who dealt with them, should not be set in an unduly long perspective. Except for the Alans and Huns, the barbarians who participated in the invasions were all neighbors of the empire; those with whom we shall be concerned had been on imperial soil, and in frequent contact with the private and public levels of Roman life, for several decades prior to the agreements and transactions that will presently be studied. If these facts deserve to be stressed, it is not in order to intimate that the barbarians had been "Romanized" either by proximity to the frontier or by almost a generation of exposure to Roman provincials. As recent authors remind us, the notion of higher and lower civilizations making contact with each other—unequally filled vessels being connected up and thus finding a common level—is an oversimplification that human experience

[48] Cf. the sentiments of Aubin quoted above, at n. 35. The Gothic blood in Jordanes no more makes his *Getica* Germanic than the Vandal blood in Stilicho altered his loyalty to the empire he served. Our most realistic image of a barbarian kingdom comes from a Gallo-Roman, Gregory of Tours.

[49] Contrast to the deeply rooted presupposition that medieval history proceeds from an equilateral trinity of Roman, Christian, and Germanic elements, or involves an "encounter of Germanity with Christianity and the inheritance of Antiquity" (H. Löwe). A history of Christianity apart from the Roman Empire would be as distorted as Aubin's "independent point of departure for German history" (n. 35). Besides, the notion of triune beginnings tacitly assumes an antecedent catastrophe, after which it was necessary to rebuild from distinct heaps of materials.

31

tends to contradict: " 'Civilisation' does not contact 'barbarism.' . . . What happens is, that men make contact with other men. Or, with other kinds of women."[50] If people meet at all, they do so as individuals, not collectivities. What they communicate to each other has less to do with the social and historical background that any individual may bring to the encounter than with elementary traits of personality and character. The most that may be said on a collective plane is that, for all the parties involved, living together modifies the quality of existence, the more so when the association is permanent.

The circumstances that brought barbarians onto Roman territory in sufficient numbers and with enough power to make a difference were not all the same. At the two extremities of Roman Europe, the island of Britain and the Balkan peninsula, the aliens who immigrated were so numerous that, by the close of the sixth century, the space inhabited by barbarians had expanded across the North Sea and the Danube, apparently dislodging and displacing the Roman provincials. Over the long stretch extending between Britain and the Balkans, the similar, but much more limited, retreat of the empire from its former bounds is delineated, rather roughly, by the modern frontier between Romance and Germanic dialects.[51] These two forms of retreat, in turn, bore little resemblance to the more spec-

[50] A. P. Thornton, "Jekyll and Hyde in the Colonies," *International Journal* 20 (1965): 226-227.

[51] Cf. the second zone described by Löwe in Gebhardt, *Handbuch*, 9th ed., vol. 1, p. 92 (the three zone scheme was proposed by Aubin). The division I suggest proceeds from what the empire did: evacuation of Britain; limited withdrawal from the Rhine and upper Danube border districts; inadequate defense of the Balkans (where the Slavs settled). Barbarian immigration into these lands was gradual and complex; e.g., the process that sent Irish and Saxons to Britain and Britons to Armorica. Löwe stressed the distinctiveness of the Germanic tribes involved, but this does not work for the Franks (see next note) and makes no allowance for the Slavs in the Balkans—an important reminder that the "fall" of the empire was not an exclusively western phenomenon.

tacular, but also more precarious, circumstances with which we shall be concerned. The fifth-century settlements in imperial territory that the present study considers were made in one piece by single bands of barbarians wholly cut off from *barbaricum*. The aliens in these instances penetrated far from the old frontier, then halted in a sea of Romans and took charge, usually by explicit agreement with the imperial government, which accepted them as military auxiliaries.[52] Their numbers are very difficult to establish; as shown in Appendix A, the one documented figure that modern historians have been ready to trust is easier to interpret as fiction than as a head count. Nevertheless, tens of thousands may have been involved in each group—enough to matter. Besides, these were armed bands under military leadership moving into open space populated by unarmed, untrained civilians. They could inspire fear and respect even if they risked being culturally swallowed up by the population amid which they lived.

The prototype for these settlements was the immigration of Gothic refugees authorized by the emperor Valens in 376, or, more precisely, the pacification of these Goths in 382. They had rebelled in 377 and won a great victory at Adrianople (378) but then had been gradually worn down by Roman arms and diplomacy to the point at which their leaders accepted an advantageous treaty. By necessity or by choice, Theodosius I and his descendants were willing to tolerate, rather than to expel or annihilate, those barbarians who rebelled within the imperial borders (like the Goths of 377 and 395) or broke across them in a massive raid (like the Vandals, Alans, and Sueves in 406/7).[53] The Ro-

---

[52] Nicely characterized by Musset, *Vagues germaniques*, p. 69 n. 1. The Merovingian kingdom resembled this type of settlement to the extent that Clovis and his successors established their capitals very far from the limits of concentrated Frankish population.

[53] The third-century empire experienced incursions that were at least as severe as those faced by Theodosius and his sons, but all the invaders were then cleared out, at the cost of a little territory: why did this not happen again? Many Roman historians currently main-

man government had long cultivated certain of its neighbors as a precious military asset usable for the benefit of
the empire and had thus convinced many barbarian leaders,
such as the Goth Athaulf, that the most advantageous
course for them and their followers was to serve and pro-
tect Romania.[54] These were fragile ideas with limited life
spans; Roman philo-barbarism was no sturdier or widespread than barbarian devotion to the public interests of
the Roman state. Historians of late antiquity have not fully
explained why the emperors since Constantine placed
markedly greater confidence in foreign troops and generals
than their predecessors had, and it is worth noting as well
the change that official opinion at Constantinople underwent in the second half of the fifth century: its mounting
hostility towards free barbarians laid the ideological basis
for Justinian's campaigns.[55] Nevertheless, the attractive

---

tain that barbarian "pressure" was too great: Piganiol, *Empire
chrétien*, p. 422; A. H. M. Jones, *The Later Roman Empire, 284-602*
(Oxford, 1964), pp. 1027-1031; J. F. Matthews, review, in *JRS* 56
(1966): 245. An alternative worth exploring is that, to the Roman
government, concessions to barbarians were safer than the domestic
risks of efficient defense (the third-century emperors Aurelian, Pro-
bus, etc. had paid a heavy personal price).

[54] Military use of barbarians: Jones, *LRE*, pp. 619-623, 199-200;
Stroheker, *Germanentum u. Spätantik*, pp. 9-29, 30-53; Manfred
Waas, *Germanen im römischen Dienst im 4. Jahrhundert n.C.* (Bonn,
1965). The famous story of Athaulf, in Orosius *Historia adversus
paganos* 7. 43. 3-6, deserves to be combined, on the one hand, with
the report of an Alamannic king who was promoted to command of
a unit in the Roman army of Britain (Ammianus 29. 4. 7), and, on
the other, with Jordanes's *Getica*, portraying service to the empire as
the historic raison d'être of the Goths. Gerhard Wirth, "Zur Frage
der foederirten Staaten in der späteren römischen Kaiserzeit," *Historia*
16 (1967): 240, cf. 236, spoke of "the customary attacks whose object
was [for the attackers] to be taken into the Empire and then give
up their own political existence in favor of the advantages offered
by service to the Empire."

[55] Alexander Schenk von Stauffenberg, "Die Germanen im römischen Reich," *Die Welt als Geschichte* 1 (1935): 72-100, 2 (1936):
117-168, attempted an interpretation. The idea of an economic

power of the empire, typified by the government's welcome to foreign military elites, had a more certain role than any impulse from the barbarian side in establishing exotic dominations on provincial soil. When set in a fourth-century perspective, what we call the Fall of the Western Roman Empire was an imaginative experiment that got a little out of hand.

The present book, to whose specific subject matter we now turn, is directly concerned with one aspect of this experiment: on what legal terms did barbarian soldiers and their dependents take root in the empire? The question must go unanswered in several regions for lack of evidence; in others, there is enough to permit at least an approximate reply. We begin with a Roman countryside whose most novel feature, instituted since the reign of Diocletian, was a high level of bureaucratic regimentation with a view to the levying of taxes and the performance of essential tasks. At the chronological close of the inquiry, the fiscal organization had shrunk and withdrawn to managing the financial interests of barbarian kings, but the countryside continued to be characterized, on the one hand, by a high level of large, absentee landownership and, on the other hand, by the presence of a servile working force whose bondage stemmed in large part from tax law. As for the barbarian settlers, some of them had been suppressed or displaced by hostile armies, whereas others endured. In either eventuality, their installation had had a real but limited effect upon the organization of landownership in the districts of settle-

---

weakening or decline of the empire is often substituted for an explanation. The distinction made by Musset, *Vagues germaniques*, pp. 224-226, between "infiltrations" (such as military recruitment) and the invasions proper is misleading. For hostility prior to Justinian: the historians Victor Vitensis, Zosimus, and Count Marcellinus (also the Gallic Chronicler of 452?); the reign of Leo I, with its campaign against the Vandals (469) and downfall of the Aspar military dynasty (471), seems important; perhaps the Vandal seizure of Carthage (439) was the turning point.

ment: much of the regimentation peculiar to late Roman life evaporated, whereas other dimensions of the age became, if anything, more deeply entrenched than ever before. It remains to be seen who the barbarians in question were and what were the technicalities of their installation in the western provinces.

In 418, the Visigoths of King Wallia accepted the settlement in Aquitaine offered them by the Roman government; in 443, the "remnants" of the Burgundians were settled by Aëtius in a part of eastern Gaul; in 476, the army of Italy, composed of various small barbarian peoples, forced the deposition of the last Western emperor and the accession of Odoacer as their king in order that they might obtain landed allotments; in the 490s, after Theodoric overthrew Odoacer, the Ostrogoths were assigned lots in Italy; and two groups of Alans accepted similar settlements in the course of the fifth century. These were all regulated operations, presupposing the cooperation of barbarian leaders with the Roman authorities, conducted according to law and intended to maintain at least relative harmony between the barbarian people being settled and the indigenous population. They were different from the arbitrary expropriations by which Geiseric provided for the Vandals in North Africa or from the prolonged depredations of the Sueves in northwest Spain. At the heart of each regulated settlement was the provision of an allotment for each qualified Goth, Burgundian, or whatever. Whether these awards were distributed as soon as the treaties with the West Roman government came into force is not known and perhaps unlikely; sooner or later, however—and almost immediately in Italy—allotments were made: barbarian warriors acquired a stake in the countryside alongside Roman landowners. Both for the beneficiaries and for the Romans who paid the bill, it was a memorable moment.

However momentous at the time, these settlements have left a very poor record, which fails to answer essential questions and leaves much to the imagination. Several chronicles devote single lines to the subject; the Burgundian laws provide intriguing but obscure evidence, which is paralleled rather than developed in the Visigothic Code; Procopius alone attests to the first settlement in Italy, and he, along with the *Variae* of Cassiodorus, offers what glimpses may be had of the scheme instituted by Theodoric.[56] Hardly any of this is descriptive or portrays human beings actually installing barbarian settlers in the Roman provinces; most of the information is inferential, and it bears on the legal or institutional technicalities of land assignment. Altogether, the relevant lines of source material would fit onto five pages or less.

This scanty evidence has been known for many decades. Gaupp's book on the subject, published in 1844, is still judged to be the indispensable point of departure, and many commentaries have followed, down to Ferdinand Lot's long article, "Du régime de l'hospitalité," published in 1928.[57] Since then, certain aspects of barbarian settlement have aroused lively discussion, but these have not included the land assignment itself, a subject that is regarded either as having been exhausted by Lot and his predecessors, or as being too poorly documented to be knowable.[58]

[56] *Chronica minora*, ed. T. Mommsen, MGH *AA*, vols. 9 and 11; *Leges Burgundionum*, ed. Ludwig Rudolf de Salis, MGH *Leges*, vol. 2, pt. 1 (hereafter *LBurg*); *Leges Visigothorum*, ed. K. Zeumer, MGH *Leges*, vol. 1 (hereafter *CE*, for *Codex Eurici*, and *LVisig*, for the main collection); for Procopius, below, Chapter III; Cassiodorus *Variae*, ed. Å. J. Fridh, *Corpus Christianorum*, ser. Lat. 96 (Turnhout, 1973), also ed. T. Mommsen, MGH *AA*, vol. 12.

[57] Ernst Theodor Gaupp, *Die germanischen Ansiedlungen und Landtheilungen in den Provinzen des römischen Westreiches* (Breslau, 1844); Ferdinand Lot, "Du régime de l'hospitalité," *Revue belge de philologie et d'histoire* 7 (1928): 975-1011.

[58] E. A. Thompson, "The Settlement of the Barbarians in Southern Gaul," *JRS* 46 (1956): 65-75; J. M. Wallace-Hadrill, "Gothia and Romania," in *The Long-Haired Kings and Other Studies in Frankish History* (New York, 1962), pp. 25-48, esp., 30-33. Thompson de-

Neither of these views is altogether correct. Earlier commentators have left many questions unsettled, and, though the thrust of Lot's investigation was admirable, the conclusions he reached were disappointing and uneven. As for the documentation, no new texts can be introduced, but the ones there are—most of all those bearing upon Italian conditions—can be better interpreted than they have been.

The present study reexamines this old subject and introduces three novelties into the discussion. To begin with, a critical appraisal will be made of the assumption that the allotments to barbarians followed Roman practices for quartering soldiers, known to moderns as "the *hospitalitas* system." Some historians have been less wedded to this notion than others, but none has established what basis there was in Roman law for assigning land, not just shelter, to barbarian soldiers. Next, the Italian evidence will be set at the forefront of the discussion, as constituting, in effect, the only body of source material that is extensive enough to illustrate the technicalities of a barbarian settlement. The other texts are late and fragmentary and should not be interpreted without the assistance of the Italian example. Finally, it will be argued that the "land" given to barbarians was not ordinary property but a special mode of ownership made possible by late Roman tax law. The allotment that a barbarian initially received consisted of tax assessment and its proceeds—a "superior" ownership that did not extinguish or supersede the private proprietary rights of the

pended essentially on Lot, "Hospitalité," without reconsidering the evidence; so also Thompson, "The Barbarian Kingdoms in Spain and Gaul," *Nottingham Medieval Studies* 7 (1963): 3-33. Wallace-Hadrill, p. 30 n. 2, ". . . we know almost nothing of [the Visigothic] settlement" (a correct appraisal of the evidence). The main expositions since Lot are: Schmidt, *Ostgermanen*, pp. 171-173, 316-317, 327-329, 362-363, 505-506 (little influenced by Lot); Wilhelm Ensslin, *Theodorich der Grosse* (Munich, 1947), pp. 94-97, 193-196, 203-205 (Italy only); and especially Musset, *Vagues germaniques*, pp. 284-288, trans. James, pp. 214-217.

Romans owning assessed land and paying its taxes. This peculiarity helps to explain why the settlements occasioned hardly a ripple of protest from the Roman provincials and why the few protests they aroused assumed the form they did.

II

****

THE ROMAN BASIS FOR
BARBARIAN LAND ALLOTMENTS

BARBARIAN settlement is almost always said to have taken place in accordance with the terms of Roman military quartering, the system for providing soldiers with shelter outside military camps.[1] There is a sound basis for this contention. The sources—though not those for Italy—use the words "hospitality," "hosts," and "guests" in speaking about the relationship between Roman provincials and the newcomers.[2] The currency of these expressions is eloquently shown by a hagiographer denouncing certain Visigoths: playing on the word *hospitalitas*, he mentions land tenure by *sors hostilitatis*, "enemy's—or alien—allotment," fully expecting that his irony would be understood.[3] It is one thing, however, to observe that the terminology of quartering was applied to the barbarians and quite another thing to conclude that their land grants were applications of the *hospitalitas* system.

Many historians have envisaged a direct and compre-

[1] The best illustrations occur in textbooks, where this doctrine is firmly anchored; for example, H. St. L. B. Moss, *The Birth of the Middle Ages, 395-814* (Oxford, 1935), pp. 64-65; R. H. C. Davis, *A History of Medieval Europe from Constantine to Saint Louis*, rev. ed. (London, 1970), pp. 32-33; Norman Zacour, *An Introduction to Medieval Institutions*, 2d ed. (New York, 1976), p. 6. The connection was originally made and elaborated by Gaupp, *Ansiedlungen*.

[2] *CE* 276; *LBurg* 13, 54, 55, 84. For other references, below, Chapter VI.

[3] *Passio s. Vincentii Aginensis* 6, ed. Beaudouin de Gaiffier, in *Analecta Bollandiana* 70 (1952): 180 (full text, Chapter VI, n. 7); Courcelle, *Hist. litt.*, pp. 344-345 n. 4.

hensive relationship between "hospitality" and a distribution of land. Dopsch is one example: "In accordance with the Roman quartering system, one-third of the Roman land and soil was transferred by [Odoacer] to [the army of Italy] as enduring ownership."[4] Ludwig Schmidt, after twice recognizing the limited extent of Roman *hospitalitas*, omitted any qualification when turning to the earliest settlement of all: "The land assignment in Aquitaine followed the principles of the Roman quartering system, such that Roman landowners were forced to yield parts of their entire immovable property, along with *coloni*, slaves, and livestock."[5] Perhaps the most complete misapprehension of what was involved is reflected by J. B. Bury: ". . . the principle of these arrangements was directly derived from the old Roman system of quartering soldiers on the owners of the land. On that system, which dated from the days of the Republic, and was known as *hospitalitas*, the owner was bound to give one-third of the produce of his property to the guests whom he reluctantly harboured. This principle was now applied to the land itself, and the same term was used."[6] Bury's explanation is a good point of departure for an account of what Roman quartering was.

To begin with, *hospitalitas* was not a technical term, but one word used among others in the relevant laws. These

---

[4] Alfons Dopsch, *Wirtschaftliche und soziale Grundlagen der europäischen Kulturentwicklung*, 2d ed. (Vienna, 1923), vol. 1, p. 203.

[5] Schmidt, *Ostgermanen*, p. 505.

[6] J. B. Bury, *History of the Later Roman Empire from the Death of Theodosius I to the Death of Justinian* (London, 1923), vol. 1, p. 206. Cf. Katherine Fischer Drew, *The Burgundian Code* (1949, repr. ed., Philadelphia, 1972), p. 62 n. 1, "the old Roman precedent of quartering soldiers on the land, allowing them one-third of the property of the original owner." Comparable misunderstandings occur in Laetitia Boehm, *Geschichte Burgunds* (Stuttgart, 1971), p. 56, and Dietrich Claude, *Geschichte der Westgoten* (Stuttgart, 1970), p. 37, according to whom the Theodosian title *de metatis* is composed of laws "die vorsahen, dass den Neuankömmlingen ein Teil der Güter der bisherigen Bevölkerung zugeteilt wurde."

laws do not occur under a heading *de hospitalitate* in the Codes of Theodosius II and Justinian; the name of the title is *de metatis*, and the householder's duty is described as the *metatorum praebendorum onus.*[7] The same duty was called *hospitalitatis munus* and, considerably earlier, *recipiendi hospitis necessitas*; another phrase is *hospitem recipere* or *suscipere.*[8] A soldier was said to sojourn *hospitali iure*, to enjoy *hospitalis commoditas*, or to occupy a *hospitium.*[9] As far as we know, *hospitalitas* did not become a technical term in the barbarian kingdoms either. The Burgundian code, which includes a famous regulation of settlement, also contains a title "on not denying hospitality to envoys of foreign peoples and travelers"; the legislator evidently did not believe that his use of "hospitality" in this title rendered ambiguous his later reference to a special *ius hospitalitatis* enjoyed by the Burgundians.[10]

Even if not technically called *hospitalitas*, there was a regulated system of quartering in the Roman Empire. Citizens had to comply; quartering was a *munus, onus, necessitas*, what we might term an obligatory requisition. The substance of the obligation was so familiar among the Ro-

---

[7] *CTh* 7. 8; *CJ* 12. 40; *NTheod II* 25 (444). *Metatum* is late Latin (not in Lewis and Short, though *metator* is), and not, I believe, attested in the West. Significantly, the word stresses the "measuring" of space for quartering, transposing to private houses the measuring formerly carried out in setting out a Roman camp. The word calls to mind the official *mensores*, subordinated to the *magister militum per Orientem* and the *magister officiorum* (*Notitia dignitatum*, Or. 7. 66, 11. 12), who carried out the division. Almost all the Eastern laws are addressed to the *magister officiorum*.

[8] *CTh* 7. 8. 3 (384); *Dig.* 50. 5. 10. 2 (Paulus); *Dig.* 50. 4. 18. 29-30 (Arcadius Charisius) and *CTh* 13. 3. 3 (333); *CTh* 16. 2. 8 (343).

[9] *CTh* 7. 8. 1 (361); *NTheod II* 25. 1. 2 (444); *HA, Aurelian* 7. 8 (in accord with the current consensus, I take the *HA* to date from no earlier than 395).

[10] *LBurg* 38, "de hospitalitate legatis extranearum gentium et itinerantibus non neganda." For *ius hospitalitatis*, *LBurg* 55. 2 (below, Chapter v n. 57).

mans that they never felt compelled to spell it out. We must turn to the Burgundian code in order to have the conditions outlined: anyone denying "a roof or fire" was fined; in other words, the host was bound to provide his guest with shelter and, perhaps, a little heat.[11] That is all. The lands, produce, or revenue of country estates were altogether excluded from Roman *hospitalitas*.

Not surprisingly, much of the quartering was expected to take place in cities.[12] The law on the subject that has drawn

[11] *LBurg* 38. 1: "Quicumque hospiti venienti tectum aut focum negaverit, trium solidorum inlatione multetur." The same was true of primitive Greek hospitality: Daremberg-Saglio, *Dictionnaire des antiquités* 3 (1899): 295. For the terms of billeting laid down to East Roman troops in Edessa (503-505), see Jones, *LRE*, pp. 631-632; they did not include food. The Byzantine troops that occupied Carthage after defeating the Vandals were assigned to houses by clerks and shopped for their food at the market: Procopius *Bellum Vandalicum* 1. 21. 10.

Ernst Levy, *Late Roman Vulgar Law. The Law of Property* (Philadelphia, 1951), p. 126, denied that the rules of *LBurg* 38 had anything to do with Roman quartering; stressing the reference to "travelers" (*itinerantes*), he derived the law from Germanic ideas of hospitality. But *legati* are just as explicitly mentioned. One might doubt that *LBurg* 38 was intended to safeguard the rights of any casual traveler on his way to anywhere. The comments about this law by Fustel de Coulanges, *Nouvelles recherches sur quelques problèmes d'histoire*, ed. Camille Jullian (Paris, 1891), pp. 314-320, are largely correct.

[12] Vegetius *Epitoma rei militaris* 2. 7: "mensores qui . . . hospitia in civitatibus praestant" (as an alternative to laying out a camp in the countryside, where *metatores* chose the site and laid out the outlines, and *mensores* measured within). The famous law of 398 (next note) begins, "In qualibet vel nos ipsi urbe fuerimus vel ii qui nobis militant commorentur. . . ." Cities are explicit in the exemption of state factories, *CTh* 7. 8. 8 (405) and in 7. 8. 9 (409); implicit in the exemption of: professors and doctors, *Dig.* 50. 5. 10. 2, 50. 4. 18. 30 (referring to Vespasian and Hadrian), *CTh* 13. 3. 3 (333), 10 (370, Rome); master painters, *CTh* 13. 4. 4 (374); clerics, *CTh* 16. 2. 8 (343); synagogues, *CTh* 7. 8. 2 (368-373); governors' palaces, *CTh* 7. 8. 6 (400). Constantinople gets special attention in *CTh* 7. 8. 3 (384), 13 (422), 14 (427), 15 (430), 16 (435), *NTheod II* 25 (444), *CJ* 12. 40. 10 (450-455); *CTh* 6. 23. 4 (437), immunity for

most modern attention was issued by the Eastern emperor Arcadius in 398 and describes how a (town) house is to be shared between the owner and his guest: it was divided into three parts (by an official *mensor* or *metator?*); the owner had first choice, then the guest, and the last third reverted to the owner; business premises were not included in the partition unless some portion of them was needed for stabling; and, if the guest was a dignitary of the highest rank (*vir illustris*), the house was shared half-and-half.[13] The pro-

houses "vel in hac sacratissima urbe vel in qualibet alia . . . civitate." By comparison, specific reference to quartering in the country (*praedia*) occurs only in *CTh* 7. 8. 7 (400) and 10 (413), both for Africa. (A further instance, from the sixth century, is cited below, n. 17.)

[13] *CTh* 7. 8. 5 (398), issued by Arcadius to the Eastern *magister officiorum*. This is a reform law, designed to repress abuses on the part of officials, in which the legislator especially insists on the owner's right to first choice after division; it is hard to tell whether the specified fractions were long established or being newly instituted. For general treatments of the subject, R. Cagnat, "Hospitium militare," in Daremberg-Saglio, *Dictionnaire des antiquités* 3 (1899): 302-303; Émilienne Demougeot, "Une lettre de l'empereur Honorius sur l'*hospitium* des soldats," *NRHD*, 4th ser., 34 (1956): 26-49, esp., 25-29, who was wrong to think that this *munus* was a fourth-century novelty. She overlooked the evidence of the *Dig.*, as does J. Gaudemet, *Institutions de l'Antiquité* (Paris, 1967), p. 724 n. 5.

On the letter of Honorius, discussed by Demougeot, see also A. H. M. Jones, "A Letter of Honorius to the Army of Spain," *Xe Congrès international des études byzantines, Istanbul 1955* (Istanbul, 1957), p. 223, and *LRE*, pp. 202, 1107 n. 44. The document would be exceptionally important to barbarian settlement if, as Jones believed, it held forth to the troops "the hope of *hospitia* on discharge" ("Letter," p. 223). Owing to the lamentable condition of the text, this possibility is not excluded, but it is very faint and improbable. The preferable interpretation is that Honorius simply confirmed the ordinary rules of military quartering: the troops were entitled to exact billets wherever they happened to be staying. Such a confirmation was not superfluous. Jones, *LRE*, p. 1099 n. 46, also proposed that certain "Goths were settled [in Macedonia] as *hospites* on the system later used in the West." He inferred this from a passage of an oration of Themistius in which these Goths are said to pay the same taxes as Roman provincials. Taxpaying, however, was not to be an obligation of barbarian *hospites* in the West, as will be seen.

portions mentioned—an ordinary rate of one-third for the guest, and a preferred rate of one-half—have aroused greater interest than the specific object shared, which was nothing more than the shelter a house affords. The "duty to receive a guest" was a *munus personale* in the strict sense of the phrase: it was an imposition upon one's personal convenience, but not a charge upon one's financial resources.[14]

The imperial government took pains to combat abuses on the part of its agents availing themselves of quarters. A whole title of the Theodosian Code is concerned with protecting hosts from forced exactions of featherbeds, wood, and oil by military travelers, and another title forbade officers, except those of the very highest rank, to requisition baths.[15] According to a literary source, the characteristic abuse of a soldier vis-à-vis his host was to seduce his wife;[16] no laws repressing this practice have come down to us. As for food, its supply to the quartered traveler was out of the

---

[14] No text in Roman law specifically classifies *hospitalitas* in this way. I draw the inference from the distinction of Arcadius Charisius between "personal" and "patrimonial" *munera* (*Dig.* 50. 4. 18. 1 and 18), which stresses the presence or absence of expenditure. Cf. *Dig.* 50. 4. 6. 3-5 (Ulpian), where the accent is rather on the relative ease of exemption; this resembles *Dig.* 50. 5. 11 (Hermogenianus), according to which the duty of receiving a guest was among the "munera, quae rei propriae cohaerent," as though affecting the house rather than its owner. Since a house can provide only shelter, such an interpretation also excludes expense.

[15] *CTh* 7. 9, "de salgamo hospitibus non praebendo"; 7. 11, "ne comitibus et tribunis lavacra praestentur." (*Salgamum*, "pickle, delicacy," used figuratively, is military slang; there is no apparent basis for the definition "food" given by Alexander Souter, *Glossary of Later Latin* [Oxford, 1949].) For a later measure repressing abusive exactions by quartered soldiers, Cassiodorus *Variae* 5. 39. 15. These exactions were not casual abuses of power; the soldiers were asking only for what had been the prerogatives of guests according to the ancient rules of hospitality: Theodor Mommsen, "Das römische Gastrecht und die römische Clientell," *Römische Forschungen*, vol. 1 (Berlin, 1864), p. 344.

[16] *HA, Aurelian* 7. 4, 8. Cf. *HA, Macrinus* 12. 4, intercourse with host's slave girl (of bad repute).

question. A Western law of 413, addressed to Africa, is explicit: "we grant *hospitalitas* alone, on the condition that nothing be demanded of the host that might be thought necessary for the sustenance of men or beasts."[17] If food and fodder had been involved, quartering would have slipped from the category of a *munus personale* to that of a *munus patrimoniale*—a charge entailing financial obligation. The government did not wish this to occur. Of course, undisciplined soldiers had the reputation of helping themselves to hens, sheep, and other comestibles, but such pilfering was understood to be at the expense of the provincials in general, not specifically to the detriment of hosts.[18]

For the government to have allowed the provision of food as a part of the quartering arrangement would have been to subvert the elaborate organization of soldiers' pay and citizens' taxes, both of which went under the same word *annona* in the later empire. The injunction to a pilfering soldier was "let him be content with his *annona*"; and, in a law of 416, "let soldiers be content with our generosity, and let the taxpayers always endure only the annual levy."[19]

[17] *CTh* 7. 8. 10 (413): "Solam sane hospitalitatem sub hac observatione concedimus, ut nihil ab hospite, quod vel hominum vel animalium pastui necessarium creditur, postuletur . . . nec ulli liceat residere, ne diuturnitas conmanentium ulla ex parte praedium vexet." In an account designed to emphasize abuses, Procopius sharply distinguished military provisioning (by forced purchases from producers reimbursed by tax credits, *Anecdota* 23. 11-12) from the billeting of soldiers (*Anecdota* 23. 22, on farms; 23. 24, in Byzantium).

[18] *HA, Pescennius Niger* 3. 6, 10. 5-6, *Aurelian* 7. 5; *CTh* 7. 4. 12 (364), "ut milites recordentur commoda sua, quae in annonarum perceptione adipiscuntur, extrinsecus detrimentis provincialium non esse cumulanda" (interestingly, the altered copy in *CJ* 12. 37. 3 is addressed to the *milites et eorum superstantes*). *HA, Alexander Severus* 47. 3 also relates that, when the emperor charged *honestiores patres familias* with the care of sick soldiers, he reimbursed their expenses.

[19] *HA, Aurelian* 7. 5, "annona sua contentus sit" (cf. Luke 3:14, the famous injunction, "contenti estote stipendiis vestris"); *CTh* 7. 9. 4 (416), "militibus nostrae sufficient largitates et conlatoribus annua

We have no precise information on how traveling soldiers and civil servants were supplied—whether, for example, they were given travel money or could draw rations from state storehouses.[20] The details are incidental. What matters is that, at all times and wherever they were, soldiers and civil servants drew salaries from the state, consisting chiefly of daily rations, simple or multiple, for their animals as well as themselves. Acknowledging this point, Ludwig Schmidt notes that the government "recovered" these rations "from the individual landed properties as a special payment."[21] There was more to it than that. The principal annual tax paid by the registered tributaries of the later empire was the *annona*, and much of the intricate bureaucracy of taxation existed in order to transfer this revenue from the citizen producers and payers to the salaried consumers.[22] Feeding soldiers was tantamount to paying them, and a host obliged to provision his military guest would have been enduring not a tolerable *munus* but the odious burden of double taxation.

The official supply of rations to soldiers and special categories of travelers did not cease when the western provinces passed to the government of barbarian kings. Several letters of Cassiodorus, in the name of Theodoric, instruct the praetorian prefect to provide *annonae* to official travelers; on one occasion, three gold pieces per "mess," in lieu of provisions, were issued to a detachment of Gepids crossing

---

tantummodo semper imminebit indictio" (with specific reference to soldiers occupying *hospitia*).

[20] Lot, "Hospitalité," pp. 1006-1007 (on the basis of Gaupp), and Musset, *Vagues germaniques*, pp. 286-287, suggested that the technicalities are more precisely and definitely known than they in fact can be. The relevant texts are under *CTh* 7. 4, "de erogatione militaris annonae." Cf. the particularly misleading exposition of Fustel de Coulanges, *Invasion germanique*, pp. 521-522, which may have influenced later French scholars. See also below, Chapter III n. 63.

[21] Schmidt, *Ostgermanen*, p. 171.

[22] For the outlines, Stein, *Bas-Empire*, vol. 1, pp. 74-76, 61-62; Jones, *LRE*, pp. 61-66, 448-461, 626-630.

northern Italy; on another, the rations of active garrisons are shown to have been dispensed by their commanding officers.[23] The Visigothic Code contains a law detailing what the soldiers of a garrison had to do if the civil authorities, charged with supplying them, failed in their task.[24] According to Burgundian law, shelter had to be granted to all travelers, but only *legati* of foreign peoples were entitled to food and, in winter, to fodder. Characteristically, however, this charge was not borne by the host alone; he shared the cost with "those who cohabit within the boundary of this villa."[25] Though somewhat crude, this rule retained the essential idea that food and fodder were an item of general taxation, whereas hospitality was a legitimate personal inconvenience. Food was one thing, shelter another.[26] Ro-

[23] *Variae* 5. 23 (young archers being escorted to their commander), 4. 45 (Herules coming to court); the Gepids, 5. 10-11; garrisons, 2. 5, 5. 13, 5. 39. 15, 10. 18; officer's role, 3. 42, 10. 18 (cf. Vegetius *Epitoma rei militaris* 3. 3 and Appendix E, below). Other letters on the issue of rations: 3. 40-42 (the army in Gaul), 3. 51, 3. 53. 5, 4. 13 (to a military *vir illustris*).

[24] *LVisig* 9. 2. 6 (*Antiqua*; for the meaning of this term, below, Chapter IV at n. 5). Cf. *Variae* 5. 13, which seems to be addressed to persons resembling the *annonarii* of the Visigothic law.

In connection with *LVisig* 9. 2. 6, it is exceptionally interesting to observe that, under Justinian, the East Roman regiments called *foederati* were headed, though not at war, by *optiones*, a title comparable to *annonarius*; see Jones, *LRE*, pp. 626, 664-665; *CJ* 4. 65. 35. 1; Justinian *Novel.* 116, 117. 11 (542); equivalence of *annonarius* to *optio*, *CTh* 8. 1. 3 (333).

[25] *LBurg* 38. 3-4. Cf. Cassiodorus *Variae* 4. 45. Governors (*iudices*) on circuit were entitled to be fed for three days but no more in the *municipia* where they stopped: *NMajor* 7. 17 (458); *Variae* 5. 14. 7, specifies that this was a charge on the *pauperes*.

[26] The classification of shelter apart from food was so deeply entrenched in custom that it passed uninterruptedly to the Carolingian period. The capitularies from 768 to 814 and beyond repeatedly affirm the prerogative of those traveling on royal business: no one may deny them a roof and fire, if the weather is inclement, or grass for their beasts; but travelers seizing anything more are subject to making multiple restitution on complaint by the victim. See MGH *Capitularia*, vol. 1, pp. 43, 116, 144, 152, 198-199, 429 (Ansegis

man quartering was concerned exclusively with providing official travelers with a roof over their heads; it had nothing to do with land or its produce.

These observations suggest that, although the laws on quartering are not irrelevant to barbarian settlement, they do not deserve the prominence they are usually accorded. The Theodosian Code contains a precedent for assigning to a soldier one-third, or even one-half, of a house, but the similarity of fraction does not help at all to explain the granting to Burgundians of "one-third of the bondsmen and two-thirds of the arable from that place where hospitality has been assigned to them."[27] The rule quoted here, and its Visigothic and Ostrogothic counterparts, can on no account

---

Capitularium 3. 39). The right of Frankish kings to exact *hospitium* for their *legatarii* from everyone was written into *Lex Ribvaria* 68. 3, ed. R. Buchner, MGH *Leges*, vol. 3, pt. 2, p. 119. This looks like a direct survival from the prerogatives of the Roman state, even though possibly related to *LBurg* 38, as proposed by Franz Beyerle, "Das Gesetzbuch Ribvariens," *ZRG, Germ.* 55 (1935): 22. The right to requisition shelter from everybody was distinct from the envoys' *tractoria*, which, in its seventh-century form, specified the per diem of remounts, food, and fodder that royal agents were to supply to the bearers by requisition from *loca consuetudinaria*: Marculf *Formulae* 1. 11, ed. K. Zeumer, MGH *Formulae*, p. 49. Such requisitions were a special tax, distinct from the general obligation to provide shelter, and they affected a limited category of the population: *Capitulare de villis* 27, MGH *Capitularia*, vol. 1, p. 85, "homines illi qui antiquitus consueti fuerunt missos aut legationes soniare."

[27] *LBurg* 54. 1 (text at the opening of Chapter v). It is astonishing to observe how casually modern authors have accepted the idea that rules for dividing a house were extended to the division of someone's complete property. For example, Otto Seeck, *Geschichte des Untergangs der antiken Welt*, vol. 6 (Stuttgart, 1921), p. 129: "A tripartition corresponding to [*CTh* 7. 8. 5] was now also introduced for the landed property that the Romans had to yield to the German being settled *aber mit dem sehr wesentlichen Unterschiede* that the latter claimed two-thirds and that only one-third was left to the former owner." If matters had taken this course, the really "essential difference" would surely have been, not the proportions, but the jump from temporary use of a dwelling to full ownership of a total estate.

be regarded as simple extensions, or broad interpretations, of an old Roman principle. If the fifth-century settlements were different from arbitrary acts of conquest and expropriation—and the circumstances in which they occurred certainly suggest a large measure of Roman consent and legality—then they must be related to something other than quartering.

The alternative is not difficult to find, and it has not completely escaped the attention of earlier commentators. Ludwig Schmidt, who (as we have seen) realized that the *annona* was collected from landowners, ventured the idea that Odoacer's soldiers demanded to have assigned to themselves "a third of the arable land destined to the delivery of the *annona*."[28] Whether or not this statement is accurate does not matter for the moment. Its value resides in Schmidt's acknowledgment that, behind the assignment to soldiers of productive land and cultivators, we must see, not the system of quartering, but the laws governing soldiers' salaries and citizens' taxes; Gaupp had also been aware of this.[29] There may have been a time, though none is documented, when the Visigoths or Burgundians quartered in a Roman province were officially supplied with rations from public storehouses; it is almost certain that the army of Italy, composed of barbarians, had been provided for in this way until the mutiny of 476.[30] The settlement of all

---

[28] Schmidt, *Ostgermanen*, p. 316.

[29] To the extent of giving a careful account of military supply and recognizing that *hospitalitas* afforded only shelter: Gaupp, *Ansiedlungen*, pp. 79-85, 88.

[30] Gaupp, *Ansiedlungen*, pp. 198-200, 317, insisted on a period of transition from the receipt of rations to the award of allotments; cf. Lot, "Hospitalité," pp. 1007-1008, and Courcelle, *Hist. litt.*, p. 143, who insisted on this point but without evidence. The Visigoths at least had experience with ration issues for many years before 418. On Italy, Lot, p. 1000; Schmidt, *Ostgermanen*, p. 316. The continued, though limited, issue of rations under Theodoric (above, n. 23) suggests that the mechanism had still been running smoothly in 476.

these peoples, when it took place, was an act of commutation—the exchange of daily rations for a permanent endowment. Moreover, if this endowment replaced rations, it had to guarantee a reliable, effort-free revenue, requiring no agricultural exertions on the part of the barbarian recipient. How could the state provide barbarians, or anyone else, with endowments of this special kind?

From the late third century onward, taxation in the empire might be said to have described a complex circuit, beginning with a landowner's declaration of private assets (*professio censualis*), continuing with the emperor's announcement of the tax rate for the year (*delegatio*), followed by the payer's tax contribution (*annona*), and ending, after suitable transport, storage, and paperwork, with the issue to soldiers, officers, and civil servants of their daily rations (also called *annona*), which varied from simple to multiple according to rank.[31] The *annona* was not the only tax, nor even alone in being levied upon the landowners' assessment declarations. Moreover, the forms of taxpaying and military issue were affected by various modifications as the fourth century went on, notably by laws tending to commute transactions in commodities into payments and issues in money. The Roman tax system in the early fifth century differed considerably from what it had been under Diocletian, and its evolution had had serious effects upon the contributors as well as upon the army. If the details of these changes were better known, the barbarian settlements in the West would be easier to explain.[32] However that may

[31] Among general accounts, that of Jones, *LRE*, pp. 448-460, has the rare virtue of not permitting the circuit of state income and expenditures to be obscured by excessive attention to assessment units.

[32] Other taxes: *CTh* 7. 6 (*vestis militaris*); the papyrus analyzed by André Déléage, *La Capitation du Bas-Empire* (Mâcon, 1945), pp. 73-74. Changes in taxation and military pay: André Cérati, *Caractère annonaire et assiette de l'impôt foncier au Bas-Empire* (Aix-en-Provence, 1969), part 1; Jones, *LRE*, pp. 629-630 (military pay); Walter Goffart, *"Caput" and Colonate: Towards a History of Late*

be, nothing had occurred to disrupt the basic circuit traced by the flow of state revenues and outlays: at one end of the line, there stood the taxpayer's *professio* of assets, at the other, the salary or rations issued to the servants of the state, or at least owed to them.

A term within this circuit deserving special attention is *delegatio*, the emperor's announcement of the tax rate. *Delegatio* in private law meant the "assignment of a debt": B owes a sum to A, and C owes the same amount to B; by "delegating" C's debt to A, B may discharge his indebtedness.[33] The modern procedure of writing a check on one's bank account offers a familiar analogy: by means of a check, the debt of the bank to its depositor is "delegated" to some person or firm to which the depositor is in debt. The system of "delegation" is adaptable to a variety of circumstances. In the public context of imperial finances, the taxpayers owed to the emperor, who owed to his salaried servants; by the annual *delegatio*, the emperor assigned the salary account to the taxpayers for discharge. Understandably, the imperial debt was not assigned to taxpayers in person. What the emperor's *delegatio* laid down was the tax rate on the aggregate assessment, that is to say, the property declared by the taxpayers in their *professiones*; if these assets, chiefly productive land, paid their tax at the announced rate, then the emperor's debt for the year was satisfied.[34]

Roman Taxation (Toronto, 1974), pp. 83-84 with n. 54. An important development from the taxpayer's standpoint was the apparent freezing of the tax rate, in lieu of annually variable *delegationes*, best attested by the establishment of a fixed charge on assessments: W. Goffart, "From Roman Taxation to Medieval Seigneurie: Three Notes," *Speculum* 47 (1972): 380-381.

[33] W. W. Buckland, *A Text-book of Roman Law*, 2d ed. (Cambridge, 1932), pp. 570, 253.

[34] For a general account of the imperial *delegatio*, Johannes Karayannopoulos, *Das Finanzwesen des frühbyzantinischen Staat* (Munich, 1958), pp. 87-90. But, to my knowledge, the significance to taxation

Such terminology presupposes (at least in our thinking) that the citizens' *professiones* itemized the capital that guaranteed the emperor's aggregate indebtedness. Citizens owned private property (*possessiones*), but, when such property was booked into a tax declaration, it took on the special character of a capital asset of the state, yielding through taxes an annual dividend or interest charge, and being at the emperor's disposal in respect to its annual tax payment.[35] The government even had ways of dividing these capital assets into official units of account—called *iuga, capita, millenae,* or *centuriae,* depending on the region —which neatly simplified the disorderly complexities of privately owned farms and expressed only those aspects of property that interested the state. These units of account were not land but, rather, "shares of assessment" in the apportioning of levies and "shares of proceeds" in the apportioning of tax yields. Naturally, a taxpayer continued to be the owner of his property and in full charge of its management; the assets declared by private owners were distinct from the public lands of the state. But the state had a claim upon the *professiones* booked in its assessment records, a claim that might be realized in other ways than by merely collecting the declarant's annual tax payment.[36]

When these mechanisms and presuppositions of late Roman taxation are kept in mind, it is difficult to escape the impression that they may have provided the legal basis for the award to (barbarian) soldiers of the arable, bondsmen, and woods of provincial taxpayers. For, if the state met its obligations to the troops by collecting the tax proceeds of citizens' *professiones,* then it was not illogical for it to discharge the same obligation by assigning to each

---

of this term—the emperor transferring his debt to the taxpayers—has never been observed.

[35] Cf. Goffart, *Caput,* pp. 105-106.

[36] For these units, Goffart, *Caput,* pp. 31-65, 91-98, and Goffart, "Three Notes," pp. 167-174.

soldier an appropriate fragment of *professio* and leaving it to him to collect the tax at its source. The citizen presumably lost nothing by the exchange: he retained ownership of his property (*possessio*) and continued to pay its tax; only his assessment declaration (*professio*) passed out of state records and into the hands of a state employee.[37] The soldier, for his part, need not have gained any increase in stipend, but he obtained permanent tenure of that stipend for himself and his descendants, and he avoided the chicanery customarily endured at the hands of those paying salaries.[38] If any party lost in the process, it was the state: fewer bureaucrats were needed to service the tax machinery, assessments were eliminated from its books, troops enjoyed security of stipend regardless of whether they fought or not. But that is precisely where one would expect the losses to have been concentrated. As we shall presently see, the barbarian settlements were carried out with little or no protest on the part of the Roman provincials. Such a result can hardly be explained unless the costs were chiefly absorbed by the state.

To sum up, Roman quartering imposed upon the owners of houses only the obligation to provide soldiers with shelter. No doubt it played a part in the barbarian settlements, but it does not help to explain their most salient feature— the assignment to each qualified Visigoth, Burgundian, Ostrogoth, or whatever of a landed allotment, an allotment, moreover, that yielded immediate and reliable returns. The legal basis for these allotments was provided partly by tax law and partly by the laws governing the

---

[37] Goffart, "Three Notes," pp. 381-386.

[38] For chicanery, Aurelius Victor *De Caesaribus* 33. 13, ed. P. Dufraigne, Budé (Paris, 1975); *CJ* 12. 37. 16 (Anastasius); Cassiodorus *Variae* 1. 10 (very eloquent); perhaps also Sidonius *Epistolae* 5. 7. 3 (*stipendia paludatis*). The hereditary obligation of military service in the later empire was at least a first step toward the permanence of stipends (though certainly not applied in this way at first; but the treatment of *res familiaris* in *CTh* 7. 22. 2, 5, 11 is suggestive, and so is *CTh* 7. 1. 11).

issue of military rations. The latter established the state's obligation to its soldiers, the former, its claim upon the taxpayers and their registered agricultural property. Together, they justified the rapprochement between taxpayers and tax recipients that the barbarian allotments principally entailed.

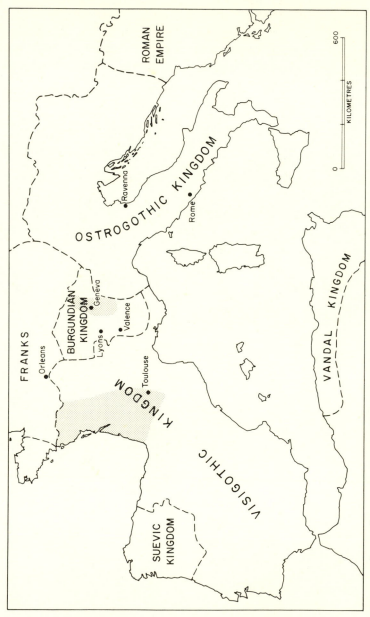

Map 1. The Barbarian Kingdoms, ca. A.D. 500

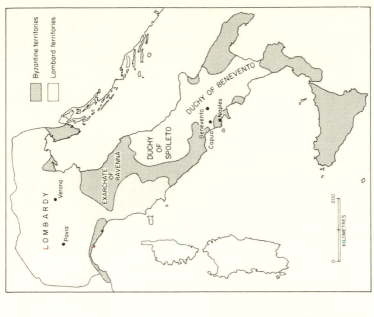

Map 2. Italy, ca. A.D. 600

Explanatory Note

The political boundaries shown are highly approximate; the maps are meant to provide only a general geographical context for the allotments to barbarians.

Orleans and Valence appear on Map 1 in order to illustrate the Alan settlements discussed in Chapter IV. The shaded portions of the same map indicate the narrower extent of Visigothic and Burgundian territories some fifty years before 500. The Italian kingdom of Odoacer (476-489) lacked the eastward extension of its Ostrogothic successor.

III

ALLOTMENTS IN
FIFTH-CENTURY ITALY

As currently explained, the installation of the barbarians in Gaul and Italy is altogether paradoxical. On the one hand, it is said to have necessitated the expropriation of one-third, one-half, or two-thirds of Roman properties in the district of settlement; and, in Italy at least, the expropriation is understood to have applied to all Roman proprietors, relieving them, without exception, of one-third of their fortunes. On the other hand, no evidence has survived to document or even to suggest a correspondingly drastic blow to private property.[1] There is no direct proof that Romans were officially deprived of their estates; expropriation itself is an inference, based principally on the misconception that Roman *hospitalitas* entailed the cession of land. The generals Constantius and Aëtius, who organized the Visigothic and the Burgundian settlements respectively (418 and 443), dealt with the barbarians from positions of strength; circumstances did not compel them to dispossess the provincials in order to accommodate the federate soldiers.[2] The only incident of landowners' resistance to barbarians about which we are informed occurs in an area of northern Gaul where Roman state control had broken down several dec-

---

[1] Delbrück, *Kriegskunst*, vol. 2, p. 346, thought that an expropriation of two-thirds of Roman lands would have been "a revolution in ownership unparalleled elsewhere in history"; Fustel de Coulanges, *Invasion germanique*, p. 537, spoke convincingly of the consequences that massive expropriations would have had if they had taken place.

[2] Thompson, "Settlement," pp. 65-67, rightly stressed the generals' initiative; these settlements "were in no sense a Roman compromise with the barbarians."

ades before.[3] In the southwest and east, there is no trace of protest, let alone of resistance, to allotment, and the major landowners are known to have retained their preeminence, without discernible loss, under barbarian rule.[4] As for Italy, where the allotment scheme affected all landowners, the good relations of the senate with Odoacer and Theodoric are a well-established fact, and we are assured by sources difficult to discount that proprietary relationships were not overturned. As Ennodius put the matter, "innumerable bands of Goths" were enriched "with the Romans hardly feeling it."[5] The contrast between the supposed rigors of settlement and its documented impact is vivid and disturbing. Once it is realized, one cannot help questioning the premise of expropriation.

Well aware of the paradox, several scholars have attempted to resolve it, usually by qualifications of various kinds, such as that the settlements affected limited areas and that only a minority of landowners lost land.[6] E. A. Thompson has argued on a more general plane that the Gallo-Romans willingly endured heavy sacrifices of property for the sake of military assistance against the internal threat of the Bacaudae.[7] Another possibility is that the barbarian settlements were calmly borne because they had little effect on

[3] Discussed below, Chapter IV at n. 14.

[4] Karl Friedrich Stroheker, *Der senatorische Adel im spätantiken Gallien* (Tübingen, 1948), pp. 43-105; Wallace-Hadrill, "Gothia," pp. 33-34.

[5] Johannes Sundwall, *Abhandlungen zur Geschichte des ausgehenden Römertums* (Helsinki, 1919), pp. 180-189; Ernst Stein, *Histoire du Bas-Empire*, vol. 2 (Paris, 1949), pp. 41-46; André Chastagnol, *Le sénat romain sous le règne d'Odoacre*, Antiquitas, 3d ser., vol. 3 (Bonn, 1966), pp. 52-56. The extract from Ennodius *Epistolae* 9. 23 is quoted in full below n. 25.

[6] For example, Delbrück, *Kriegskunst*, vol. 2, pp. 346-347; Lot, "Hospitalité," pp. 989-993; Thompson, "Settlement," pp. 68-69. An earlier authority, Karl Binding, *Das burgundisch-romanische Königreich (von 443-532 n. Chr.)* (1868; repr. ed., Aalen, 1969), pp. 34-35, was unperturbed by the idea of massive expropriations.

[7] Thompson, "Settlement," pp. 70-74.

private fortunes.[8] The hypothesis of the present study is that it was not *hospitalitas* but the tax system, through the mechanism already described, that permitted the Roman state to provide for the barbarians and to require no more from Roman subjects than the taxes they were accustomed to contribute; the allotments that the barbarians were awarded consisted of existing tax assessments and the revenues they yielded, and not of private property wrested from its owners. It will later be argued that an allotment scheme of this kind was instituted in Gaul. In Italy, its existence can be positively documented, but not without a complete reappraisal of the evidence.

With minor variations, the accepted account of the Italian settlement is as follows (the applicable sources are indicated in parentheses): In the days of Romulus Augustulus, the barbarians forming the army of Italy mutinied when their demand for "one-third of the land of Italy" was denied; they overthrew the emperor, under the leadership of Odoacer, who granted their wish (Procopius). Every Italian landowner either relinquished one-third of his estates to one of Odoacer's soldiers or paid the government a new tax—the *illatio tertiarum*—consisting of one-third of his revenue (Cassiodorus). This arrangement underwent little change when Theodoric installed his rule: the old allotments were redistributed to the Ostrogoths (Procopius), and the tax was continued. The fact that the expropriation had occurred under Odoacer explains the contemporary allegation that Theodoric's allotments were hardly felt by the Italians (Cassiodorus, Ennodius). Allot-

[8] A form of this argument was developed by Fustel de Coulanges, *Nouvelles recherches*, pp. 279-305, where he also took into account the criticism addressed to an earlier version of his views by Julien Havet, "Du partage des terres entre les Romains et les barbares chez les Burgondes et les Visigoths," *Revue historique* 6 (1878): 87-99. The strength of Fustel's case resided in its insistence that there had been no expropriation (pp. 293-294); he himself was less than satisfied with the alternative interpretation he proposed of how the settlements had taken place.

ments were awarded by *delegatores*, issuing a *pittacium delegationis* to each qualified barbarian (Cassiodorus). Because the Ostrogoths, like their predecessors, received fractions of variably sized private estates, there was no uniformity whatever in allotments. As far as the Italians were concerned, a mitigating circumstance was that Theodoric, and probably Odoacer as well, forced the barbarians to continue paying the normal tax on the lands they received (Cassiodorus).[9]

There would be little to change in this account if the sources justified the inferences drawn from them. But they do not. Procopius, whose testimony is accorded extreme importance, lived two generations after Odoacer and portrayed his usurpation in a context that one is better advised to doubt than to believe. The stellar witness, Cassiodorus, does not tell us that Ostrogoths were taxed on their allotments; he does not describe the *illatio tertiarum* of the Romans as a confiscatory surtax; and he never hints that the "thirds" were a holdover from Odoacer's regime. Finally, an important item has been neglected: in the *Variae* of Cassiodorus, Gothic allotment holders are once called *millenarii*, "holders of *millenae*," that is to say, holders of a "unit of tax assessment"—a direct indication not only of the composition of allotments but also of their being of standard size. These various items will be examined one by one.

We learn from Cassiodorus that the distribution of Gothic allotments was called *deputatio tertiarum*, and that the tax paid by Romans in lieu of allotment was the *illatio ter-*

---

[9] The interpreters differ little among themselves over this account: Ludo Moritz Hartmann, *Geschichte Italiens im Mittelalter*, vol. 1 (Gotha, 1897), pp. 93-94 (authoritative); Giulio Romano and A. Solmi, *La dominazione barbariche in Italia (395-888)* (Milan, 1940), pp. 114, 123-125, 167-168; Heinrich Brunner, *Deutsche Rechtsgeschichte*, 2d ed. (Leipzig, 1906), vol. 1, p. 77; Schmidt, *Ostgermanen*, pp. 316-317, 327-329, 362-363; Ensslin, *Theodorich*, pp. 94-97, 205; Stein, *Bas-Empire*, vol. 2, pp. 41-43, 119; Giovanni Tabacco in *Storia d'Italia*, vol. 2, *Della caduta dell' Impero al secolo XVIII* (Turin, 1974), pp. 23, 33.

tiarum. Thus the term *tertiae*, "thirds," regardless of precisely how it must be defined, is central to the allotments carried out in Theodoric's time. A major dignitary, Liberius, serving as praetorian prefect, was charged with providing for the Goths and gained high praise for acquitting himself ably of an arduous task.[10] Neither Cassiodorus nor Ennodius suggests that the "thirds," as allotments or as tax, had been a part of the Italian scene for some twenty years prior to Theodoric, or that Liberius simply transferred the losers' holdings to the winners.[11] The silence of these authors does not, of course, exclude the possibility of institutional continuity from Odoacer (Liberius himself was a holdover). It is odd, however, that the early sources fail to confirm Procopius. If his story is to be believed, it must stand on its own.

The credibility of Procopius in this instance should not be evaluated in isolation from the other information of the same sort that he supplies; the issue raised here is a fragment of a much larger problem confronting modern users of the *History of the Wars.* Along with the many chapters that Procopius wrote as a strict contemporary, carrying out the role of a reporter and often an eyewitness, he is also responsible for chapters of a very different kind that set out historical and ethnographic background.[12] Modern histo-

[10] *Variae* 2. 16. 5 (*deputatio*; also Liberius); 1. 14, 2. 17 (*illatio*). Several authors have understood *deputatio* as a "commission" or "board" presided by Liberius: Felix Dahn, *Die Könige der Germanen,* vol. 3 (Würzburg, 1866), p. 5; Bury, *Later Roman Empire,* vol. 1, p. 453; Romano and Solmi, *Dominazione barbariche,* p. 167; Ernesto Pontieri, *Le invasioni barbariche e l'Italia del V e VI secolo* (Naples, 1960), p. 162. The correct meaning is almost certainly "assignment"; see *Variae* 3. 35, where Liberius *constiterit deputasse* pursuant to the king's *ordinatio.*

[11] For Ennodius, below n. 25.

[12] Berthold Rubin, "Prokopios von Kaisareia," in *PW* 23 (1957), the currently authoritative treatment, recognized the distinctive character of the introductory chapters (cols. 309, 359-360), but did not class with them the ethnographic sections like *Bell. Goth.* 1. 12 (the Franks), 2. 14-15 (the Heruli), 4. 5 (the Huns).

rians value these chapters of background very much, for ethnographic information is rare, and Procopius's historical introductions are chiefly about the otherwise badly documented fifth century. Our books accord a place of honor to his testimony on these subjects and hinge some very important notions upon his word alone. In the matter of most immediate concern, we would not prize his version of Odoacer's usurpation if the older testimony available to us were wholly satisfactory.[13] Now, Procopius has an enviable reputation for excellence and veracity as a reporter, but does this reputation carry over to the nonreportorial chapters? Can their contents be cited with confidence, as though reliably factual? No sustained and comprehensive attempt has yet been made to supply an authoritative answer; even Rubin's voluminous commentary offers little guidance.[14]

[13] Major generalizations in Germanic *Frühgeschichte* depend on *Bell. Vandal.* 1. 22. 1-12 (emigrants kept in touch with tribesmen who stayed behind) and *Bell. Goth.* 2. 15 (some east Germans returned to Scandinavia in the sixth century): Schmidt, *Ostgermanen*, pp. 107, 548, 535-555; Schwarz, *Germ. Stammesk.*, pp. 51-52, and *Zur germ. Stammesk.*, p. 295. (Modern users suppress Procopius's own qualifications: contact between the two groups of Vandals had long been lost; far from the Heruli's having any primitive associations with Thule, their ancestral homes were just north of the Danube.) Odoacer alone is at the center of early accounts of 476; only Procopius states that an army mutiny overthrew Orestes. See Bury, *Later Roman Empire*, vol. 1, pp. 405-406; Jones, *LRE*, pp. 244, 1114 (n. 13); Stroheker, *Germanentum und Spätantike*, pp. 98-99, none of whom intimates that the testimony of Procopius—which they prefer to any other—is less trustworthy than that of the other authorities.

[14] Rubin, "Prokopios," col. 309, specified that, though surpassed by contemporaries as an antiquarian, Procopius is unrivaled as an historian of his time. The distinction is well established: Edward Gibbon, *A History of the Decline and Fall of the Roman Empire*, ed. J. B. Bury (London, 1896-1900), vol. 3, p. 479 n. 76, with Bury's appendix, ibid., vol. 4, pp. 515-516; Averil Cameron, ed., *Procopius*, Great Histories Series (New York, 1967), p. xviii. Although Rubin, col. 360, recognized that, in the introductions, Procopius was not narrating early history for its own sake, his comments on individual chapters miss many details and presuppose, in general, that errors were unintentional, the result, for example, of defective extracts from

Yet guidance is badly needed, for Procopius is anything but a reporter when he looks beyond the experiences of his time and place. This trait is well known to modern users. Ludwig Schmidt, for instance, noted that what Procopius wrote about periods earlier than his own "is often unreliable and of an anecdotal character."[15] The point that needs clarification is whether innocence or conscious choice lies behind such passages: did Procopius unintentionally reproduce the errors of defective sources, or did he select, arrange, and alter a rich fund of information into forms that suited his purposes?

When innocence and sincerity are assumed, Procopius is trusted to have collected and passed on as much accurate matter as came to hand. His accounts are thus believable unless demonstrably false, and fragments of fact may be confidently extracted even from visibly fictional contexts.

Priscus (col. 309). Also along these lines, Jakob Haury, *Zur Beurteilung des Geschichtsschreibers Procopius von Cäsarea* (Munich, 1896), pp. 20-27.

What may be in question here is, not Procopius's credibility as such, but a precise definition of the genre that these introductory chapters and digressions belong to. Cf. Arnaldo Momigliano, "Some Observations on the *Origo gentis Romanae*," in Momigliano, *Secondo contributo alla storia degli studi classici*, Storia e letteratura 77 (Rome, 1960), p. 166, "A brief 'mythical' preface to monographs on recent history (an 'Archaeologia') was in style" (with reference to the late Roman Republic). There would be an exact parallel if Procopius were taken, as he might be, to write a succession of monographs on recent history.

[15] Schmidt, *Ostgermanen*, p. 30. As observed by Leopold von Ranke, *Weltgeschichte*, vol. 4 (Leipzig, 1883), pp. 288-289, Procopius made mistakes when dealing with distant places as well as with distant times. Alfred Schulz, *Procopius, de bello Vandalico Lib. I, 1-8, Eine historische Untersuchung* (Berlin, 1871), took the right critical direction, particularly in downplaying Priscus as a source. I have not been able to consult M. Brückner, *Zur Beurteilung des Geschichtsschreibers Procopius von Caesarea* (Ansbach, 1896), who (according to Bury, appendix to Gibbon, *History of the Decline and Fall*, vol. 4, p. 516) taxed Procopius in these chapters with "want both of historical sense and of conscientiousness."

Without being spelled out, this doctrine seems to have generally guided the historians who mine Procopius for information on subjects outside his field of direct vision, such as the regime of Odoacer.

Yet the presumption of innocence hardly does justice to the contemporary evidence potentially available to Procopius if he had meant to be meticulous in recreating the recent past. Neither does it take sufficient account of the wide scope of the fictions embodied in his works. For example, Procopius turns the Persian king into the guardian of Theodosius II, eliminates the Huns (though not Attila) from the fifth-century invasions, has Aëtius die earlier than Attila, and adapts to the assassination of Aëtius a saying that had been formerly applied to a less famous general.[16] These are not casual errors in otherwise trustworthy narrative; on the contrary, the glue that holds the larger narratives together often consists of misinformation, without which the coherence of the story would vanish. An outstanding instance occurs in the brilliant sketch of Gothic wanderings that opens the *Vandal War*—probably the first general history of the barbarian invasions, foreshadowing the syntheses that are still attempted today. Although wholly admirable from a literary standpoint, Procopius's sketch is misleading history, carried along by anachronism, tele-

---

[16] *Bell. Pers.* 1. 2. 7-11 (to 1. 2. 4, cf. the equally fanciful account of John Malalas *Chron.*, ed. L. Dindorf [Bonn, 1831], p. 350, according to which Honorius went East to make his nephew coemperor); roughly speaking, *Bell. Vandal.* 1. 3-5 cover the period from 395 to the 460s, but, although Attila appears at 1. 4. 24, he merely heads "a great army of Massagetae and the other Scythians"—vague Herodotean names (in the Hunnic ethnography of *Bell. Goth.* 4. 5, the motifs usually associated with fourth-century Huns are transposed to those of the sixth century); *Bell. Vandal.* 1. 4. 27-29 (a famous error, attributed by Rubin, "Prokopios," col. 405, to poor sources, but cf. Schulz, pp. 4-5); *Bell. Vandal.* 1. 4. 28, cf. Damascius *Life of Isidore* 91 (pre-526, see c. 64) = Photius *Bibliot.* cod. 242, ed. R. Henry, *Photius*, Budé, vol. 6 (Paris, 1971), p. 27, the comment of the Vandal Geiseric on the treacherous death of Marcellinus in 468.

scoped chronology, *suppressio veri*, and outright legends.[17] His objective in these chapters was not to portray the past with fidelity but to provide a firm and compendious background to sixth-century events; he assembled and edited the facts in whatever ways seemed best to attain this goal. The resources of accurate information he could draw upon were incomparably richer than the debris available to us, but this consideration is merely frustrating to the modern user of the *Wars*, for a Procopian statement may be wholly false and yet be composed almost entirely of unimpeachable fact. To take an imaginary instance, there would be a world of difference between the mutineers' demanding "one-third of the land of Italy" in 476 and their asking for the same fraction of (shall we say) public land. Yet Procopius cannot be trusted to have included the adjective or other little qualifier that distinguishes truth from fiction: the operative criterion was his convenience, a matter that is almost wholly beyond our ken.[18]

[17] Rubin, "Prokopios," col. 402, insisted on Priscus as source (perhaps on the premise that Priscus is the single source independently used by Procopius, Theophanes, and Nicephorus Callistus—a premise that needs very careful testing). The contents of Procopius's sketch, e.g., the suppression of the Huns (common to the later texts), make Priscus unlikely: he would have known better. Eustathius of Epiphania (ca. 518) may be preferable, but there are other possibilities. For anachronism, *Bell. Vandal.* 1. 2. 6 (the Gepids); telescoped chronology, *Bell. Goth.* 1. 1. 9 (the Ostrogoths); *suppressio veri* (treatment of Attila's Huns, as n. 16); legends, e.g., *Bell. Vandal.* 1. 2. 25-26 (Honorius's reaction at Rome's fall to Alaric). No one seems to notice that at ibid. 1. 2. 10, Procopius rejects in a few words the magnificently distorted legend of Rome's fall told by John Malalas, ed. Dindorf, pp. 349-350 (much copied in later Byzantine chronography); he objects to the story because it is out of keeping with Honorius's character, his own knowledge of which is spelled out in the very dubious *Bell. Vandal.* 1. 2. 25-26.

[18] For a parallel instance: Procopius reports a law issued for the benefit of Spanish landowners in the early fifth century (*Bell. Vandal.* 1. 3. 3); this might be true, though basically anachronistic in the context supplied by Levy, *Law of Property*, pp. 184-190; as Schulz (above, n. 15) cogently argued, Procopius is more likely to be trans-

Procopius was in Italy from 536 to 540 and wrote the *Gothic War* in the mid-540s. It would have been possible, though not necessarily easy, for him to gather precise information about Odoacer's usurpation and the land settlement it occasioned more than sixty years before. The question is whether or not he took the trouble to do so: "Procopius is a fabulous writer for the events which precede his own memory."[19] One thing is obvious about the chapters that interest us, namely, that Procopius was not primarily concerned with supplying a dispassionately exact report of what happened in 476. The account of the barbarians' demand to be given "one-third of the land of Italy" occurs in an introductory chapter and is deployed to best dramatic advantage: the soldiers' ultimatum in 476 was the culminating point in a pattern of increasingly outrageous barbarian behavior, the deplorable result of a series of misfortunes reaching back "some time earlier"—by our chronology, as far back as to the late fourth century—when the Romans first committed the error of entering into alliance with barbarians. This sad tale of mounting barbarian insolence could hardly be better climaxed than with a call for the expropriation of a full third of all Italian land; a Constantinopolitan audience that might be indifferent to distant wars and ravages might personally identify with the confiscation of private property.[20]

---

posing to Spain a favor granted to dispossessed African landowners: *NValent III* 35. 1. 12 (452), cf. ibid. 12 (443), 34 (451). This was also the view of Ludwig Schmidt, *Histoire des Vandales,* trans. H. C. Del Medico (Paris, 1953), pp. 31-32.

[19] Gibbon, *History of the Decline and Fall,* vol. 3, p. 479 n. 76. The *Wars* were written between 542 and 545 but published only in the spring of 551: Rubin, "Prokopios," col. 354.

[20] *Bell. Goth.* 1. 1. 2-8 (cf. especially *Bell. Vandal.* 1. 2-8, whose tales of Alaric and Attila are specifically evoked in *Bell. Goth.* 1. 1. 3). The commentary of Rubin, "Prokopios," col. 428, does not go far enough (e.g., nothing about the demand for land). Procopius states that a little before Augustulus the Romans had first made alliances with barbarians, to wit, Alans, Sciri, and other Gothic peoples. Be-

How indulgently should this narrative be read? Procopius was in a better position than we to know that Roman alliances with barbarians were not a novelty that began with the emperor Arcadius (395-408); like us, he could easily have recognized that the link between Alaric and Odoacer was tenuous and that the latter's usurpation was a consequence of the decades of Italian instability after the murder of Valentinian III, rather than of barbarian arrogance. We are right to applaud Procopius for writing a short and highly effective assessment of the course of events leading to the overthrow of Romulus Augustulus, but the literary skill he manifests ought not to be confused with

---

cause of the immediate connection made to Alaric, this might refer to the time of Arcadius (as in *Bell. Vandal.* 1. 2. 7), but the names themselves rather precisely suggest the peoples associated with Odoacer in other sources (*Excerpta Valesiana* 37, ed. J. Moreau [Leipzig, 1968]: Sciri; Marcellinus Comes *Chron.* a. 476 [MGH *AA*, vol. 11, p. 91]: Goths; Jordanes *Romana* 344, *Getica* 242: Torcilingi [=Alans?], Sciri, Heruli). Another instance, it would seem, when Procopius deliberately telescoped chronology.

The reference to a demand for land is not isolated. Cf. *Bell. Vandal.* 1. 3. 3, about Spain (above, n. 18); and ibid. 1. 5. 11-15, about Geiseric's confiscations in Africa. (Neither is commented on by Rubin, cols. 403, 406.) Procopius only implies expropriation in Italy, whereas his account of partial dispossessions and confiscatory taxation by the Vandals is altogether explicit. The Vandal passage deserves more critical handling than it got from Courtois, *Vandales*, pp. 276-283, who, however, assembled much relevant information. The measures described by Procopius are too loosely dated (ostensibly after 455, but not necessarily) and they compare poorly in precision to the settlement detailed by Victor Vitensis *Historia persecutionis Vandalicae* 1. 12-14, ed. C. Halm, MGH *AA*, vol. 3, p. 4, which may be precisely identical. Victor is not a cool narrator, but Procopius exceeds him in darkly coloring the facts. It is interesting, for our purposes, that Victor speaks of Geiseric's dividing one province among his army *funiculo hereditatis*; since provinces are public districts and since Procopius says that the grants to the soldiers were tax free (*Bell. Vandal.* 1. 5. 14), Geiseric seems to have carried out something very similar—as will be seen—to the allotments in Italy and Gaul. One would have difficulty inferring this from Procopius alone, whose language persistently evokes private property.

historical precision. The impressionistic inaccuracy of the context hardly lends credibility to his report of the culminating act.[21] Procopius also prefers Theodoric to Odoacer and calls on the allotments a second time in order to give point to the contrast between the two barbarian leaders. Theodoric allegedly abstained from all injustice, "except that the Goths divided among themselves the part of the land which Odoacer had given to his followers";[22] in other words, it was too much to expect that Theodoric should have undone the damage perpetrated by his predecessor, but at least he bore no responsibility for the initial outrage.

Three points merit special attention: in keeping with Byzantine tradition, Procopius despised Odoacer as a tyrant and respected Theodoric's character and achievements; the alleged role of the army in 476 and the forthright implication that Italian landowners were obliged to yield one-third of their real estate are new in the history available to us; the wider context is a criticism of the ostensibly novel Roman practice of cooperating with barbarians. The Italian allotments in Procopius are not a neutral fact, therefore, but a dramatic highlight. We stand on more solid ground in doubting the substance of his narrative than we would in accepting it as historically true.

There is no scientific way to extract nuggets of fact from basically dubious but unique information. We can choose to believe some parts of Procopius's report and would probably be hypercritical not to do so, but anyone's choice is no better than a personal guess. A cautious selection would be that the soldiers insisted on allotments in 476, that Odoacer satisfied their demand, and even that Odoacer's grants were later redistributed among the more numerous Ostrogoths.

[21] M. A. Wes, *Das Ende des Kaisertum im Westen des römischen Reiches* (The Hague, 1967), pp. 71, 81, pointed out that Procopius is the unique source for the *Bodenreform* (as he called it), and he praised the vision (*durchdringsten Blick*) Procopius manifests in interpreting the incident. Procopius's vision merits praise, but it does not authenticate his facts.

[22] *Bell. Goth.* 1. 1. 26-31 (esp., 27-28).

Since one or more of these points may be quite false, it seems irresponsible to extract more from these chapters of the *Gothic War*. Present views based on Procopius are, in effect, that the Ostrogothic settlement was anticipated in every detail by that of 476; that the soldiers of Odoacer were allotted one-third of the land of Italy, in the literal sense of privately owned land; and that Theodoric's allotments caused little stir because they were essentially at the expense of Odoacer's followers.[23] It should now be apparent that such ambitious inferences are unwarranted; they call for greater fidelity and accuracy from Procopius than the literary context and date of his account allow us to expect.

In turning to the earlier sources on the Italian settlement —chiefly, Cassiodorus's *Variae*—it is appropriate to begin with two letters whose tenor is altogether surprising if expropriations took place. Where Gaul is concerned, the absence of complaints or resistance (except in one case) is inferred from silence; in Italy, not only is there no protest, but "on the contrary the land settlement was warmly praised by contemporaries."[24] Ennodius wrote to Liberius: "You have enriched the countless hordes of Goths with generous grants of lands, and yet the Romans have hardly felt it. The victors desire nothing more, and the conquered have felt no loss."[25] Jones perceptively observed that, though this is

---

[23] Anticipation in every detail (notably the *illatio tertiarum*, about which Procopius says nothing), Hartmann, *Geschichte*, vol. 1, pp. 93-94; Brunner, *DRG*, vol. 1, p. 77 n. 22; Bury, *Later Roman Empire*, vol. 1, p. 453, "exactly similar." Schmidt, *Ostgermanen*, p. 327, circumstantially described the composition of the grant, as though there were a basis for doing so: ". . . from the belongings of the *possessores* [=Italian landowners], the Germans received one-third of the townhouse, the lands, slaves, *coloni*, and livestock"; he reinforced these unfounded statements by cautioning that the barbarians' share in woods and waste lands is unknown. On Theodoric's allotments, Courcelle, *Hist. litt.*, p. 205, "Libérius avait eu l'art, en effet, d'établir les Ostrogoths de préférence sur les tierces qui appartenaient précédemment aux soldats d'Odoacre."

[24] Jones, *LRE*, p. 251.

[25] Ennodius *Epistolae* 9. 23, p. 245: "quid quod illas innumeras

flattery, Ennodius "would hardly have introduced the topic at all if it had been a painful one."[26] Cassiodorus was equally panegyrical in speaking about Liberius to the Roman senate:

It gives us pleasure to refer to the way in which in the assignment of the thirds he united both the possessions and the hearts of Goths and Romans. For though men usually quarrel when they are neighbours, the sharing of estates seems in this case to have produced harmony. For the result has been that both peoples, by living together, have achieved concord, an unprecedented and altogether praiseworthy accomplishment. By the division of the soil the hearts of the owners have been united, the friendship of the people has grown by their losses, and at the cost of a part of the land a defender has been acquired, so that the security of the estate is wholly preserved.[27]

Again, Jones stressed that these lines cannot be discounted as mere flattery. "It would hardly have been tactful to use such language to an assembly of landowners, if they had felt bitterly resentful at their losses."[28] The two contempo-

---

Gothorum catervas vix scientibus Romanis larga praediorum conlatione ditasti? nihil enim amplius victores cupiunt et nulla senserunt damna superati." The translation is by Jones, *LRE*, p. 251.

[26] Jones, *LRE*, p. 251.

[27] *Variae* 2. 16. 5: "Iuvat nos referre quemadmodum in tertiarum deputatione Gothorum Romanorumque et possessiones iunxit et animos. Nam cum se homines soleant de vicinitate collidere, istis praediorum communio causam videtur praestitisse concordiae: sic enim contigit, ut utraque natio, dum communiter vivit, ad unum velle convenerit. En factum novum et omnino laudabile: gratia dominorum de cespitis divisione coniuncta est; amicitiae populis per damna creverunt et parte agri defensor adquisitus est, ut substantiae securitas integra servaretur. Una lex illos et aequabilis disciplina complectitur. Necesse est enim, ut inter eos suavis crescat affectus, qui servant iugiter terminos constitutos." Translation by Jones, *LRE*, p. 251; the last two sentences omitted.

[28] Jones, *LRE*, p. 251.

rary observers certainly make it sound as though something had been sacrificed, but could that something have been as much as one-third of the landed fortune of every proprietor? Italians would have had to be a strangely resigned breed if they had unprotestingly endured losses on such a scale as that.

Intent on their praise of Liberius, neither Ennodius nor Cassiodorus explained what the "assignment of thirds" precisely involved. Some have thought that, if Liberius collectively distributed plural "thirds," then a singular *tertia* must be synonymous with a single Gothic allotment (*sors*).[29] Yet the equivalence of *tertia* with *sors*, though logical, is nowhere confirmed, and, contrary to the widespread belief that every Goth received one-third of a Roman estate, there is no basis for assuming that a Gothic allotment consisted of one-third of anything: its size was probably determined in a different and less capricious way, as will be seen.[30] According to both authors, the operations Liberius conducted had to do with land; Ennodius mentions *praedia*, "estates," and Cassiodorus marshals a string of words suggestive of private property, *possessiones, praedia, cespes, ager, termini*, in order to produce his miraculous paradox that, in the case of these two nations, the fact of becoming neighbors has created concord rather than the usual enmity. But, in view of the intent of Ennodius and Cassiodorus to muster all the resources of panegyric to celebrate Liberius's

[29] Brunner, *DRG*, vol. 1, pp. 77; Lot, "Hospitalité," p. 1002; Ensslin, *Theodorich*, p. 94. For another, but also mistaken, view of what *tertia* meant, Schmidt, *Ostgermanen*, p. 329.

[30] When directly referred to, the Gothic lot is always called *sors*: *Variae* 2. 17, 8. 26. 4. Note also the two papyri bearing on these institutions: *PDipl* 115 (540) establishes that some lands being sold are free from every "nexus fisci deviti populi pribati . . . nec non et a sorte barbari. . . ."; *PDipl* 138, a list of acknowledgments of debt (mainly called *cautiones*) bearing various dates, includes an entry for a *pittacium de titulis tertiarum* (503), clearly referring to money payments in respect to the *illatio tertiarum* (these papyri are to be *PItal* 31 and 47-48A).

achievements as prefect, should this terminology be taken literally? The words used are the common, not necessarily legal, terms that, in epideictic contexts like these, might be applied with equal accuracy to a slave tenure, a freehold farm, or a tax assessment. There is no doubt that the Goths were awarded "land"; the problem is to discover the legal regime of their award. It hardly seems wise to rely upon these letters to provide a factual account of legal technicalities.[31]

The best approach to an understanding of the Italian *tertiae* is by an examination of the *illatio tertiarum*, a tax discussed in some detail in two of Cassiodorus's letters. As stated before, the current doctrine with regard to this tax— set out principally by Hartmann, who believed he could find precedents for it—is that Romans paid it in lieu of allotment and that it amounted to one-third of the revenue of their lands. Hartmann attributed the institution of the tax to Odoacer, as being a necessary complement to assigning "one-third of the land of Italy" to his soldiers. All the landowners of the peninsula, he supposed, were deprived of a third of their estates, some by direct assignment to a barbarian, the others by taxation of an equal amount of their revenues.[32] Now, confiscation of property on such a massive

---

[31] *Variae* 2. 16 is the only text from anywhere that might sustain the assertion that barbarian allotments were composed of portions (*pars agri*) detached from the estates of Roman landowners (*praedia, substantiae*) by a process of dividing the soil (*cespitis divisio*). I am satisfied, however, that a literal reading of this kind is incorrect. The panegyrical effect sought by Cassiodorus was obtained by describing the *tertiarum deputatio* in the language of private property: in this language it was a miracle, whereas in reality—i.e., the possibilities afforded by tax law—there was nothing miraculous about it.

[32] Hartmann, *Geschichte*, vol. 1, pp. 94, 124 n. 6, prefigured by Gaupp, *Ansiedlungen*, p. 489, and Dahn, *Könige*, vol. 3, pp. 143-145. The Roman precedent Hartmann alleged was the *fiscus barbaricus* mentioned in *PItal* 1 of 445 or 446 (note also the "Gothic treasury" mentioned in Malchus, fragm. 18); he was following Theodor Mommsen, "Ostgotische Studien," *Neues Archiv* 14 (1889): 501 (=*Gesammelte Schriften*, vol. 6, pp. 439-440). This *fiscus* is too poorly doc-

scale may or may not be regarded as believable. The actual number of allotments, at least to Odoacer's troops, is thought to have been rather small and concentrated in a limited area of northern Italy.[33] The tax, however, is thought to have been generally applied, and it severely strains the imagination. Suddenly, the government would have been pocketing one-third of the revenues of every landowner in Italy, small and large, in addition to continuing to levy the normal land tax on the other two-thirds of their property. There is no firm information about tax rates, but it seems fair to assume that the imposition of the *illatio* (on the terms proposed by Hartmann) would have meant almost doubling every landowner's tax bill.[34] The lavish returns of the new tax would have dwarfed the proceeds of the ordinary land tax, turning the *illatio* into the

---

umented to merit a place in discussions of the *illatio*; even *PItal* 1, the key text, attests to a sum no longer being paid to it. Rather than relating this "treasury" to a particular tax, I am inclined to connect it to the *scrinia barbarorum* in the *officium* of the *magister officiorum*; see William G. Sinnigen, "*Barbaricarii, barbari* and the *Notitia dignitatum*," *Latomus* 22 (1963): 806-815, and especially p. 812 n. 1; the circumstances described in Ammianus Marcellinus 26. 5. 7 make it likely that the *scrinia* had a financial side. If this conjecture is correct, the passages involved are relevant to state outlays rather than to its income.

Where Hartmann and others had the *illatio* consist of a fraction of revenue (*Ertrag*), possibly meaning the harvest (thus Romano and Solmi, *Dominazione barbariche*, p. 168), Jones speaks of it as a fraction of estate rentals (*LRE*, p. 250). The distinction, if any, is not worth discussing, since either interpretation lacks a documentary basis.

[33] On the geographic distribution of allotments (of no interest here), Ensslin, *Theodorich*, p. 96; Volker Bierbrauer, "Zur ostgotischen Geschichte Italiens," *Studi medievali*, 3d ser., 14 (1973): 10-26.

[34] If the rate was under 25%, the total tax would more than double (e.g., at 20%, the rise would be to 46.6%); if more than 25%, then the proportionate increase would be somewhat less (e.g., at 33%, the rise would be to 55.5%). We can visualize the demoralizing impact of such a measure by assuming that our income tax calculations began with a deduction of one-third in the government's favor and went on from there as an ungraduated percentage of the balance.

pillar of state finance; the treasury, under Theodoric as well as Odoacer, would have been perhaps a hundred percent richer than under the last Western emperors, with no corresponding increase in expenditures.[35] Besides, how would the "revenue" of landowners have been determined and checked? Did every piece of Italian property have an officially known rental (in money) of which one-third could have been levied? No such procedure was involved in the land tax. Were new procedures instituted and, if so, why have they left no trace?[36] Even if Odoacer's government had been able to carry through this draconic and technically

[35] There is no evidence that such was the case. Stein, *Bas-Empire*, vol. 2, p. 43, conjectured that the effect of the *illatio* would have been tax decreases "in other regards," notably the cancellation of recruit supply and its commutation (but had these been levied after *NValent III* 6. 3 [444]?). Even more curiously, Jones, *LRE*, p. 251, commented: "It was thus possible to meet increases in expenditures without increasing the land tax, and this was no doubt some consolation to landowners for their losses." Those subjected to an *illatio* of the kind supposed by Hartmann (and Jones, *LRE*, p. 250) would have been astonished to hear that their land tax had not been increased (see the details in n. 34). Jones probably had in mind *Variae* 2. 16. 4; but this passage, which is unrelated to *tertiae*, says simply that Liberius avoided tax increases by recovering "illa quae consueverant male dispergi." Cf. Ennodius *Epistolae* 9. 23: "tu solus dissipata conponas . . . lapsa exusta perdita, cum te aspexerint, convalescunt."

Some further consequences of an *illatio* on Hartmann's terms (i.e., one-third of the revenues of all Italian land) deserve to be mentioned: prior to the distribution of allotments, its proceeds would have exceeded those of the ordinary land tax unless the latter was charged at a rate higher than 50% (!); even if as much as half these lands (i.e., one-sixth of Italy) had been distributed in individual allotments, the *illatio* from the balance would still have yielded the government a revenue at least equal to what remained of the ordinary tax. Neither Hartmann nor anyone else appears to have thought through the implications for state finance of an *illatio* on the terms he proposed.

[36] For revenue and rentals, above, n. 32. At best, the existing public tax registers recorded the declared inventory of estates and their tax charge: Goffart, "Three Notes," pp. 376-377, 380-386. The "revenue" (harvest?) or rental of land was not a matter of public record, nor did it become so.

difficult measure, its consequences for Italy would have been devastating: anyone able to emigrate would have done so, and those staying behind would have included enough literate men to have thoroughly blackened the barbarian regime. Instead, the stones of the Coliseum disclose that the Roman senatorial families thought the time appropriate for the refurbishment of their reserved seats.[37] The predictable consequences of such a tax are wholly out of keeping with everything else we know about the tranquility and modest well-being of Italy under Odoacer. Hartmann's interpretation of the *illatio* was consistent with the premise of expropriation, but the implications of such a tax are dizzying and wholly unconfirmed. And, if the tax cannot have been a proportionate confiscation of revenue, then perhaps the barbarian allotment was also rather different from what has been imagined.

Cassiodorus himself gives us no reason to suspect that the *illatio* was a crushing and confiscatory burden. In *Variae* 1. 14, we see the Catalienses petitioning Theodoric that the payment that the *illatio* called for should cease to be a separate item of accounting and should instead be consolidated with the tax total (*tributaria summa*). Their reason for making this request was that the *illatio* was a *nomen suspectum*, an occasion for mistrusting the government. It would appear that they did not mind the amount of the tax but were apprehensive about its eventually being converted into Gothic allotments (as illustrated by *Variae* 2. 17). Theodoric granted their request on the grounds that it cost him nothing and would save him from *competitiones*, which presumably means solicitations at court in regard to the *tertiae* of Catalia.[38] It is difficult to infer from these

---

[37] Chastagnol, *Sénat romain*, pp. 42-44, but rather shabbily, p. 36.

[38] *Variae* 1. 14: ". . . nec decet esse difficile beneficium, quod non patitur largitate detrimentum. Et ideo praecelsa magnificentia tua [= the praetorian prefect], quod a Cataliensibus inferebatur genere tertiarum, faciat annis singulis in tributaria summa persolvi, nec post super hanc partem patiantur supplices aliquam quaestionem. Quid

circumstances that, over and above the normal tribute weighing on Italian landowners, the *illatio* was an onerous additional tax. Far more likely, it was merely a slice of the normal land tax. It required a special name because it formed the distinct account by means of which one could identify the local assessment that was available, if necessary, for allotment to Goths. The request of the Catalienses was for restoration of the *status quo ante*: tax payment in a single consolidated account. Theodoric, no longer thinking it necessary to safeguard the separate *nomen*, could easily grant their wish.

This interpretation of the *illatio* is confirmed by *Variae* 2. 17, in which Theodoric instructs the local authorities of Trent to cancel the taxes due from the allotment that he has just awarded to a Goth:

> We do not wish our generosity to be damaging to anyone, lest what is granted to one person should be turned to the expense of another. Know, therefore, by the present authority, that no one should pay any tax (*functio fiscalis calculi*) in regard to the allotment (*sors*) we have granted to the priest Butila by our generosity; know, rather, that whatever gold pieces (*solidi*) are comprised in that payment are to be relieved to you from the *tertiarum illationes*. Neither do we wish anyone to contribute what, by our humanity, we have remitted to another.[39]

enim interest, quo nomine possessor inferat, dummodo sine imminutione quod debetur exsolvat? Ita et illis suspectum tertiarum nomen auferimus et a nostra mansuetudine importunitates competentium summovemus." Fridh treats "Quid enim interest" as a complete sentence; I prefer Mommsen's punctuation. "Compententium" in Fridh is a typographical error.

[39] *Variae* 2. 17: "Honoratis possessoribus defensoribus et curialibus Tridentinae civitatis Theodericus rex. Munificentiam nostram nulli volumus extare damnosam, ne quod alteri tribuitur, alterius dispendiis applicetur. Et ideo praesenti auctoritate cognoscite, pro sorte quam Butilani presbytero nostra largitate contulimus, nullum debere per-

No document brings us closer than this one to the process of Ostrogothic allotment. The following features stand out: the government was concerned that giving something to a barbarian should occasion no loss to Romans; the ordinary tax payable to the state in regard to the allotment was completely abolished; the local officials, who kept the tax records, were instructed that the gold pieces equivalent to the tax payment of the allotment were stricken from a part of the records, namely, the account of *illatio tertiarum* (the plural seems insignificant); and, in a final, and somewhat obscure, injunction, the municipality appears to have been told that the remission of tax-in-gold must be passed on to exactly the right taxpayer(s), that is, the one or several formerly paying gold with respect to the assessment that had now been allotted.[40] The basic idea justifying the claim that allotments entailed no sacrifice by Romans was that tax remission fully compensated for whatever was lost.

---

solvere fiscalis calculi functionem, sed in ea praestatione quanti se solidi comprehendunt, de tertiarum illationibus vobis noveritis esse relevandos. Nec inferri a quoquam volumus, quod alteri nostra humanitate remisimus, ne, quod dictu nefas est, bene meriti munus innocentis contingat esse dispendium." The last clause is not translated above.

Theodoric's cancellation of tax has no apparent connection to Butila's being a priest. Leilia Cracco-Ruggini, *Economia e società nell'Italia annonaria* (Milan, 1961), p. 334, maintained the contrary.

[40] The final sentence could be, and probably is, no more than a repetition of the introductory sentence. But this reading presupposes that *alteri nostra humanitate remittere* is synonymous not only with *alteri tribuere* in the first sentence but also with *sortem Butilani nostra largitate conferre*—a possible but odd equivalence, since Theodoric's "remission" of tax was only to the Romans of Trent. There is a faint possibility, therefore, that *quisquam* and *alter* in the final sentence both refer to Roman taxpayers, one of them continuing to pay while the other enjoys exemption. On this interpretation, Theodoric was demanding strict honesty from the local authorities: no surreptitious advantage was to be taken by those in close contact with the tax machinery; the cancellation must benefit no one except the payer(s) responsible for the *professio* conferred upon Butila. It is more likely, however, that Cassiodorus was merely repetitious.

Prior to the assignment to Butila, that which became his allotment was subject to ordinary taxation, but those taxes were recorded in a special account; once in Butila's possession, the *sors* was tax free, at least as far as Trent and the royal government were concerned. Finally, it is worth observing that Theodoric addressed himself only to taxation in gold: someone who had formerly contributed gold to the state would no longer have to pay it either to the government or to anyone else.[41]

When dissociated from the influence of Procopius, Cassiodorus's evidence on the *illatio tertiarum* leads to a considerably modified interpretation of the Italian "thirds." Rather than being an additional and crushing levy on Roman estates, the *illatio* was nothing more severe than one-third of the ordinary land tax paid as a separate account. The point of collecting it in this way was to denote that one-third of the declared property of any given tax district formed a special category of assessment, distinct from the assessment upon which the ordinary tax was levied; the rate was the same, the accounts were different. As long as the tax was collected as a separate item, there was no need for the authorities to identify the assessments giving rise to the *illatio tertiarum* and to demarcate them, even on paper, from those contributing the ordinary tax; the allocation of one-third could remain theoretical as long as the tax was being paid to the state. But, once an allotment was award-

---

[41] There is an underlying hypothesis here, namely, that the tax-in-gold owed by someone in behalf of a *professio* in the municipal records was not identical to the tax proceeds of the private lands and cultivators to which the *professio* referred; in other words, the tax system was double-tiered, with the state being directly interested primarily in proceeds in gold. A full study of fifth and sixth-century taxation would be needed to establish whether this hypothesis is correct, and this is not the place for it; my firm impression is that a double-tiered system, or something very like it, had long prevailed, as the basic condition for the commutation of state revenues to gold. Important in this connection is Hans Geiss, *Geld- und naturwirtschaftliche Erscheinungsformen im staatlichen Aufbau Italiens während der Gotenzeit* (Stuttgart, 1931).

ed, and part of the tax ceased to be paid, then a corresponding segment of assessment had to be carved out of the tax registers and conveyed to its barbarian recipient.[42] On this interpretation, the word *tertiae* is best understood as an abbreviated form of *tertiae professionum*, "thirds of assessment declarations." In any given tax district, one could speak of the "one-third of assessments," *tertia professionum*, either allotted to individuals or occasioning a specially collected tax; the government, from its perspective (which is that of Cassiodorus), could refer collectively to the "thirds," meaning one-third of the *professiones* of every Italian tax district. Because the objects declared for assessment were agricultural property, there was no contradiction in using such a word as "estates" in their regard, or even in speaking of "one-third of the land of Italy." But there was a world of difference between *tertiae* so understood and a catastrophic confiscation of private property.

The most direct proof that the Italian allotments were composed of tax assessment, requiring no dispossession of Roman owners, is supplied by *Variae* 5. 27, in which Theodoric calls the Goths *millenarii*, "holders of *millenae*"— the *millena* being specifically a "unit of tax assessment." Although the place of these units in the tax system has already been briefly described, it is appropriate to pause for a few more words of explanation. No earlier commentator of *Variae* 5. 27 understood the term *millena* in quite the same way as it can now be interpreted.

The late Roman units of tax accounting date back to the age of Diocletian, when, in the absence of a stable cur-

---

[42] *Variae* 1. 14 and 2. 17 imply that the *nomen tertiarum* was a distinct account only from the standpoint of payment. For the assignment of allotments, cf. Goffart, "Three Notes," pp. 174, 381-382. Brunner, *DRG*, vol. 1, p. 77 n. 22 inferred from *PDipl* 115 (above, n. 30) that the award of a *sors* liberated other Roman lands *a sorte barbari*; this makes too much of the coincidental detail that the papyrus documents the sale of *portiones*. The initial allocation, if worked out in the registers, would distinguish assessments subject to the *illatio* from those subject to ordinary taxation.

rency, the government was forced to devise a method for setting a definite value upon the diverse agricultural assets declared by taxpayers for purposes of assessment. Schedules were drawn up of the various types of assets, animate as well as real, in such a way that they indicated what quantity of each type of asset "paid the tax-in-kind (*annona*)" of one abstract unit of assessment. By sifting the individual property declarations through the schedules, the authorities were able to rate the taxable wealth of each proprietor in terms of homogeneous units of account. The institution of these abstract units, in lieu of valuations in depreciating coin, provided a device by which the annual tax levies could again be fairly apportioned among the payers in proportion to their assets.[43] The *millena* was a unit of this kind. It was peculiar to Italy, notably to the center and south, and is first documented in 440.

Cassiodorus refers to the *millena* in the *Variae* independently of the letter under discussion, and he also mentions the *iugum*, a more anciently attested unit of the same kind.[44] These letters, as well as other evidence, illustrate a little-known aspect of these assessment units: in Theodoric's Italy, and probably much earlier, the government used them as a device not only for apportioning tax levies among taxpayers, but also for measuring the generosity of the state toward those institutions and persons that it favored with the direct grant of tax proceeds. For example, Theodoric instructed his praetorian prefect to assign one *millena* "additional to the customary number" to the public baths of Spoleto; the baths, therefore, had an allotment of

[43] Goffart, *Caput*, pp. 32-34, 41-52, 60-63, 141-143. It is particularly important to understand that these units are abstractions, a simplified quantification of *professiones*; they refer to real assets but are not identical to them.

[44] *NValent III* 5. 1. 4 (440); *NMajor* 7. 1. 16 (458); Cassiodorus *Variae* 2. 37, 4. 20 (*iugum*). An old, mistaken conception of the *millena* was rectified by Ferdinand Lot, "De l'étendue et de la valeur du *caput* fiscal sous le Bas-Empire," *NRHD*, 4th ser., 4 (1925): 13-15; but it still occurs in Sidonius *Carmina*, ed. Loyen, p. xv n. 2.

several *millenae*. In a case like this, the *millena* was a unit of tax proceeds. It would seem that what the government did when wishing to bestow a benefit of this kind was to consult the official registers of tax declarations (*professiones*), identify within them private agricultural property up to the value of the one or several "units" that were to be given, and convey to the beneficiary a suitable document recording the composition of the allotment and the name of its private-law owner(s). On the basis of this document, the state-designated recipient of the *millena*—either a person or an institution—could hereafter collect at source the tax payments of his "unit."[45] Since such an allotment consisted of tax proceeds, it was necessarily tax free.[46]

Mommsen related the *millenarii* of *Variae* 5. 27 to the tax *millena* but did not elaborate.[47] Subsequent commentators have differed from him. Their contention has been that the word signifies "thousandmen," or chiliarchs, on the model of *centenarius*, "hundredman"; Theodoric, therefore, was not addressing the Goths in general, but only their officers of that rank. It has also been inferred that the "thousand" was a basic subdivision in the Gothic army.[48] A close reading of the source suggests that Mommsen was right.

[45] The baths of Spoleto: Cassiodorus *Variae* 2. 37. For a fuller discussion in the context of Roman precedents, Goffart, "Three Notes," pp. 167-174.

[46] This anticipates the discussion below of whether the Ostrogoths were taxed.

[47] Mommsen, "Ostgotische Studien," p. 499 n. 3 (= *Gesammelte Schriften*, vol. 6, p. 438). Mommsen translated *millena* as *Steuerhufe* (comparable to Old English "hide" or Frankish *mansus*) and thus regarded *millenarius* as equivalent to *possessor*, on the understanding that the Ostrogoths paid taxes just like the Romans. He was followed by Hartmann, *Geschichte*, vol. 1, p. 129 n. 9, who did not elaborate; and by Rietschel (next note).

[48] More correctly, the identification of *millenarius* with a military thousand antedated, and was not dislodged by, Mommsen's discreet observation (full documentation in Rietschel, below). After Mommsen: Ernst Mayer, review of Hartmann, *Geschichte*, in *Göttingische gelehrte Anzeigen* 165 (1903): 202; Brunner, *DRG*, vol. 1, p. 181

The reference to Gothic *millenarii* occurs in one of a pair of letters concerning the distribution of a royal donative to the troops. The wider context is supplied by *Variae* 8. 26, in which Theodoric's successor declares to his Germanic subjects, "Allotments of your own (*sortes propriae*) nourish you and, with the Lord's help, our gifts enrich you." In other words, all qualified Goths had two official sources of support: a basic salary in the form of their allotment and, in addition, a donative in money.[49] Theodoric's first letter about the donative is addressed to "all the Goths residing in Picenum and Samnium" and summons them to Ravenna to be awarded their gifts by the king in person.[50]

---

n. 7; M. Krammer in *Neues Archiv* 32 (1907): 538-539; Ludwig Schmidt, "Die *comites Gothorum*. Ein Kapitel zur ostgotischen Verfassungsgeschichte," *Mitteilungen des Instituts für österreichische Geschichtsforschung* 40 (1924): 132; Ernst Stein, "Untersuchungen zur spätrömischen Verwaltungsgeschichte," *Rheinisches Museum für Philologie* 74 (1925): 387-388, and *Bas-Empire*, vol. 1, p. 384, vol. 2, p. 121; Lot, "Hospitalité," p. 1003; Ensslin, *Theodorich*, pp. 195-196; Jones, *LRE*, p. 256.

With Mommsen (but disregarded by all the above except Krammer), Siegfried Rietschel, "Die germanische Tausendschaft," *ZRG*, Germ. 27 (1906): 234-252, who convincingly demonstrated that there was no such thing as a primitive Germanic thousand; the theory of its existence was developed only by Wilhelm Sickel (1879), on a priori grounds. It now appears that the hundred was not a primitive Germanic institution either (below, Chapter VIII n. 6).

[49] *Variae* 8. 26. 4: "Nam quae necessitas ad iniusta compellat, cum vos et sortes alant propriae et munera nostra domino iuvante ditificent? Nam et si cui aliquid expetendum est, speret de munificentia principis quam de praesumptione virtutis, quia vobis proficit, quod Romani quieti sunt, qui, dum aeraria nostra ditant, vestra donativa multiplicant." In *Variae* 5. 26, *munera* (= "gifts") is also used as synonym for the *donativum* mentioned in 5. 27.

[50] *Variae* 5. 26, "Universis Gothis per Picenum et Samnium constitutis." Ensslin, *Theodorich*, p. 196, maintained that the trip to Ravenna was a military march, on which the Goths were supplied with rations, as though on active service. This is a misunderstanding of the phrase *exercituales expensae* in 5. 26. It is true that, in *Variae* 3. 42. 2, these words refer to rations. In 5. 26, however, the sense of the passage is identical to the line of 8. 26 quoted in n. 49: since the

The second one, which opens with the passage that interests us, is to a *saio*, charged with communicating the royal summons:

Consuetudine liberalitatis regiae commonemur, ut Gothis nostris debeamus solemnia dona largiri. Et ideo devotio tua millenarios provinciae Piceni et Samnii sine aliqua dilatione commoneat, ut eos, qui annis singulis nostrae mansuetudinis praemia consequuntur, pro accipiendo donativo ad comitatum faciat incunctanter occurrere, quatinus, qui bene nobis meriti fuerint, maiore munificentia gratulentur.[51]

The current interpretation of these lines calls for us to believe that the *millenarii* are a category of officers, that the rewards received "each year" signify the donative, and that the "greater generosity" denotes something additional to the donative. Each of these readings is difficult to sustain. Even in Procopius's lengthy account of the Gothic wars, there is no trace of Ostrogothic "thousands" or "thousand-men," and, if the *millenarii* are understood as officers, they cannot be identical to "all the Goths" of *Variae* 5. 26, as there is every reason to think they are. Donatives were approximately quinquennial in the late Roman army, and nothing (outside this letter) allows us to suppose that they were annual in Ostrogothic Italy. On the contrary, Athalaric's reference to "the Lord's help" in *Variae* 8. 26 underlines their adventitious nature: far from being reliably annual, they were distributed when the government could afford them. As for a payment in excess of the donative, none is otherwise attested or need be imagined, provided "greater generosity" is understood to mean the donative itself.[52]

Goths receive regular pay from the king, they should not despoil the unarmed Romans. If there had been question of special rations, *Variae* 5. 27 would have approximated the wording of 5. 10.

[51] *Variae* 5. 27, ed. Fridh, p. 204.

[52] On *millenarii* as officers, Rietschel, pp. 244-245, "sonst unter den

Of these readings, only the first deserves further attention, for there were "thousandmen" at least among the Vandals and the Visigoths.[53] Stein sought to buttress this interpreta-

---

ostgotischen Beamten- und Offiziertiteln der des millenarius nirgends vorkommt," and next note.

The other two points hinge on reading the text roughly as follows (from *eos qui* and omitting nonessentials): "so that [your devotion] might make those who obtain annual rewards come to receive [this] donative [and] so that those who are specially deserving might rejoice in [even] greater generosity." For Roman donatives, Jones, *LRE*, pp. 623-624. That Ostrogothic donatives were annual is invariably maintained: Dahn, *Könige*, vol. 3, pp. 74-75; Mommsen, *Gesammelte Schriften*, vol. 6, p. 436; Ensslin, *Theodorich*, p. 195; Jones, *LRE*, p. 256; but the doctrine rests on the inference that *praemia = donativum* in this letter. (A subsidiary argument might be derived from the adjective *solemnia* in the phrase *solemnia dona*, since *solemnis* can mean "annual" and often does in the context of state finances. Here, however, it need only parallel *consuetudinariae res* later in the letter. Donatives could be customary, a consecrated item of military pay, without being annual.) Procopius *Bell. Goth.* 1. 12. 47-48 is sometimes cited in connection with Theodoric's donatives, but it refers to Ostrogothic rule in Gaul and Spain and need not describe a donative. For generosity additional to the donative, Ensslin, p. 196. It is a logical way to dispose of *maior munificentia*, but only if *praemia* really were in apposition to *donativum*.

It should perhaps have been noticed long ago that two rather important, and anomalous, Ostrogothic institutions—"thousandmen" as officers and annual donatives—were based only on this difficult sentence of *Variae* 5. 27.

[53] For the evidence, Rietschel, pp. 241-244; also Courtois, *Vandales*, pp. 216-217, 231-236, and Dietrich Claude, "*Millenarius* und *thiufadus*," *ZRG*, Germ. 88 (1971): 181-190. Unlike Rietschel, I am disinclined to accept Mommsen's suggestion that the documented Vandal *millenarius* was the holder of an ordinary *sors*, like the Ostrogothic one ("Ostgotische Studien," p. 499 n. 4). For an aspect of this subject, see Appendix A.

It is worth noting that *millenarius* occurs in lieu of *tribunus* in Cassiodorus-Epiphanius *Historia tripartita* 6. 35, 7. 1 (ed. R. Hanslik, *CSEL* 71), and that the old *cohors milliaria* is called *millenaria* in a seventh-century MS fragment of Vegetius (*Codices Latini antiquiores*, vol. 1, no. 114); also, "Tribunus qui super duos vel tres pagos vel super mille," in the Merovingian "Traktat über Ämterwesen," ed. M. Conrat, *ZRG*, Germ. 29 (1912): 248. Rietschel's interpretation of

tion by a syntactical argument. In his view, the sentence as it stands has an unendurable "Härte der Konstruktion" that would be avoided by emending *faciat* to *faciant*. Changing the subject of this verb from the singular *saio* to the plural *millenarii* would result in a chain of command—Theodoric ordering the *saio* to summon, the *saio* passing the word to the "thousandmen," and the "thousandmen" notifying *eos qui*, namely, "all the Goths."[54] On this interpretation, it is absolutely necessary for the "annual rewards" to be the donative and for some other meaning to be found for the "greater generosity." As far as the sentence structure is concerned, Stein's objection has some merit, but his emendation is by no means mandatory, since, from the standpoint of syntax, *faciat* will do just as well.[55] The main issue continues to be whether *millenarii* are a select group of officers or "all the Goths."

The quotation lends itself to a straightforward reading provided no extraneous "thousandmen" are introduced. In accordance with Cassiodorus's practice in pairing letters, the *millenarii* of Picenum and Samnium can hardly be anyone else than "all the Goths" of the same province in *Variae* 5. 26.[56] All the plural nouns of 5. 27—"our Goths,"

---

millenarius from Romanist premises, though incomplete, is almost certainly correct.

[54] Stein, "Verwaltungsgeschichte," pp. 387-388. Dahn, *Könige*, vol. 3, pp. 77-78 n. 6, had also proposed this emendation.

[55] In response to my inquiry drawing attention to Stein's emendation, Professor Åke Fridh of Göteborg University, the editor of the *Variae*, had the kindness to reply as follows: "From the purely syntactical point of view, it would certainly not be impossible to retain *faciat*" (letter of 31 January 1974). I am very thankful for his thoughtful consideration of this problem.

[56] *Variae* 1-10 (the royal letters) contain about sixty groups of two or more letters. The standard pair notifies a dignitary of his appointment to an office and then conveys the same news to the Roman senate. The pair most closely resembling *Variae* 5. 26-27 are 5. 10-11, to a detachment of Gepids marching to Gaul and to the *saio* escorting them. It appears to me that there is no parallel in these letter groups for the abrupt change of subject implied by having the

"the *millenarii* of Picenum and Samnium," "those who obtain annual rewards," and "those who are well deserving"—
are synonymous references to the same people. The first
relative clause (*eos qui*) speaks of the summoned Goths
from the standpoint of the *millena*, defined as that which
provided them with annual rewards from the king; the
second (*qui bene meriti*) describes them from the standpoint of the donative, the reward "greater" than, and additional to, their annual salary that they earned by active
military service. To put the matter another way, the quoted
lines elaborate upon the two Gothic sources of support outlined in *Variae* 8. 26: precisely because the Goths were
holders of *millenae*, they "obtain each year the rewards of
Our Mildness" ("*sortes propriae* nourish you"), and the
donative they were to hasten to receive was the "greater
generosity" earned by their merits ("our gifts enrich
you").[57] In sum, *Variae* 5. 27 tells us that "all" the Goths
resident in Picenum and Samnium who were entitled by
their military service to receive an occasional donative from
Theodoric could also be collectively referred to as *millenarii*—beneficiaries of annual salaries composed of tax revenues collected at source.

So interpreted, *Variae* 5. 27 decisively complements the
other Cassiodoran evidence on Ostrogothic allotments.
Millenae, or their north Italian equivalent—units of tax
assessment and their proceeds—provided the "military outlays" given to the Goths so that they would maintain
civilitas, outlays that continued even when the recipients

---

millenarii of 5. 27 be only the leaders of the Goths in 5. 26. Dahn,
Könige, vol. 3, pp. 77-78, 80, was troubled by the discrepancy;
Schmidt, "Comites," p. 132, thought there was a deliberate contrast.

[57] On the same abbreviated basis as in n. 52, the translation is: "so
that [your devotion] might make those who each year obtain the
rewards of Our Mildness [that is to say, from their *millenae*] come
. . . to receive a donative, whereby they who have deserved well of us
might rejoice in greater generosity [that is, than the annual rewards]."
The balance of the letter shows that all the summoned Goths were
understood to be *bene meriti*.

retired from active service and were no longer eligible for a donative.[58] One-third of all Italian *professiones* formed the fund placed at the disposal of Liberius for distribution among the Ostrogoths, and he apportioned it in individual lots consisting of one *iugum* or one *millena* per qualified Goth. The basis of qualification is unknown to us, and awards of several units must surely have been possible, but allotments to barbarians were basically identical to the revenue awarded to the baths of Spoleto—an assignment by the praetorian prefect of tax proceeds and of the property declaration pledged to their annual payment.[59] The tax-in-gold weighing upon these assessments, and due to the state, was forgiven to whoever paid it; to that extent, the transfer of *professio* from its former holder to a Goth was fully compensated and entailed no loss to a Roman. What remained as revenue for the *millenarius* was the tax contribution of the land, in whatever form it had customarily been paid.[60]

[58] For *exercituales expensae* (5. 26), see above, n. 50. *Variae* 5. 36 grants a discharge for infirmity and terminates the donative; since the recipient was "solvent in [his] own right," he should not, while *otiosus*, receive the *res laborantium*. Theodoric's reference to royal generosity in paying troops does not contradict the idea that he meant *sortes*; he also said, "praestante tempore munificentia sit pro lege" (*Variae* 3. 39. 2), and cf. Symmachus *Relatio* 3. 18, "quod a principio beneficium fuit, usu atque aetate fit debitum."

[59] Cf. Schmidt, *Ostgermanen*, p. 327, "Since the properties to be partitioned cannot have had the same size, the individual lots cannot have had the same extent; without doubt, the larger and better *Landstücke* fell to the leaders"; the same on p. 363; Stein, *Bas-Empire*, vol. 2, p. 119. Schmidt was consistent with the premise of expropriation. The idea that *millenae* of standard size were awarded obviates the need to imagine that gross inequalities were involved in the *deputatio tertiarum*. Schmidt, *Ostgermanen*, p. 362, affirmed that *sortes* went to "every independent free man"; on the question of the personal qualifications for an award, see below, Chapter VIII at n. 24 and Appendix E.

[60] See above, n. 41. On the hypothesis stated there, the award of an allotment wiped out the upper tier of taxation, leaving the *millen-*

Thus far we have considered allotments from the lofty eminence of the government, a perspective that Cassiodorus, not surprisingly, tends to favor. Among matters more directly relevant to the recipients than to the donor, we should most like to know what happened when a Goth obtained his *sors* and precisely what kind of revenue he derived from it, but we are left guessing. Nevertheless, the *Variae* do supply information on three points additional to those already covered: the documentation of allotments, the taxation of Goths, and the occasional expropriation of Roman landowners by barbarians after the allotments had been made. More has been made of the first two of these than the evidence allows; the third point, however, which is paralleled in Gaul, is a valuable complement to the scheme of allotment whose outlines we have now been able to discern.

It has been said that the Goths were given their *sortes* by officials called *delegatores*, charged with issuing "assignment warrants" (*pittacia delegationis*).[61] A *delegator*, however, was not an official, but anyone engaged in assigning a debt (*delegatio*): Caesarius, bishop of Arles, "assigned" when he gave property by *pittacium*; Cassiodorus as praetorian prefect acted as a *delegator* when he paid members of his staff with *delegatoria*, authorizing them to draw their salaries on the tax receipts of a designated province; and a curial, an accountant, or a receiver of taxation might discharge a debt he was being hounded for by "delegating" a fiscal debtor from whom he had been unable to collect.[62]

arius to benefit from the lower tier (very possibly, payment in kind; cf. the allotments mentioned in *NValent III* 5. 1. 4 [440]).

[61] Gaupp, *Ansiedlungen*, p. 474; Hartmann, *Geschichte*, vol. 1, p. 94; Alfred von Halban, *Das römische Recht in den germanischen Volksstaaten*, vol. 1, Untersuchungen zur deutschen Staats- und Rechtsgeschichte, ed. O. Gierke, 58 (Breslau, 1899), p. 112; Ensslin, *Theodorich*, p. 94; and Jones, *LRE*, p. 250, specified *delegatores*; many others (Brunner, Lot, Schmidt) mentioned *pittacia*.

[62] For the procedure of *delegatio*, above, Chapter II at n. 33. Cae-

When amended in this way, the idea that each Ostrogoth was issued a *pittacium* remains possible but lacks positive proof. The context where the term occurs has no specific reference to an allotment; on the contrary, the letter implies that what a barbarian had seized "without warrant (*pittacium*)" was private-law property.[63] As just established, the Gothic *sors* was composed of assessment and its proceeds. If so, then a *pittacium* giving title to property went one step beyond the allotment itself; somewhat like a foreclosure, the issue of a *pittacium* by the appropriate authority converted the Goth's (or anyone's) tenure of an abstract *professio* into direct ownership of the property declared and, possibly, of its bankrupt taxpayer. But even this interpretation is hardly certain, since the procedure of

---

sarius of Arles *Opera omnia,* ed. G. Morin, vol. 2 (Maredsous, 1942), p. 285; Cassiodorus *Variae* 11. 33, 35-38; *Edictum Theodorici* 126, particularly important (the *Edictum* is in *FIRA* 2, pp. 684-710).

[63] *Variae* 1. 18. 2: "Si Romani praedium . . . [since 489] . . . sine delegatoris cuiusquam pittacio praesumptor barbarus occupavit, eum priori domino summota dilatione restituat." (Letters in Bks. 1-3 are dated between 507 and 511.) If, as argued here, allotments consisted of tax units (*millenae* or *iuga*) rather than *praedia,* then *Variae* 1. 18 refers to the acquisition of private ownership, and not of an allotment. Another assignment by *pittacium* occurs in *Variae* 3. 35, addressed to Romulus; since this is believed to be the deposed emperor (whose mother is also mentioned), the award can hardly be a barbarian allotment. Even so, 3. 35 is a better basis than 1. 18 for the idea that *sortes* were documented by *pittacia.*

The special interest of the word *pittacium* in the context of barbarian "hospitality" is that, in *CTh* 7. 4, it denotes the warrant or chit delivered by military *actuarii* to keepers of tax stores in return for ration supplies; that is to say, the *pittacium* documented the moment at which the tax *annona* turned into the ration *annona.* But it is not established that *pittacium* retained this narrow definition in the sixth century: in *Variae* 12. 20, it has the general sense of an "acknowledgement of debt" (*obligatio chirographi*)—by the pope; the same in *PDipl* 138 (503), where it appears to be a synonym for *cautio;* Ennodius *Vita Epiphanii,* ed. Hartel, p. 375, mentions *pictacia ad clusuras,* meaning "passports" or "exit permits."

delegatio by *pittacium* is only sketchily known.[64] It is enough to observe that, although the issue of *pittacia* was common within Italian public finance, we cannot affirm that it had a mandatory relationship to the distribution of barbarian allotments.

Three letters of Cassiodorus specify that certain Goths, and non-Gothic "old barbarians" with Roman wives, had to pay tax or "due obligations" (*fiscus, debitae functiones*) in respect to their farms and estates (*casae, praedia*); unless they did, others would be unjustly obliged to bear the charge in their stead.[65] If these letters are understood to refer to barbarian allotments, they prove that the Goths were assigned taxable property and received it on precisely the same terms of tax payment as had applied to its former Roman owners. Reasoning in this way, almost all modern commentators have agreed that the Goths were taxed just like the *possessores* they replaced.[66] Such a conclusion, however, is hasty and mistaken. The word *sors* never occurs, nor is implied, in the texts ordering barbarians to pay taxes; the letter about Butila (*Variae* 2. 17) plainly indicates that his allotment ceased to be subject to taxation, and *Variae* 6. 24 contrasts the Goths "who obey our commands" to the Romans "who pay annual tribute." The correct interpretation of this evidence was given long ago by Fabien Thibault.[67] Gothic *sortes* were tax exempt (indeed, as we have

---

[64] Cf. Goffart, "Three Notes," p. 174, where I spoke more confidently about awards by *pittacium* that I would now. For an interesting case of bankruptcy (by a lessee of public lands), *Variae* 5. 6-7. More relevant perhaps is the procedure of *Edictum Theodorici* 127.

[65] *Variae* 1. 19, 4. 14, 5. 14. 6.

[66] Gaupp, *Ansiedlungen*, pp. 481-482; Dahn, *Könige*, vol. 3, pp. 141-143; Ensslin, *Theodorich*, p. 96; Jones, *LRE*, p. 251. This was Mommsen's basis for identifying the *millenarii* with "steuerpflichtigen *possessores*" ("Ostgotische Studien," p. 499 n. 3).

[67] Taxes payable on account of *possessiones, casae* (4. 14), or *praedia* (5. 14. 6); "nullum debere persolvere fiscalis calculi functionem" (2. 17; fuller, above n. 39); "Tributa quidem nobis annua devotione persolvitis . . . ut vos . . . defendant qui nostris iussionibus

91

now seen, they mainly consisted of tax proceeds), but Goths with allotments were free to acquire additional property out of their personal resources. As Theodoric took pains to point out, the king's periodic distribution of donatives in gold to his Goths enabled them to invest in real estate if they chose to do so. When they did, the property they bought continued to bear its normal assessment, in accord with the rule that assessment was necessarily conveyed with ownership. Very properly, therefore, Theodoric forced those Goths owning property on the same terms as Romans did to assume responsibility for the normal taxes.[68] Exemption was not a matter of nationality but an incident of tenure; just as churches held some tax-free property but were taxed on whatever additional lands that they were given, so were Gothic beneficiaries of tax-exempt allotments obliged to pay tax on whatever ordinary Roman property they acquired.[69] In principle, though, the Goths were

---

obsecundant" (6. 24. 1). Fabien Thibault, "L'impôt direct dans les royaumes des Ostrogoths, des Wisigoths et des Burgondes," *NRHD*, 3d ser., 25 (1901): 700-709. Thibault also, and rightly, drew attention to the contrast between *Variae* 6. 21 and 7. 3 (which shows that, whereas a Roman rector collected taxes, the Gothic count had no such obligation), and to *Variae* 8. 26. 4, "quia vobis proficit, quod Romani quieti sunt, qui, dum aeraria nostra ditant, vestra donativa multiplicent."

[68] *Variae* 4. 14. 2, "Qui enim debent ad fiscum celerius esse devoti, nisi qui capiunt commoda donativi, quando amplius de nostra humanitate recipiunt quam stipendii iure praestetur?" See above, n. 41: anyone with a reliable income in gold was in a good position to situate himself in the upper tier of taxpayers. Obligatory transfer of tax liability: *Fragmenta Vaticana* 35 (ca. 330; *FIRA* 2, pp. 469-471); *CTh* 11. 3. 5 (391); *PItal* 10-11 (489); *Lex Romana Burgundionum* 40; *Variae* 4. 14, "is solvat tributum, qui possessionis noscitur habere compendium." There is no basis for supposing that the receipt of a *sors* obliged an Ostrogoth to enroll his name in the Roman tax records.

[69] *Variae* 1. 26. 2-3 (a Gothic church): "quatinus superindicticiorum onera titulorum praefata ecclesia in ea summa non sentiat, qua usque a magnifici viri patricii Cassiodori . . . temporibus est soluta. Ea vero quae a tempore beneficii ad ecclesiam nostram ab aliquibus est translata professio, commune cum universis possessoribus onus

immune from taxation. If they were content to live off their *sortes*, their obligation was to serve the king as soldiers, and not to contribute to his treasury. The Gothic taxpayers were only that minority who, by deciding to invest in land, incurred the same burdens as Roman *possessores*.

In the arguments just developed concerning "assignment warrants" and Gothic taxation, the lack of specific references to *sortes* in the relevant letters of Cassiodorus has been the basis for a negative conclusion: the letters are not about allotments since none is mentioned. The same silence is observable in the letter we come to now. On the other hand, this letter documents a relationship between two Romans and a Goth that is hard to account for otherwise than by the assumption that an allotment is tacitly involved: the Goth was trying to transform his *sors* into private-law property—expropriation after the fact. The text, dated ca. 527, reads:

King Athalaric to Cunigast, *vir illustris*. [We] are moved by the pathetic complaint of Constantius and Venerius, who allege that a farm (*agellum*) called Fabricula, belonging to them, with everything upon it, has been taken away by Tanca; they add that, unless they sue for recovery of their property, the status of ultimate servitude will be imposed upon their free persons.

[The addressee is to call Tanca before his court, hear the case, and pronounce judgment:] for, just as it is a serious matter to deprive owners of their rights, so is it

---

solutionis agnoscat et illius subiaceat functioni, cuius nacta est iura dominii. Alioquin grata nobis augmenta eius esse non possunt, qui fisci damno proficiat. Sufficiat possessori compendium pensionis: tributa sunt purpurae, non lacernae." The last line is presumably a negative response to the claim of the church to be tax-exempt because clerics were forbidden to fight. The whole passage is important for stressing the distinction between the tax yield of landed property and its private revenue. (For the coupling of basic tax with liability to *superindicta, Variae* 5. 14. 6.)

unfitting to our age to depress free necks with the yoke of servitude.

If the rules for immediate recovery of possession (*momenti iura*) are applicable, let the seized property be restored at once, but only if [the defendant or his agent] has attended the trial. Let violent seizure cease, and either let [Tanca] possess convicted slaves with the goods he is entitled to, or let him relinquish free men who have been proved unimpaired and sound [that is to say, with respect to their liberty].

[Tanca should be grateful that the king allows him the benefit of a trial and excuses him from the penalty for seizure of property before a trial.][70]

Like many others of the *Variae*, this letter documents a type of transaction, not just an isolated instance, and, though we cannot be sure about the rights and wrongs of the case reported, the eventuality that the appeal was justified may be seriously entertained.[71] Boëthius bears witness to comparable situations: "How often have I protected, by putting my authority in danger, such poor wretches as the unpunished covetousness of the barbarians harassed with unending accusations."[72] The Roman appellants whom Cassiodorus shows us were free men and landowners. Their dispute with Tanca was not just over the ownership of some land, as though between neighbors, but also over their per-

[70] *Variae* 8. 28. In strict law, seizure of property prior to final judgment of a dispute (signified by the widely used terms *invasio*, *pervasio*, and *praesumptio*) resulted in the loss of the case; Athalaric excused Tanca from the application of this rule.

Ostrogoths did not reduce only Romans to servitude; *Variae* 5. 29-30 show it being done to other Goths, but without reference to land.

[71] For a timely warning that pleas need not be truthful, H. Idris Bell, *Egypt from Alexander the Great to the Arab Conquest* (Oxford, 1948), pp. 24-25.

[72] *De consolatione philosophiae* 1. 4. 35, trans. H. F. Stewart, Loeb (London, 1918), p. 145. See also the sermon (probably applicable to Visigothic territory) cited below, Chapter VI n. 7.

sonal status—an unambiguous sign that the Goth was, in some respect, their "superior." This "superiority" of a Goth over Roman landowners is precisely the sort of relationship that would exist between someone holding a tax declaration, and benefiting from its annual proceeds, and the owners of the declared property. It is not surprising that the latter were in some jeopardy: a free *possessor* paying "taxes" to the beneficiary of a Gothic *sors* need not have looked very different from an agricultural bondsman paying rent to his owner, and, in the cases involving accumulated debts, the margin must have seemed very thin indeed.[73] Expropriation was not a prerequisite of Gothic allotment, but, over the years, it was a consequence that being allotted might have for those Romans who fell into arrears of payment or had the misfortune of having a rapacious Goth as their "superior."

Italy was not the only arena for oppression of this kind; various Visigoths in Gaul acted in the same way. Such at least is the contention of a pair of hagiographies, both of the sixth-century but relating events that supposedly happened in the time of the kingdom of Toulouse. Although these texts have the usual shortcomings of their genre as historical documents, the portrayal of institutional conditions cannot be far wrong.[74] The shorter passage reads: "One 'dominate' above all from the nation of Gothic origin had, by virtue of the alien allotment (*sub sorte hostilitatis*), deprived all the inhabitants of the place of all their rights of property, and, for a long time, the rapacity of that family danced about here and there, feasting on the goods of vari-

[73] The Roman *possessor* whose *professio* had been awarded as an allotment was subject to being squeezed between the Goth, who might justly foreclose his property for arrears of payment, and the state, whose assessment registers kept him personally responsible for the tax payments of the land: to be obliged to payment without owning one's land added up to servitude.

[74] Courcelle, *Hist. litt.*, pp. 339-347; Thompson, "Settlement," p. 65 n. 3.

ous persons without becoming sated. . . ."[75] By formally associating allotment and dispossession, the hagiographer establishes a point that is only implicit in *Variae* 8. 28: the *sors hostilitatis*—as noted earlier, an ironical pun on *hospitalitas*—was the specific platform from which these Visigoths went on to deprive free Romans of their property and otherwise to plunder them.

The second text varies on the same theme:

> . . . in the time of the Goths, when [King Theodoric II, 456-466] was ruling, an unbearable order (*iniunctio*) was laid upon the citizens of Saintes, such that they would lose their properties and would be subjected most of all to losing their free condition. And when [the Goths] had taken away the riches of ordinary men (*mediocres*) but, aroused by the torch of greed, were also lusting after the wherewithal of all the well born (*nobiles*), they laid down that all of them should be dragged in chains with unrestrained harshness to the city of Toulouse, so that, by wresting the life [of the men of Saintes], they might with unendurable usurpation fulfil the full scope of their plunders: with the residents eliminated, the barbarians might own (*possiderent*) whatever they lusted after.[76]

Lot's interpretation, centered on the term *iniunctio*, was that the passage had something to do with taxation; but this calls for *iniunctio* to carry a technical sense that it does not have.[77] The noteworthy points are, rather, that the in-

[75] *Passio s. Vincentii* 6, ed. de Gaiffier (cited Chapter II n. 3), p. 180; Latin text below, Chapter VI n. 7.

[76] *Vita s. Bibiani Sanctonensis* 4, ed. B. Krusch, MGH *Script. rer. Merov.*, vol. 3, p. 96.

[77] Ferdinand Lot, "La *Vita Viviani* et la domination visigothique en Aquitaine," in *Mélanges Paul Fournier* (Paris, 1929), pp. 467-477; on *iniunctio*, p. 470, where Lot merely built on Krusch's statement that *iniunctio* meant *tributum* (MGH *Script. rer. Merov.*, vol. 3, p. 96 n. 2). Thompson, "Settlement," p. 68 n. 22, repeated Lot without further argument.

cident opposed a group of Goths, and not the king, to the *cives* of Saintes, that it occurred many decades after Gothic allotments were distributed (the assignment of allotments is not in question), and that the threat hanging over the Romans, and perhaps realized in the case of the *mediocres*, was the loss of their properties and personal freedom. Except for the dangers incurred by the *nobiles*, the situation is the same as the other two we have seen, in which settled Goths strove to seize Roman property and sometimes succeeded. Boëthius must have had something like this in mind when he wrote about covetous barbarians harassing poor wretches with unending accusations. The *nobiles* were the main obstacle to the Goths' emerging as the unchallenged seigneurs of Saintes, and they could not easily be reduced to bondage. They were, therefore, dragged in chains to the royal court, probably on the pretext of some capital crime, which the hagiographer does not specify; it was expected that they would be put to death. The intercession of their bishop prevented this outcome and also restored them to the king's favor. The hagiographer then lost interest. Perhaps the expectation was that, under royal protection, the *nobiles* would be safe for a while from further assaults on the part of their Gothic rivals.

That there are only three documented episodes of this kind seems less important than that they all involve the same circumstances. They are valuable for illustrating the point that, in Gaul as well as Italy, the expropriation of Roman property was not the condition for barbarian allotments but a consequence that they might have. We would be wrong to suppose, moreover, that the oppressive behavior described by Cassiodorus and the hagiographers was peculiar to barbarous Goths. Another hagiographer tells us

---

In thirty-two instances of *iniungere* and forms in *CTh*, the word never occurs in a context of taxation. The instances that are at all relevant to the *Vita Bibiani* involve an official order to perform an occasional task: *CTh* 13. 4. 1, 5. 7 (334), 6. 22. 3 (340), 11. 10. 2 (370), 15. 3. 3 (387), 6. 23. 2 (423, possibly costly).

how a saintly abbot successfully interceded before the Burgundian king Hilperic (ca. 467) against a Roman "puffed up with an office at court" who had subjected *pauperes* to slavery by high-handed means.[78] Salvian of Marseille, writing in the 440s in the part of Gaul still under Roman control, describes a more complex pattern of conduct that had much the same results: poorer landowners, hard pressed by the tax machinery, turned to the rich for protection; they made over their whole property to their protectors but—the essential point—they continued to bear the fiscal burden of their lands. They or their heirs, now threatened by private seizure of their property as well as by the public tax collectors, were eventually forced to flee their holdings and to lose the basis of their free status. Their remaining option was to become the bondsmen of the rich.[79] The thrust of Salvian's argument should not mislead us into thinking that he was portraying an abuse of law on the part of the greedy rich. In order to stress that the outrageously uncharitable behavior of protectors toward their protégés was a matter of individual moral responsibility, Salvian avoided mentioning the role of the state in making

[78] *Vita ss. patrum Iurensium* 92, 95, ed. and trans. François Martine, Sources chrétiennes 142 (Paris, 1968), pp. 336, 338, 340: "dum pro adflictione pauperum, quos persona quadam, honore dignitatis aulicae tumens, vi pervasionis inlicitae servitutis iugo subdiderat, coram . . . Hilperico . . . nititur defensare. . . ."; "regii sententia promulgata, liberos restituit libertati." In the light of ibid. 94, Martine (p. 336 n. 2) is unquestionably right to identify the *persona* as a Gallo-Roman, rather than a Burgundian, as believed by Courcelle, *Hist. litt.*, p. 168. This *Vita* is roughly contemporaneous—early sixth century—to the *Vita Bibiani* and *Passio Vincentii*. In regard to all these hagiographers, see the suggestive observations of Arnaldo Momigliano, "La caduta senza rumore di un Impero nel 476 D.C.," *Rivista storica Italiana* 85 (1973): 10-14.

[79] *De gubernatione Dei* 5. 38-45. The latest edition is by Georges Lagarrigue, Sources chrétiennes 220 (Paris, 1975), pp. 340-346 (with French translation). For an earlier denunciation of greedy landowners, Cyprian *Ad Donatum* 12 (owners adding *saltus* to *saltus*, a theme also found in pagan literature). Only in Salvian is tax law presupposed by the whole transaction.

these transactions possible. Disembodied taxation plays a sinister part in the exposé, but Salvian had no intention of shifting the blame to the government and supplying rich landowners with the excuse that their conduct toward the *pauperes* was entirely within the law.[80] Regardless, however, of Salvian's innuendos to the contrary, the rich acted in enforcement of their legal rights. So, at a later date, did the barbarians in Gaul and Italy.

Similar results—loss of property and freedom—suggest similar premises. The protectors portrayed by Salvian underwrote the tax assessments of their protégés vis-à-vis the state. The barbarians to whom the government gave allotments consisting of tax assessment were in the same position, except that they were exempt from the monetary obligations that Roman protectors assumed. From this platform of "superiority" guaranteed to them by the state, the holders of assessments, regardless of nationality, had the capability of expropriating and enslaving the *possessores* subject to them. Neither the protectors nor the Goths manifested extraordinary harshness; they were, more or less severely, exercising legitimate rights to exact revenue from their personal taxpayers. These incidents may, therefore, be less significant for what they tell us about friction between Goths and Romans than for showing the success of the government's system of allotment in locating the barbarians within the upper stratum of provincial landowners.

The appeal of Constantius and Venerius against Tanca—Roman *possessores* contending against the Goth who, in all likelihood, held their assessment as his allotment—brings to an end our examination of the evidence bearing upon the settlement in Italy. Their case, and the others like it, illus-

---

[80] Although often cited to illustrate fifth-century, or even late Roman, conditions (e.g., Stein, *Bas-Empire*, vol. 1, pp. 344-347), the passage has not, to my knowledge, received a detailed commentary explaining the legal basis of the situation, such as the paradox, "cum rem amiserint, amissarum tamen rerum tributa patiuntur" (5. 42); Lagarrigue's annotation is elementary, but he is hardly to blame. For a possible approach, see above, nn. 41, 60, 74.

trate that expropriation, even of minor landowners, leaves traces in the historical record. A correspondingly greater outcry would have been heard if the very mode of allotment had been based, as was once supposed, on the dispossession of Roman proprietors. There was no need for the government to resort to such draconic measures. The tax system was so ordered as to make barbarian settlement a comparatively simple and, at least initially, painless matter, as Ennodius and Cassiodorus attest. On the basis of the texts that have now been reappraised, the facts of the Italian case can be set out in summary form.

What occurred under Odoacer can be only incompletely known from Procopius. However probable it is that Odoacer's troops insisted on allotments and that he satisfied their demands, nothing certain may be said about what he allocated to this purpose or how the allotments he made were later treated by Theodoric. We reach solid ground only with the testimony of Cassiodorus. The point of departure of the Ostrogothic settlement was a special allocation, or fund, segregated from the total tax assessments of Italy. A one-third share of these assessments was made available for distribution, and its availability was affirmed by collecting one-third of the ordinary tax from each district as a separate account, the *illatio tertiarum*.[81] Out of this allocation of assessments, Liberius made his individual assignments, using the unit of tax assessment, *iugum* or *millena*, as the minimum standard for an award to each qualified Goth.[82] As soon as allotments were assigned, the

81 If the word *tertiae* in *Variae* 1. 14, 2. 16, and 2. 17 is understood as a short form of *tertiae professionum*, i.e., the total allocation, it might well be the precise concept underlying Procopius's phrase "one-third of the land of Italy."

82 *Variae* 8. 26 establishes that the king's Gothic subjects held *sortes* and received donatives; "all the Goths" summoned to receive a donative in 5. 26 are called *millenarii* in 5. 27; thus, in the parts of Italy where *millenae* were the units of tax accounting, each Gothic *sors* was composed of one *millena*. Presumably, the corresponding unit of allotment in the north was the *iugum* (4. 20).

state cancelled the corresponding amount of tax-in-gold from the local accounts of *illatio tertiarum*; this compensated the previous (Roman) holder of the assessment for his loss.[83] When Liberius completed his work, a considerable part of the allocation must have been used up, because it had become *sortes Gothicae*. Whatever balance was left continued to pay its tax as a distinct account and remained at the king's disposal if he needed to provide a previously overlooked Goth with an allotment. Alternatively, a tax district could be allowed to eliminate its balance of the allocation and to resume paying the whole of its tax under a single heading.[84]

Just like the institutions receiving state subsidies in the form of *iuga* and *millenae*, the holders of Gothic lots obtained the tax proceeds of their awards and were, naturally, tax-exempt in their regard. Presumably, they were supplied with an extract from the public tax registers, itemizing the concrete components of the *iugum* or *millena* of assessment that was now theirs, and also specifying the proprietors owing the tax of the assessment and the amount of tax due. This document, which may or may not have been a *pittacium delegationis*, was their warrant for collecting the annual proceeds of their allotment from the Roman *possessores*.[85] In theory, the relationship of the Goths to their individual taxpayers was supposed to remain on an abstract and public level. Some Goths, however, not content with their state-derived "superiority," contrived to turn them-

---

[83] *Variae* 2. 17. If the compensated Roman suffered a real loss, it consisted in the difference between the tax-in-gold he had paid to the state and the (presumably more valuable) tax payments of the land and its cultivators—the payments that now passed from him to the Goth.

[84] *Variae* 2. 17 illustrates the first eventuality, and 1. 14, the second.

[85] No example has survived. The suggestion here is that such documents were in the form of the *polyptyca exactorum* referred to in the *Interpretatio* to *CTh* 11. 26. 2 or the *breves* in Gregory the Great *Registrum* 14. 14 (cf. 9. 48, 199); Goffart, "Three Notes," pp. 381-382.

selves eventually into private-law owners of the Roman tributaries and their lands.[86] Individual cases of this kind, which lacked official sanction, were the only element of expropriation that the Ostrogothic settlement entailed.

Cassiodorus never mentions the precedents upon which the allotments were based. The Goths are never called "guests," and there is no information on how they were provided with shelter. Although the fraction one-third is reminiscent of the proportion of a house allotted to a military traveler, it is too common a fraction to be associated exclusively with one institution. Rather than being derived from the laws on billeting, the fraction may have simply been an estimate of the proportion of state revenue spent on maintaining the standing army. The essential point is that the government, at least in Italy, acquitted its debt to the barbarians in a more edifying and legal way than by high-handedly stripping its subjects of a large fraction of their wealth. The Gothic allotments, like military expenses in general, were a public expenditure, met out of the resources at the disposal of the state; just as rations were issued out of tax proceeds, so were the *sortes* assigned out of tax assessments, with a corresponding loss of revenues, since the former payers of tax-in-gold were indemnified. The result of the operation was somewhat different from turning the Goths into landowners. Instead of becoming simple proprietors, they acquired a privileged position in the Italian countryside, similar to that of any person or institution drawing income—effortlessly—from tax proceeds. Their private interests were intimately associated, not just with something so elementary as private property, but with the state-instituted system of privilege on which their annual salaries depended.

[86] *Variae* 8. 28.

IV

****

SETTLEMENTS IN GAUL.
THE VISIGOTHS

ITALY is the model case of barbarian settlement. Only there can we know more or less precisely who conducted the allotments, what resources were allocated to this purpose, how the allocation was administered, how much each Goth was given, and even what kind of oppression a Goth could exercise upon the Roman taxpayers assigned to him. The Italian example offers modern imaginations a firm guide to the course that a fifth-century settlement in Roman territory might take; and more, it documents an instance where allotments could be made without expropriation of private property because tax assessments were awarded instead.

It is tempting to assert flatly that the procedures used in Italy had been adopted at an earlier date by the Roman authorities when they established the Visigoths in Aquitaine and the Burgundians in Sapaudia. Such a view would have the advantage of eliminating the various difficulties that the currently accepted interpretation of the settlements in Gaul presents. The hard part is to tailor the evidence of the Visigothic and Burgundian laws to the Italian pattern. It is not as though these sources are more favorable to the traditional interpretation; for example, the "one-third" of Roman *hospitalitas* bears little relation to the "two-thirds" of the land and "one-half" of the woods, house, and gardens stipulated in some texts from Gaul. The fundamental problem is that the Visigothic and Burgundian laws speak at a great distance in time from the original allotments and that they say very little. There is, in fact, only one substantial text for Gaul, namely, title fifty-four of the Burgundian

103

code, itself bristling with difficulties. All the rest are odds and ends, of little independent value. The kind of conclusions attainable with the help of Cassiodorus's *Variae* are beyond reach in Gaul. The best that can be hoped for is an approximation, compatible both with the evidence that there is and with the lessons of Ostrogothic Italy.

A closer look at the sources for Gaul illustrates their shortcomings. The chroniclers tell us no more about the original Visigothic settlement in 418 than that it was initiated by the patrician Constantius, who assigned to King Wallia a territory for his people to inhabit.[1] The church historian Philostorgius adds details drawn—we cannot tell how accurately—from Olympiodorus: the Visigoths were granted both rations and land for tillage.[2] There are also the personal reminiscences of Paulinus of Pella, largely confined, however, as regards this topic, to the period when the Visigoths were temporarily in Bordeaux (413-414).[3] In short,

[1] Prosper *Chron.* a. 419, "Constantius patricius pacem firmat cum Wallia data ei ad inhabitandum secunda Aquitanica et quibusdam civitatibus confinium provinciarum" (MGH AA, vol. 9, p. 469); Hydatius *Chron.* a. 418, "Gothi intermisso certamine quod agebant per Constantium ad Gallias revocati sedes in Aquitanica a Tolosa usque ad Oceanum acceperunt" (MGH AA, vol. 11, p. 19). The Chronicle of 452 has "Aquitania Gothis tradita" under 413 (MGH AA, vol. 9, p. 654), where the others note Athaulf's seizure of Narbonne. Jordanes *Getica* 160-165 and Isidore of Seville *Historia Gothorum* (MGH AA, vol. 11) add nothing. See also Thompson, "Settlement," pp. 65-67; J. F. Matthews, *Senatorial Aristocracy and Imperial Court, A.D. 364-425* (Oxford, 1975), pp. 318-319.

[2] Philostorgius *Historia ecclesiastica* 12. 4. On relations to Olympiodorus, J. F. Matthews, "Olympiodorus of Thebes and the History of the West (A.D. 407-425)," *JRS* 60 (1970): 81, 91. Olympiodorus is discernible at two removes: Philostorgius's adaptation and Photius's ninth-century summary of Philostorgius. The chronology of Philostorgius's account (as we have it) is completely confused, and the grant of rations was probably unrelated to the settlement in Aquitaine. All in all, the reference to land "for cultivation" offers little guarantee of accuracy. Jones, *LRE*, pp. 202 and 1109 n. 65, may have taken Philostorgius more seriously than he deserves.

[3] Paulinus *Eucharisticus* lines 282-290 (ed. H. G. Evelyn-White,

we are denied the slightest glimpse at the distribution of allotments and cannot even tell precisely when it took place. The first text documenting the existence of Visigothic *sortes* occurs in the Code of Euric (hereafter *CE*), whose date is about 475, and, at any rate, in Euric's reign, 466-484/5.[4] Two extracts bear on the subject, and the more circumstantial of them lacks the opening lines that are indispensable to its interpretation. For further information, we must turn to the mid-seventh-century collection of Reccesvinth (hereafter *LVisig*). Under the rubric *Antiqua*, it reproduces accurate extracts from the second Visigothic codification, the *Codex revisus* of Leovigild, drawn up in Spain between 568 and 586. In keeping with the role of a reviser, Leovigild modernized whatever laws of Euric he incorporated into his code.[5] Four or five *Antiquae* contain unmistakable references to the allotments, but they can

---

Loeb, *Ausonius*, vol. 2): his favorite dwelling, the only one of his houses without a Gothic *hospes*, was plundered; in several cases, Gothic guests saved the houses they were in from damage. For the date, Matthews, *Aristocracy*, p. 317 (who, however, confuses guests with "settlement"). Paulinus later lost his extensive property, but for political and family reasons (*Eucharisticus* lines 503-515). Nothing more in his autobiographical poem can be definitely related to the special circumstances of Visigothic settlement, including lines 575-579, which record the voluntary purchase by a Goth of one of his estates (it is tempting, though, to explain why the price was, in Paulinus's estimation, "scarcely just" by conjecturing that the Goth already had rights to the estate by virtue of allotment, and that what he paid represented only Paulinus's share; but Paulinus's words permit only speculations). See also Chapter VI n. 27.

[4] Rudolf Buchner, *Die Rechtsquellen*, Wattenbach-Levison, *Deutschlands Geschichtsquellen im Mittelalter. Vorzeit und Karolinger*, Beiheft (Weimar, 1953), p. 7 with n. 16.

[5] Ibid., with n. 18.

There is a tendency, in discussions of *hospitalitas*, to equate *Antiquae* with laws of Euric (e.g., Lot, "Hospitalité," p. 988 n. 4, on p. 989); as a comparison of *CE* 276 with *LVisig* 10. 3. 5 shows (see Appendix B), the revision was considerable, and in most cases there is no way to establish its extent.

hardly be taken to document fifth-century conditions.[6] With the exception of CE 276 and 277, therefore, the Visigothic information available to us is more indicative of how the old settlement looked, or was understood, at the close of the sixth century in Spain, than of how it had been in Gaul under Euric, let alone at its inception some fifty years earlier.

The information that the chronicles supply about the Burgundians is no more detailed than that about the Visigoths. It is noted under 443 that the "remnants" of the Burgundians—after the destruction in 436 of their kingdom in northern Gaul—were given Sapaudia "to divide with the natives"; the patrician Aëtius promoted their relocation. Then, in 457, the Burgundians enlarged their territory: with the assent and support of the Visigoths, King Gundioc "entered Gaul with his people and all their goods in order to reside."[7] There are also later accounts of these events.

[6] LVisig 10. 1. 8, 9, 16, 10. 3. 5 (opening lines); moreover, 10. 1. 6 (an Antiqua emendata, i.e., revised a second time for inclusion in Reccesvinth's collection) seems relevant because of its resemblance to LBurg 31. Antiquae mentioning consortes (e.g., LVisig 8. 5. 5, where, exceptionally, one reads consortes vel ospites) might be pertinent, since the revisers may have substituted consors for hospes (10. 1. 6); but partnership was too common an institution to be exclusively between Romans and Visigoths (e.g., 10. 1. 3, 7).

[7] Chron. of 452, a. 443, "Sapaudia Burgundionum reliquiis datur cum indigenis dividenda" (MGH AA, vol. 9, p. 660). On the localization of Sapaudia—not identical to modern French Savoy—see Pierre Duparc, "La Sapaudia," Académie des inscriptions et belles-lettres, Paris. Comptes rendus (1958), pp. 371-383 (with map). Auctarium Havniensis Prosperi a. 457, after the death of the Suevic king Rechiarius (Dec. 456), "Gundiocus rex Burgundionum cum gente et omni praesidio annuente sibi Theodorico ac Gothis intra Galliam ad habitandum ingressus societate et amicitia Gothorum functus" (MGH AA, vol. 9, p. 305). (An entry for 455 records that the Burgundians repulsed a Gepid attack on Gaul; after 457 there is a large hiatus until substantive entries resume.) Although the Auctarium Havniensis was assembled in early seventh-century Italy, its fifth-century entries are now believed to stem from contemporary or near-contemporary sources, notably the Ravenna Annals: Wes, Ende des Kaisertums,

At the close of the sixth century, Marius of Avenches portrayed Gundioc's move as involving the Burgundians' "dividing the lands with the Gallic senators." Finally, in the mid-seventh century, Fredegar tells us that, much earlier, under Valentinian I (363-375), the Gallo-Romans invited the Burgundians to immigrate so that their sponsors might be able to stop paying taxes to the imperial government.[8] Although Marius and Fredegar valuably illustrate how the epoch of each one wished to remember the original settlements, they are without standing as witnesses to fifth-century conditions.[9] The contemporary chronicles, for their

---

pp. 57-58. But critical analysis of the *Auctarium Havniensis* is still in flux.

For the circumstances of Gundioc's move, which was hardly so final as the chronicle suggests, see Schmidt, *Ostgermanen*, pp. 140-141.

[8] Marius *Chron.* a. 456, "Eo anno Burgundiones partem Galliae occupaverunt terrasque cum Gallis senatoribus diviserunt" (MGH *AA*, vol. 11, p. 232); Fredegar *Chron.* 2. 46, "Et cum ibidem [that is, ad Renum] duobus annis resedissent, per legatis invitati a Romanis vel Gallis, qui Lugdunensium provinciam et Gallea comata, Gallea domata et Gallea Cesalpinae manebant, ut tributa rei publice potuissent rennuere, ibi cum uxoris et liberes visi sunt consedisse" (MGH *Script. rer. Merov.*, vol. 2, p. 68).

[9] Marius (d. 581) was a contemporary of Gregory of Tours; on the date and authorship of the Fredegar chronicle (ca. 660), W. Goffart, "The Fredegar Problem Reconsidered," *Speculum* 38 (1963): 206-241. Marius's account has been accepted without question by most authors (e.g., Thompson, "Settlement," p. 65; Lot, "Hospitalité," pp. 989-990, with small reservations); it constitutes the chief prop for the idea that barbarian settlements were at the expense of rich men only—even though Marius leaves unclear whether the *terrae* that the *senatores* divided were their own. Sparsely informed about early Burgundian history, Marius must have drawn upon a source for this, his unique entry for the Burgundians in the fifth century. But he seems to have rewritten the information in his fashion; note, for stylistic comparison, *partem Galliae* under the year 509, and *senatores* under 538. His entry is best understood as a late sixth-century interpretation of distant events. Not surprisingly, its spirit anticipates that of Fredegar's migration legend.

As regards Fredegar, Thompson, "Settlement," p. 66: "although

part, establish that there was settlement and "division" in 443 and 457. "Division" might signify a fifty-fifty partition (a ratio also suggested by the laws, as will be seen), but of what? On the precise terms of allotment and the date when *sortes* were distributed, the chronicles are silent.

The Burgundian legal sources, however, markedly surpass the Visigothic ones in length and intelligibility. Inspired by Euric's Visigothic code, King Gundobad (ca. 480-516) caused the Burgundian laws to be collected, and his code has been more fully preserved than Euric's. Its condition, however, is by no means ideal: Gundobad's collection survives only in the enlarged edition issued by Sigismund (517-523) and in ninth-century manuscripts at that.

---

this is absurdly dated . . . the tradition itself seems genuine"; in the same way, Schmidt, *Ostgermanen*, pp. 140-141, believed he could transpose a conjectured authentic core of the passage to the events of 457; literal acceptance by Boehm, *Geschichte Burgunds*, p. 58; Lot, "Hospitalité," pp. 990-991 n. 3, was more prudent. The historicity of the passage was argued by Gabriel Monod, "Sur un texte de la compilation de Frédégaire relatif à l'éstablissement des Burgondions dans l'Empire romain," *Mélanges publiés par la section historique et philologique de l'École des Hautes-Études pour le Xe anniversaire de sa fondation*, BEHE, vol. 35 (Paris, 1878), pp. 229-239; he was followed by Léonzon le Duc, "Le régime de l'hospitalité chez les Burgondes," *NRHD*, 3d ser., 12 (1888): 232-247. Monod's astonishing premise—that Fredegar was incapable of invention—is unacceptable. Fredegar's account partly depends on Cassiodorus-Epiphanius *Historia tripartita* 12. 4. 11-14 (cited above, Chapter III n. 53) and was deliberately interpolated into Jerome *Chron. a.* 373; it has obvious affinities to the "origin" legends then being developed by Fredegar himself, the *Liber historiae Francorum* 2 (where Valentinian also occurs), the *Passio s. Sigismundi* 1-2, and others. The reference to taxation is a characteristically Fredegarian touch (cf. Goffart, "Three Notes," p. 379 nn. 140-141), and so is the verb form *visi sunt consedisse*.

For an idea of how Romans perceived the Burgundian settlement in the decades after it occurred, *Vita patrum Iurensium* 94-95 (cited above, Chapter III n. 78): a mysterious (and presumably unwelcome) decree of Providence.

In Sigismund's edition, the Burgundian code is formed of an original core (*LBurg* 1-36), attributed to Gundobad's initiative, that includes several articles pertinent to the status of barbarian *sortes*. The core was then augmented by a series of Gundobad's new laws, of which some are dated, but none, apparently, is earlier than 501; these *novellae* are of considerably greater interest to allotments than are the original series. Moreover, one Burgundian law transmitted outside the code (*lex extravagans*), and dated 524, contains a clause relevant to our subject.[10] The information on allotments that the Burgundian laws supply is thus comparatively abundant but difficult to date and, in any case, it is far removed from the events of 443 and 457. The crucial text, *LBurg* 54, frequently and extensively commented upon by modern historians, is an added law of Gundobad, almost certainly issued later than 501. In sum, a few Burgundian laws permit inferences to be made about the original conditions on which allotments were made, but, since such inferences are possible only after lengthy textual interpretation, their validity is much less certain than if the sense of the laws were self-evident.[11]

Early or late, none of the texts just described provides a narrative account of the Visigothic or Burgundian settlements, not even one comparable to Procopius's tale of Odoacer's land grants. The versions in our manuals are modern reconstructions, based chiefly on three laws. Of these, *CE* 277 juxtaposes Gothic *sortes* to the "third of the Romans"; *CE* 276 mentions some Goths entering the "place of the hosts (*locus hospitum*)" in order to supervise a boundary delimitation; and *LBurg* 54 records, among other things, a recent ordinance that allowed a Burgundian to claim

---

[10] Buchner, *Rechtsquellen*, pp. 11-12.

[11] Lot, "Hospitalité," p. 977, disregarded the discrepancy between the date of Burgundian settlement and that of *Lex Burgundionum*; *LBurg* 54 is treated as though it applied to 443. So also Stein, *Bas-Empire*, vol. 1, p. 331.

"one-third of the bondsmen [and] two parts of the lands from that place in which hospitality had been assigned to him."[12]

Two features of these extracts—the terminology of *hospitalitas* and the explicit or implicit fraction two-thirds—occupy center stage in modern syntheses. A typical version is as follows (though limited, in the event, to the Visigoths, it might easily be extended to the Burgundians):

As allies of Rome, the Goths based themselves primarily on the Roman regime of military quartering (*hospitalitas*). According to it, the military *hospes* received a *tertia* (*tertia hospiti deputata*) of the country estate in which he took up residence . . . At some time after the Gothic occupation of Aquitania II and Novempopulonia . . . a new system of sharing, more favorable to the Goths, was put into practice; by virtue of it, only one-third of the cultivated land went to the Roman proprietor, and the two other parts to the Gothic partner (*consors*).[13]

An admirable effort has been made here to expand scanty data; yet there are serious problems. We are asked to believe that the barbarian allotments entailed expropriation on a large scale of Roman property, without its being shown, however modestly, that any Romans were in fact dispossessed. Moreover, the legal basis for these expropriations is derived from Roman *hospitalitas*, even though the military quartering of the Theodosian Code had nothing to do with agricultural assets or the income from land. These flaws are decisive. Our chances of reconstructing precisely how the settlements in Gaul were organized may

---

[12] *CE* 277 is dealt with at length below, and *LBurg* 54 in Chapter v. For *CE* 276, see Appendix B.

[13] Alvaro d'Ors, *Estudios Visigoticos*, vol. 2, *El Codigo de Eurico.* Instituto Juridico Español, *Cuadernos* 12 (Rome-Madrid, 1960), p. 173; the word I translate as "country estate" is *finca* (cf. Gaudemet, *Institutions*, p. 724 n. 5, "domaine"). Along the same lines, Gaupp, *Ansiedlungen*, pp. 394-403; Schmidt, *Ostgermanen*, pp. 505-506; Levy, *Law of Property*, p. 84; Jones, *LRE*, pp. 249, 251-252.

be remote, but we may be close to certain that they happened in some other way than is currently supposed.

There is a documented occasion, almost contemporary to the introduction of the Burgundians into Sapaudia, when the settlement of a barbarian people in Gaul resulted in the forthright expropriation of Roman landowners: "The [body of] Alans to whom the patrician Aëtius had given the lands of farther Gaul to divide with the inhabitants subdued resisters with their weapons and, after expelling the owners, gained possession by force."[14] Though sometimes taken to demonstrate the ferocity of the Alans (as, one suspects, the chronicler intended it to be), the incident has special value for the history of orderly barbarian settlement. For one thing, it again illustrates that the dispossession of Roman landowners was sufficiently scandalous to win a place in even a thin historical record. A less obvious implication of the Alan seizures is that the Roman government played a crucial part in the process of smoothly distributing allotments among barbarians. Here, the governmental role is demonstrated by the lamentable consequences of its absence. For reasons of political geography, it is hardly surprising that, in this instance and none other, Roman provincials physically resisted a barbarian settlement: the area in question had, for many years, been under only intermittent central control and even occasionally in rebellion.[15] Were there any assessment registers left? Was any proprietor regularly paying tax on his land? Where the regimenta-

---

[14] *Chron.* of 452, a. 442, "Alani, quibus terrae Galliae ulterioris cum incolis dividendae a patricio Aetio traditae fuerant, resistentes armis subigunt et expulsis dominis terrae possessionem vi adipiscuntur" (MGH *AA*, vol. 9, p. 660).

[15] *Gallia ulterior* was the region that withdrew from Roman *societas* under the leadership of Tibatto in 435 (*Chron.* of 452, MGH *AA*, vol. 9, p. 660); for earlier unrest in the region, Thompson, "Settlement," pp. 70-71 and Wallace-Hadrill, "Gothia," pp. 27-28. It might be conjectured that the Alan settlement of 442 was Aëtius's solution to the rising of 435, recovering something for the central government from a region that was lost to it anyway.

tion of Roman citizens had lapsed, any program for dividing lands inevitably required expropriation. Outright resistance was the natural response of owners who, in the absence of regular taxation, could hardly be compensated for their losses by mere tax relief. The course of events in "farther Gaul" is indicative of what might have happened elsewhere if the subtleties of the tax machinery had not been present to cushion the confrontation between provincials and barbarians.

For some reason, the chroniclers entered into greater detail when relating Alan settlement than when concerned with Visigoths or Burgundians. A second report happens to supply the only unambiguous evidence that tax assessments were mobilized in Gaul, as they later were in Italy, for the assignment of barbarian allotments: "The deserted countryside (*rura*) of the city of Valence was handed over for partitioning to the Alans commanded by Sambiba."[16] When Musset suggested that these Alans were given "deserted" lands because they were nomads needing nothing better to wander over with their flocks, he assumed that the adjective conveyed topographical or agrarian information.[17] In all probability, however, the chronicler's usage is identical to that of late Roman law, in which the term *agri deserti* signifies, not abandoned or barren lands, but, rather, property entered in the public assessment registers that, for whatever cause, was not paying its tax. What we can know to be "deserted" is the tax debt, and not the land itself, which continued to be occupied (especially by slaves and tenants who were immovable because registered) and more

[16] *Chron.* of 452, a. 440, "Deserta Valentinae urbis rura Alanis, quibus Sambiba praeerat, partienda traduntur" (MGH *AA*, vol. 9, p. 660).

[17] Musset, *Vagues germaniques*, p. 286 n. 1. His interpretation of *deserta* conforms to the common modern practice; e.g., Lot, "Hospitalité," p. 1010, "parties dévastées," and the discussion of *agri deserti* in Jones, *LRE*, pp. 812-823, 1039-1040 (note that the index entry "deserted land" also includes pp. 774-775, presumably as an explanation of how desertion took place).

or less cultivated.[18] Settling Alans on these lands was the alternative to giving the property to whatever entrepreneur would assume the tax burden; either way, the occupants would fall to more exacting masters. The attribution of delinquent assessments to the Alans is a typical expression of late Roman paternalism. A grant of this kind meant not only that the solvent taxpayers of Valence would lose nothing, but also that their liability for the shortage represented by these bad debts was completely relieved.[19] The objective, as in Theodoric's Italy, was to inconvenience the provincials as little as possible.

At a distance of a half century or more from 418 and 443, the Visigothic and Burgundian laws had no reason to feature the Roman refinements that entered into the original distribution of allotments. A barbarian *sors*, regardless of

[18] The important study of C. R. Whittaker, *"Agri deserti,"* in M. I. Finley, ed., *Studies in Roman Property* (Cambridge, 1976), pp. 137-175, 193-200 (notes), is an effective attack on the widely held modern view that *"agri deserti* are to be regarded as a malignant growth of the later Roman Empire, with a datable origin into the bargain." Whittaker's well-documented demonstration of the continued vitality of agriculture offers a strong incentive for a reassessment of the legal texts, on which he prudently commented (p. 138), "How one should interpret those regulations is a problem which I must confess I regard with uneasiness." For provisional remarks on these texts, Goffart, *Caput*, pp. 67 n. 4, 137 n. 4. Note the sense of "desertion" in the phrase "ne sub praetextu militiae privatum seu publicum debitum deseratur" (*NTheod II* 7. 1. 2 [439]). The best indicator of the tendency of these laws occurs in those that facilitate the substitution of solvent owners for bankrupts: *CTh* 12. 1. 161 (399), *CJ* 11. 59. 11 (405s), *CTh* 13. 11. 13 (412), 16 (417). Where assessment registry is intermittent and less than meticulous, there will be a discrepancy between the static records and the actual vicissitudes of taxable owners and cultivable lands. This discrepancy, rather than agriculture, is what the laws on *agri deserti* are chiefly about. They bear witness to the dynamics of the tax system, rather than to the realities of rural life.

[19] A severe burden of being a late Roman *curialis* was to make up for deficits in tax payments, and, in the longer run, the deficit was to be shared with the other taxpayers (*CJ* 11. 59. 1 [312-337]).

how it was initially constituted, was property from the standpoint of its recipient, and landed property at that; it was bound, as time went on, to look increasingly like an ordinary private estate. It is only to be expected, therefore, that the two codes should seem to be dealing with mere property when they regulate allotments. Be that as it may, we have now found that, in Italy, tax assessments were the assets distributed to the Ostrogoths; we have examined two hagiographies in which Visigoths behave like their Italian counterparts, and probably for the same reason; and we also know that, in Gaul, a group of Alans was assigned a category of assessments to share out among themselves. It remains to be seen whether the Visigothic and Burgundian laws, though ostensibly alien to such schemes, contain passages and provisions suggesting that the original awards consisted of a state-derived "superiority" over land rather than of (expropriated) private property. Only then will it be possible to consider what relationship the rules of Roman billeting may have had to the installation of the barbarians.

The tax machinery of Roman Gaul was in working order when the Visigoths and Burgundians were settled; Salvian bears witness to its ravages, and even Sidonius felt its impact sufficiently to ask for a little relief in 459.[20] What became of this lucrative resource when whole districts were

[20] Salvian, as above, Chapter III at n. 79; Sidonius *Carmen* 13 (459); ibid., 5. 446-448 (Panegyric of Majorian, 458): though wearied by continual tributes, Gaul gladly endures a tax for building a fleet against the Vandals. Also Sidonius *Epistolae* 5. 13 (460s), and 3. 6. 3: "It is a common saying with provincials that a good year depends less on ample crops than on a good administration" (trans. O. M. Dalton [Oxford, 1915], 1: 73). Operations of tax machinery in the Visigothic kingdom: Cassiodorus *Variae* 5. 39, and the *Testamentum s. Caesarii Arelatensis*, cited and discussed in Goffart, *Caput*, p. 131 n. 26. *LRB* 40, on the transfer of tax liability, reiterates an old fiscal rule. The very categorical and circumstantial statement on the continuity of Roman taxation in the fifth-century kingdoms by Musset, *Vagues germaniques*, p. 282, is based, tacitly, on Merovingian evidence (below, Chapter VIII n. 33).

114

made available to barbarians "for residence"? Little is known about the forms of government in the earliest barbarian kingdoms of Gaul. Nevertheless, it is unlikely that the apparatus of Roman taxation was simply dismantled. What evidence there is suggests that, however altered taxation may have been, it certainly was not suppressed. As far as the Roman tax officials were concerned, the hypothesis that they became answerable to the barbarian kings, Visigothic or Burgundian, is preferable to the alternative that they continued to render account, even for a while, to the prefecture at Arles (that justice over the Roman population followed the latter course for a time is at least conceivable).[21] In Italy, the usurpation of Odoacer involved a reorganization of public finance; in effect, the proceeds of tax assessments were divided between the new king and his followers: the former retained two-thirds, and the latter were

[21] Stein, *Bas-Empire*, vol. 1, pp. 382-386 (too categorical in view of the evidence); A. Loyen, "Les débuts du royaume wisigoth de Toulouse," *Revue des études latines* 12 (1934): 406-415; Heinrich Mitteis, *Der Staat des hohen Mittelalters*, 7th ed. (Weimar, 1962), pp. 31-39 (imaginative rather than reliable); Jones, *LRE*, p. 257 (questionable handling of the evidence); Musset, *Vagues germaniques*, pp. 281-284; Herwig Wolfram, *Intitulatio*, vol. 1, *Lateinische Königs- und Fürstentitel bis zum Ende des 8. Jahrhunderts*, Mitteilungen des Instituts für österreichische Geschichtsforschung, Ergänzungsband 21 (Graz-Vienna, 1967), pp. 32-89 and, esp., 44-56. One of the most explicit statements about royal rights in Roman lands ceded to barbarians occurs in Claudian *De bello Gothico* line 539, about Alaric in Illyricum: "oppida legitimo iussu Romana coegi." This provides an excellent gloss to the *leges Theudoricianae* mentioned by Sidonius *Epistolae* 2. 1. 3 (see Appendix D n. 10).

Claude, *Westgoten*, pp. 43-44, stated that the Romans remained subject to Arles but surmised that the links of the financial personnel to Arles must have been severed by about 440, when Salvian noted flight from Roman fiscality to Gothic territory. The real question, however, is whether any exercise of authority by Arles in Visigothic territory after 418 (even by way of appeal) may be positively documented. To that extent, G. Kaufmann, "Über das Foederatverhältniss des tolosanischen Reichs zu Rom," *Forschungen zur deutschen Geschichte* 6 (1866): 443, 458, was right to insist on the internal autonomy of the Visigothic kingdom.

allocated the balance, as the fund from which their *sortes* were awarded.[22] If something of the same kind took place in Gaul with the advent of the Visigoths and Burgundians, it would partly explain the fate of the Roman tax machinery under new management.

Although expressed in terms of Romans and barbarians, rather than king and followers, a division is basic to our knowledge of the settlements in Gaul. The chronicles mention it, and, by the terms of *CE* 277 and *LBurg* 54 (leaving details aside), the shares appear to be two-thirds for the barbarians and one-third for the Romans. The phraseology of the texts is vague or ambiguous in regard to the main object of division. Modern commentators have no choice but to be more specific than their sources. The usual surmise has been that the division applied to private property—the estates of the Roman *indigenae*.[23] These estates, however, had more than one dimension. Where private property in land, expressed by the word *possessio*, coexisted with taxes assessed on landowners' declarations of their resources, called *professiones*, the ownership of land and the rents arising from it had to be distinct from the property assessments that brought annual returns to the state. Since taxes assessed in this way were levied in fifth-century Gaul, the productive lands of the districts occupied by the Visigoths and Burgundians must have yielded two forms of revenue: the private rents of landlords and the taxes col-

[22] As above, Chapter III at nn. 81-84, where this aspect of the Italian settlement is not mentioned. It is true, however, that whatever part of the *tertiae* was not distributed as *sortes* paid its taxes to the royal government, not to the Ostrogoths, and there is no indication that the proceeds of the *illatio tertiarum* were treated otherwise than as general royal revenues.

[23] Since the division of private estates is asserted without reservations in the literature (e.g., Gaupp, *Ansiedlungen*, p. 394), it is worth observing that no source applicable to Gaul specifies that *praedia, fundi*, or the like were divided; the closest is *LVisig* 10. 1. 8 (text in n. 26 below)—a late law and still not explicit. Cf. Chapter III n. 31.

lected by the state. Both stemmed from "the land" and, for all one knows, they were much the same in composition. Yet they were separate entities.

As soon as this distinction is recognized, the award of barbarian allotments is bound to look like a more complex process than the mere partition of ownership between Romans and newcomers. One is forced to confront and answer the question whether the division embraced only the private category of revenue (rents), or the public category (taxes), or both. One apparent certainty is that neither Visigoths nor Burgundians paid taxes to their kings; another is that Roman landlords kept at least a fraction of their property, together with whatever tax liability it used to bear.[24] Let us suppose, then, for the sake of argument, that all taxable Roman property in the district of settlement was subject to division, and that the distribution was made on such a basis that the tax-exempt barbarians acquired ownership of two-thirds of these properties, whereas the balance was left to the Romans, whose taxes now went to the king. On this hypothesis, the troops would seem to have been decidedly overadvantaged: as recipients of allotments consisting of expropriated estates, they would have pocketed both the private and the public revenues of their double share, whereas the barbarian king was limited to collecting only the tax revenues of his portion—the properties left in Roman hands. Once the fact that Roman landowners regularly

[24] The idea that the barbarians were taxed has a much weaker basis in the sources for Gaul than in those for Italy. Although the *Variae* permit a plausible argument that only closer study proves to be mistaken (above, Chapter III at nn. 65-66), nothing comparable exists in Gaul. Several modern authors have maintained that, sooner or later, the Visigoths and Burgundians were subject to taxation: Gaupp, *Ansiedlungen*, pp. 403-406; Dahn, *Könige*, vol. 6 (Würzburg, 1871), pp. 261-262; Fabien Thibault, "Les impôts directs chez les Visigoths et les Burgondes," *NRHD*, 3d ser., 26 (1902): 35-38; Stein, *Bas-Empire*, vol. 1, p. 383. But none of the evidence they cite sustains such a conclusion. As regards the taxation of Roman property, *LVisig* 10. 1. 16 and, perhaps, *LRB* 40.

paid taxes is injected into the story, it becomes apparent, first, that a division between king and followers was necessarily implied by any sharing out of "lands"; and, second, that an interpretation of the texts regarding Visigothic and Burgundian divisions cannot disregard the tax value of property. The understandable forgetfulness or vagueness of the Visigothic and Burgundian codes concerning such bygone conditions has to be compensated for by our efforts.

The texts themselves, to which we now turn, present arresting oddities. Let us begin by examining *CE* 277:

[1] Gothic allotments (*sortes*) and the third (*tertia*) of the Romans that have not been recovered within fifty years are on no account to be reclaimed. [2] The same holds for fugitives: it is not allowed to recall to service those who were not found within fifty years. [3] We order, indeed, that ancient boundaries shall be firm, just as our father of good memory ordered in another law. [4] And all other cases—regardless of whether good or bad . . . and regardless of whether they are slaves placed in dispute or debts that have not been collected—shall on no account be pursued if they have not been terminated within thirty years. [5] If anyone, after this number of thirty years, attempts to plead a case, let that very number oppose him, and let him be forced to pay a pound of gold to that person whom the king will order.[25]

The first sentence is of most immediate interest to us but

[25] *CE* 277: "[1] Sortes Gothicas et tertiam Romanorum quae intra L annis non fuerint revocate nullo modo repetantur. [2] Similiter de fugitivis qui intra L annis inventi non fuerint, non liceat eos ad servitium revocare. [3] Antiquos vero terminos sic stare iubemus sicut et bonae memoriae pater noster in alia lege praecepit. [4] Et alias omnes causas, seu bonas seu malas aut etiam criminales quae intra XXX annis definitae non fuerint, vel mancipia quae in contemptione posita fuerant, sibe debita quae exacta non fuerint, nullo modo repetantur. [5] Et si quis post hunc XXX annorum numerum causam movere temptaverit, iste numerus ei resistat, et libram auri cui rex iusserit coactus exsolvat" (ed. d'Ors, p. 21). See also next note.

deserves to be seen in context. In *LVisig* 10. 1. 8—from Leovigild's *Codex revisus*—one finds a heading "about the division of lands made between a Goth and a Roman" followed by a provision on dividing the "two parts of the Goth" from the "third of the Roman"; hence, an easy gloss for *CE* 277. 1: that the parts consisted of land.[26] But if this assistance from the late sixth century is dispensed with, the meaning of *sortes* and *tertia* is anything but obvious. The main problem is this: according to the standard interpretation (that private property was the object of division), *sortes* plus *tertia* (that is, the two-thirds allotted to the Goths plus the one-third left to the Romans) had to have embraced the totality of landed estates in the Visigothic kingdom; if so, then the fifty-year prescription edicted by *CE* 277. 1 necessarily applied to the totality of lawsuits over the recovery of property. But a prescription of this length— ostentatiously exceeding the, by then, consecrated thirty years—is altogether extravagant.[27] Why would Euric have applied it to something so commonplace as the recovery of all real estate? It is true that the same is done with regard

[26] *LVisig* 10. 1. 8: "De divisione terrarum facta inter Gotum adque Romanum. Divisio inter Gotum et Romanum facta de portione terrarum sive silvarum nulla ratione turbetur, si tamen probatur celebrata divisio, ne de duabus partibus Goti aliquid sibi Romanus presumat aut vindicet, aut de tertia Romani Gotus sibi aliquid audeat usurpare aut vindicare, nisi quod a nostra forsitan ei fuerit largitate donatum. Sed quod a parentibus vel a vicinis divisum est, posteritas inmutare non temtet."

Lot, "Hospitalité," p. 998, and d'Ors, *Codigo*, pp. 200-201, were mistaken in stating that *CE* 277. 1 sets a time limit on disputing the division of *sortes* from *tertia*. They disregarded the obvious parallel with *CE* 277. 2 and failed to observe that Leovigild's revised version of *CE* 277. 1 (= *LVisig* 10. 2. 1-2) is entered under the title "de quinquagenarii et tricennalis temporis intentione," and not under "de divisionibus" (*LVisig* 10. 1). *CE* 277. 1 is about the "recovery" of both *sortes* and *tertia*—whatever that may mean—and not about their delimitation.

[27] On time prescription, Levy, *Law of Property*, pp. 184-190. See also *LBurg* 79. 2-5, where Euric's example was not followed.

to fugitives. But here, too, a prescription of such inordinate length, safeguarding an owner's title for almost two generations as then counted, calls for explanation. As it happens, fugitives subject to *servitium* were a complex category. They included not only private law slaves (comparable to private law property), but also bound tenants—*coloni*—whose *servitium* was a matter of fiscal or public law, rather than of private ownership; even slaves were partly in the public sphere, provided they were registered in tax declarations.[28] We would be mistaken to think that the prescription laid down in *CE* 277. 2 was meant to defend only a private right.

These observations suggest a way out of the difficulties of *CE* 277. 1. A prescription of fifty years reeks of special privilege; it reminds one of the hundred-year prescription that Justinian—briefly—lavished upon ecclesiastical property.[29] That Euric casually granted a fifty-year prescription to all owners of lands and bondsmen is too unnecessarily generous to be believable. On the other hand, by instituting a time limit of this length with regard to something fiscal,

[28] Counting of generations, Levy, *Law of Property*, pp. 186-187. The western laws on fugitives descend from a law of Constantine (*CJ* 6. 1. 4, fugitive slaves) and, less clearly, from one of Valentinian III (*NValent III* 31, esp., parag. 5-6); but there are significant novelties, especially in the provision for nonslave fugitives and the requirement to declare strangers, which are unparalleled in East Roman legislation. See *LVisig* 9. 1. 1, 3, 6, 8; *LRB* 6. 1-2; *LBurg* 6, 39. 1-3; *Edictum Theodorici* 80, 84; *Fragmenta Gaudenziana* 18 (MGH *Leges*, vol. 1, pp. 471-472), where *tributarius*, rather than *colonus*, is coupled with *servus* and the latter term is often used to mean both. See also Sidonius *Epistolae* 5. 19. (The substitution of *tributarius* for *colonus* is of exceptional interest, since it may indicate the wholesale assimilation of taxpaying Roman *possessores* to the level of *coloni*, thus explaining the absence of *coloni* from the later Visigothic kingdom, as mentioned below, Chapter v n. 66.) On the public dimension of late Roman servitude, Goffart, *Caput*, pp. 66-90 (on slaves in particular, p. 79) and "Three Notes," pp. 182-187.

[29] Nicolaas van der Wal, *Manuale novellarum Iustiniani* (Groningen, 1964), nos. 668-669, about Justinian *Novel.* 9 (535) and 111 (541).

he may have met a genuine and urgent need to safeguard the title of those persons having enjoyment of originally governmental rights (or revenues) or, alternatively, to defend the public from abuses on the part of such persons. Euric's intent, as the phraseology suggests, may indeed have been to offer protection to those against whom claims were being pressed, rather than to assist claimants. And, if this is so, then the *sortes* and *tertia* of *CE* 277. 1, without ceasing to be property or land, would be essentially a fiscal entity, as fiscal as the *servitium* of the assessed slaves and tenants of *CE* 277. 2.[30] The terms would refer, not to *possessiones*, but to something whose proceeds were comparably lucrative, namely, the *professiones* of lands subject to taxation.

The argument for identifying the original Visigothic *sortes* and Roman *tertia* with tax assessments states a possibility rather than a firm conclusion; yet it does not lack at least partial confirmation. Another oddity encountered in the Visigothic texts is that two laws from Leovigild's *Codex revisus* portray the Roman "third" in the guise of direct royal domain:

[*LVisig* 10. 1. 8] [After formal partition has taken place, a Goth must usurp nothing] from the *tertia* of the Roman, except that which perchance has been given him by our [royal] generosity.[31]

[*LVisig* 10. 1. 16] Let the officials of each city, the reeves

---

[30] The tradition of special privilege in favor of the imperial fisc was firmly anchored (see the titles "de iure fisci," *Dig.* 49. 14, *CJ* 10. 1-7, *CTh* 10. 1); e.g., it had priority over private creditors in the collection of debt. When Reccesvinth abolished Euric's fifty-year prescription, in favor of thirty years, he excepted royal slaves: they could be recovered *absque temporum preiudicio*—fiscal privilege again (*LVisig* 10. 2. 4). A good illustration of the privilege extended to a "private" *dominus* occurs in *Fragmenta Guadenziana* 16: a slave or *tributarius* indebted to a third party must fully acquit *tributa de labore suo* to his master before satisfying his other debt.

[31] Above, n. 26.

and provosts, take away the *tertiae* of the Romans from those who hold them by occupation and return them by their efforts, without delay, to the Romans, so that nothing might be lost to the fisc—provided [however, that they are not excluded by the fifty-year prescription].[32]

To repeat a point made in regard to *CE* 277. 1: if *tertia(e)* signifies the private lands left in Roman hands after expropriation of two-thirds in favor of the Goths, then the term, at least by Euric's time and thereafter, had to mean the totality of Roman estates. It would appear, therefore, that the Visigothic king of the 570s could give away any Roman property he wished to a fellow Goth. Furthermore, there would have been a standing order to royal officials to safeguard all these Roman properties from encroachment, presumably on the part of non-Romans; the owners could rely on the state, rather than on their own efforts, to maintain them in secure possession. A recent commentator has suggested that the royal prerogative expressed in *LVisig* 10. 1. 8 was derived from an overriding right of the Roman emperor to provincial land, but this will not do at all.[33] The existence of such a prerogative in *LVisig* 10. 1. 8 is the best reason for deciding that the Roman *tertia* in the Visigothic kingdom was not ordinary private law property but a more restricted and strictly regulated category of ownership: the king could give it away because it was his. The same reasoning applies to *LVisig* 10. 1. 16: that which public officials can be expected to safeguard is royal domain, and

---

[32] *LVisig* 10. 1. 16: "Ut, si Goti de Romanorum tertiam quippiam tulerint, iudice insistente Romanis cuncta reforment. Iudices singularum civitatum, vilici adque prepositi tertias Romanorum ab illis, qui occupatas tenent, auferant et Romanis sua exactione sine aliqua dilatione restituant, ut nihil fisco debeat deperire; si tamen eos quinquaginta annorum numerus aut tempus non excluserit."

[33] D'Ors, *Codigo*, p. 176, on the basis of the famous statement (Gaius *Institutes* 2. 7, cf. 2. 21) that *dominium* over provincial land pertained solely to the *populus Romanus* or the emperor. But on the inapplicability of this dictum, A. H. M. Jones, "In eo solo dominium populi Romani est vel Caesaris," *JRS* 31 (1941): 26-31.

not the farms of any Roman subject. These laws should not be understood to mean that the "third" had always been royal property; they provide a hint about what became of the "third" in the sixth century, rather than information about what it was in the fifth. Nevertheless, they confirm the fiscal dimension of the original *tertia Romanorum* that was detected in *CE* 277. The *tertia*, though rightly associated with Romans, was the king's share of a division between himself and the other Visigoths.

Although these analyses of Visigothic texts fall short of establishing certainties, they permit at least a hypothetical account, along new lines, of what occurred in 418. The "system" or "principle" or "regime" of Roman military *hospitalitas* had little relevance to the installation of Wallia and his people in southwestern Gaul. The officials who presided over the arrangements of 418 may have availed themselves of the ancient *munus hospitalitatis* as the legal pretext for requisitioning houses from the population in order to shelter the Goths, but this was a subsidiary (and undocumented) matter. The key economic provision of the settlement—the one that assured the Goths of sustenance—consisted in the surrender to them of all the public revenues in the district. These resources of the Roman state, rather than private Roman property, composed the total, or basic, barbarian "land grant." From this grant, by appropriate adjustments over the years, there would devolve the king's domain as well as the Gothic *sortes*.

The initial award of all Roman taxpayers' assessments and payments was subjected to an immediate division between the Visigothic king and his people. We do not know at whose behest, Roman or Visigothic, or by virtue of what principle this largely theoretical apportionment took place. According to our rather late information, it called for one-third to fall to the king and two-thirds to the troops. If the tax machinery was concentrated in royal hands and kept in working order, the troops' share could have been dispensed to them as salaries, in whatever portions were set down in the muster rolls. But the occurrence of the term "allotment," and the proprietary orientation of Euric's Code, imply that, sooner or later after 418, the soldiers' two-thirds of tax proceeds were converted to individual awards of tax assessment whose yield each beneficiary collected at its source.[34] If *hospitalitas* played a part in this process of individual apportionment, it must have been in a subtler way than is suggested by the terms of Arcadius's law of 398. Neither a house nor a set fraction had anything to do with the matter. Instead, a Goth received as his allotment the full tax payments of one or more Roman taxpayers, together with the detailed inventory of assessed property (*professio*) on whose basis the tax was paid. The useful function that *hospitalitas* might serve in these arrangements was to establish a legally definable relationship between the two parties who had been assigned to one another, the Roman (singular or plural) as "giver," the Goth as "receiver"; the relationship between them was not of patron to client or of victim to thief, but of host to guest.[35] Thus, quarters in a Roman house became coupled with the receipt of revenues from a definite quota of land, probably of uniform quantity per Visigoth, and not necessarily belonging to the same host as the one providing shelter.[36]

Additional aspects of these, admittedly hypothetical, events are uncovered by considering the situation from the perspective of the Gallo-Romans. If all that the Visigoths

[34] The date of the allotments is uncertain. Brunner, *DRG*, vol. 1, p. 74; Alfonso Garcia Gallo, "Notas sobre el reparto de tierras entre Visigodos y Romanos," *Hispania* 1, no. 4 (1941): 40-41; and others have maintained that the prescription of *CE* 277. 1 documents the antiquity of the assignment of *sortes*: fifty years before Euric's accession or the issuance of his code, thus, between 419 and 431. The deduction may be correct, but, as shown here, other reasons may be imagined for the choice of a fifty-year prescription.

[35] Fuller discussion of this aspect, below, Chapter vi.

[36] There is no Visigothic evidence bearing on the size of allotments or on whether the allotment-hosts were identical to the house-hosts; for discussion of the Burgundian case, below, Chapter v at nn. 35-37.

obtained (aside from shelter) was the tax value of the district, there obviously was no need to overturn proprietary relationships by expropriation: ownership was undisturbed. But the division of tax proceeds, if combined with allotments, implied that a certain group of Romans paid taxes hereafter to the Visigothic king, whereas all other Roman landowners were mediatized, apportioned individually or in small groups to pay the tax on their properties directly to a Visigoth. It would not be surprising if an element of status entered into this distinction; one recalls the story of the *nobiles* of Saintes in the *Vita Bibiani,* whom the Goths had a harder time dispossessing than the *mediocres.*[37] Might not the obstacle to the Goths' ambitions have been that the *nobiles* were the king's own taxpayers? By virtue of contributing directly to the monarch (in gold?), the Romans who underwrote the *tertia* look as though they formed a minority comparable in status to those other direct contributors to royal needs, namely, the Visigoths whose military service was compensated by the (tax) proceeds of their *sortes;* together, they would have formed a privileged category by comparison with ordinary Roman *possessores.*[38] The process of allotment located the Visigothic recipients at an honorable social level, much as would later happen to the barbarians in Italy.

An account of the Visigothic case is necessarily limited by the dearth of source material. The various laws suggesting that the barbarian *sortes* included woods and other resources not registered for taxation are best reserved for the next chapter, where the richer Burgundian evidence

[37] Above, Chapter III at n. 76.

[38] Sidonius wrote to two distinguished Romans in Visigothic territory who were serving the king in military capacities (one of them participated on the Gothic side in the siege of Sidonius's Clermont): *Epistolae* 5. 12, 8. 6. If the lands of these men had originally been reckoned among the *tertia Romanorum,* it is at least doubtful, in view of the owners' military service in the 470s, that they were still taxpayers.

125

permits a more comprehensive exposition. As for *CE* 276—the only passage of Euric's Code in which the Romans are called "hosts"—its fragmentary state and uncertain interpretation make it suitable only for discussion in an appendix.[39] Nevertheless, the few texts examined here justify our concluding that state resources, rather than those of the provincials, paid the cost of the Visigothic settlement. The tax burden, as it weighed on the payers, need not have been reduced; but, with two-thirds of the proceeds of the land tax passing out of central control and into the hands of individual Visigoths, the apparatus of fiscality was more drastically dismantled than it would be in Italy. From its beginnings, the Visigothic kingdom was fated to be a different kind of state from that which it more or less hesitantly replaced.

[39] Woods and wastes, below, Chapter v at n. 26. For *CE* 276, Appendix B.

V

****

THE BURGUNDIANS:
FROM ALLOTMENT TO OWNERSHIP

HOWEVER similar the Burgundian experience seems to that
of the Visigoths, the details are nevertheless quite different,
perhaps because of the evidence available for study. As
mentioned before, the crucial text here is *LBurg* 54, whose
engaging intricacies are so numerous that they call for many
pages of commentary (Ferdinand Lot spent over half his
article of 1928 doing this).[1] Its lines are the most detailed
source on barbarian settlement after the *Variae*, and what
they reveal about circumstances in the Burgundian kingdom is of more than local interest. At the risk of trying the
reader's patience, *LBurg* 54 will be quoted in full and then
subjected to a long analysis, in whose course the other texts
pertinent to the Burgundian case will all be deployed.

DE HIS, QUI TERTIAM MANCI-	ABOUT THOSE WHO, CONTRARY
PIORUM ET DUAS TERRARUM	TO PUBLIC PROHIBITION,
PARTES CONTRA INTERDICTUM	ILLEGALLY SEIZED ONE-THIRD
PUBLICUM PRAESUMPSERINT.	OF THE BONDSMEN AND
	TWO-THIRDS OF THE LANDS.

[1]Licet eodem tempore, quo
populus noster mancipiorum
tertiam et duas terrarum

[1] Although, at the time
when our people received
one-third of the bondsmen

---

[1] The most eloquent tribute to its importance is that Gaupp began
his account of the settlements with the Burgundians, rather than, in
chronological order, with the Visigoths: *Ansiedlungen*, pp. 317-371.
Also, Delbrück, *Kriegskunst*, vol. 2, p. 337; Lot, "Hospitalité," pp. 977-
997. To Lot's list of special commentaries evoked by *LBurg* 54 (p. 976
nn. 4-7), add now Odet Perrin, *Les Burgondes* (Neuchâtel, 1968),
pp. 354-369.

partes accepit, eiusmodi a nobis fuerit emissa praeceptio, ut quicumque agrum cum mancipiis seu parentum nostrorum sive nostra largitate perceperat, nec mancipiorum tertiam nec duas terrarum partes ex eo loco, in quo ei hospitalitas fuerat delegata requireret, tamen quia complures comperimus, inmemores periculi sui, ea quae praecepta fuerant excessisse, necesse est, ut praesens auctoritas, ad instar mansurae legis emissa, et praesumptores coerceat et hucusque contemptis remedium debitae securitatis adtribuat.

and two-thirds of the lands, we issued an order to the effect that whoever had obtained a field with bondsmen by the gift of our parents or ourselves should not claim the one-third of bondsmen or two parts of the lands from that place in which hospitality had been assigned to him: nevertheless, since several men, as we see, disregarding their peril, transgressed these things that were ordered, it is necessary that the present order, issued as an enduring law, should coerce those who seize illegally and should offer a remedy of due security as regards whatever has been illegally seized up to now.

[2] Iubemus igitur: ut quidquid ab his, qui agris et mancipiis nostra munificentia potiuntur, de hospitum suorum terris contra interdictum publicum praesumpsisse docentur, sine dilatione restituant.

[2] We therefore order that those who are in possession of fields and bondsmen by our generosity should restore without delay whatever lands of their hosts they are shown to have seized contrary to public prohibition.

[3] De exartis quoque novam nunc et superfluam faramannorum conpetitionem et calumniam possessorum

[3] By this law we also order that the new and superfluous claim and allegation of the *faramanni*

gravamine et inquietudine hac lege praecipimus sub-moveri: ut sicut de silvis, ita et de exartis, sive anteacto sive in praesenti tempore factis, habeant cum Burgundionibus rationem; quoniam, sicut iam dudum statutum est, medietatem silvarum ad Romanos generaliter praecipimus pertinere;

[= Burgundians] regarding clearings be now removed from the burden and disturbance of the landowners: let [the latter] hold an account with the Burgundians about clearings, both past and present, as [they do] about woods, since, as has already been laid down, we order in general that half the woods should pertain to the Romans.

[4] simili de curte et pomariis circa faramannos conditione servata, id est: ut medietatem Romani estiment praesumendam.

[4] The same stipulation is laid down to the *faramanni* regarding the house and the gardens, namely, that the Romans may have possession of one-half.

[5] Quod si quisque huiuscemodi praeceptionis excesserit et non a vobis fuerat cum districtione repulsus, non dubitetis commotionem iracundiae nostrae in vestrum periculum esse vertendam.[2]

[5] If anyone transgresses the letter of this command and is not repelled with severity by you [= royal officials], do not doubt that the transports of our anger will be turned to your peril.

Gundobad issued *LBurg* 54 between 501 and 516 in order to repress certain abuses arising from a previous law of his, an ordinance "about bondsmen and lands" (*de mancipiis et terris*). The terms of *LBurg* 54. 1 suggest that Gundobad's ordinance was the first measure giving shares

[2] *LBurg* 54, ed. de Salis, pp. 88-89. I follow an older edition in dividing the law into five paragraphs rather than the three of de Salis. As usual, the translation is mine.

of "bondsmen and lands" to the Burgundians, but the implication may be unintentional, and hardly any commentator has believed that such was the case.[3] A widely held hypothesis (endorsed by Brunner and Ludwig Schmidt) is that Gundobad's ordinance *de mancipiis et terris* enlarged the allotments then existing, and did not create them de novo.[4] The question whether this hypothesis is completely correct or not may be suspended for the time being. Its immediate value resides in showing us that *LBurg* 54 documents three different moments; in reverse chronological order, they are that of the abuses dealt with by *LBurg* 54; somewhat earlier but still in Gundobad's reign (from ca. 480 on), an ordinance *de mancipiis et terris* that either instituted Burgundian allotments or, more likely, modified them in certain specific ways; and, behind that, the earliest form of Burgundian allotment that we are in a position to perceive.

The historians who have realized the existence of this palimpsest have been too few to create a consensus about

[3] In arguing that it was the first measure, Gaupp, *Ansiedlungen*, pp. 317-322, showed more sensitivity to the text than did Lot, "Hospitalité," p. 977 n. 77, when he abruptly dismissed such an idea. Like Lot and Stein (above, Chapter iv n. 11), Dopsch, *Grundlagen*, 1:221-222, treated *LBurg* 54 as though it directly documented the original partition. *LBurg* 54. 2-3, referring to "new" abuses by Burgundians, are the best basis for concluding that an older rule of partition was revised by Gundobad. The unsatisfactory alternative is to suppose that, until Gundobad, the Burgundians were allocated houses and woods, but no *terrae*.

[4] Brunner, *DRG*, 1:76; Schmidt, *Ostgermanen*, p. 172; in agreement with Gaupp, *Ansiedlungen*, pp. 323-331, and Binding, *Königreich*, pp. 262-269; so also Coville, *Recherches*, p. 188, and Raymond Saleilles, "De l'établissement des Burgondes sur les domaines des Gallo-Romains," *Revue bourguignonne de l'enseignement supérieur* 1 (1891): 59-66. The most determined argument against this view was formulated by G. Kaufmann, "Kritische Erörterungen zur Geschichte der Burgunder in Gallien," *Forschungen zur deutschen Geschichte* 10 (1870): 355-396; followed by Delbrück, *Kriegskunst*, vol. 2, p. 342 n. 1.

what the three layers reveal. Among the interpretations proposed, that of Schmidt seems most faithful to the text: the "original" (or earliest attainable) rule on allotments laid down a half-and-half division between Burgundians and Romans but left all bondsmen (*mancipia*) in Roman possession; Gundobad's ordinance kept the old quota in regard to houses and woods, but it increased the Burgundian share of lands (*terrae*) from one-half to two-thirds and, for the first time, awarded the barbarians one-third of bondsmen.[5] One more detail should be observed. The "original" allotments had been given to all the Burgundians whom Gundobad calls *faramanni*, but by the time of Gundobad's ordinance, the *faramanni* fell into two groups: those who held only their *sortes*, and a more favored few whose allotments the Burgundian kings had, over the years, augmented by gifts of "fields with bondsmen" (*agri cum mancipiis*). LBurg 54 insists that Gundobad's enlarged allotments were meant only for those *faramanni* who had not received royal gifts.[6]

[5] Schmidt, *Ostgermanen*, p. 172, following Gaupp and Binding; also Halban, *Römische Recht*, pp. 248-249. On the basis of a subtle observation, Brunner, *DRG*, vol. 1, p. 76 n. 14, held that the first grant also included one-third of the *mancipia*, but he did not take into account that *mancipia*, far from being a discrete entity, were inseparable from *terrae*. Jones, *LRE*, p. 251, believed that the original quota for Burgundians (and Visigoths as well) was one-third and cited *LBurg* 57 as a vestige of this arrangement (for a similar view, Brunner, *DRG*, vol. 1, p. 77). But, as correctly recognized long ago by Binding, *Königreich*, p. 33, the *tertia* of *LBurg* 57 is a rent (or an ordinary agrarian tenancy called after its rent of one-third the harvest), as in *LBurg* 79. 1 (reading *tertiis* instead of *testiis*) and *LVisig* 10. 1. 15 (cf. 5. 5. 9).

[6] The *faramanni* of *LBurg* 54 were the ancestors of the *Burgundofarones* in Fredegar *Chron*. 4. 41, 44, 55; see also Marius of Avenches *Chron*. a. 569 (MGH *AA*, vol. 11, p. 238), noting that the Lombards invaded Italy *in fara*, and Paul the Deacon, *Historia Langobardorum* 2. 9 (in MGH *Script. rer. Lang.*). The word has often, but wrongly, been taken to denote a specific type of family or kindred organization. I understand *fara* (in this context) to signify "detachment, ex-

131

Nowhere in the Burgundian code are the barbarian allotments obviously connected to taxation or fiscality. The assets listed in *LBurg* 54—houses and gardens, lands, woods, and slaves—seemed so concretely agrarian to Lot that he launched at once into an exposition of how the division between a Roman and a Burgundian would have worked in practice if the estate being divided had resembled a ninth-century bipartite seigneurie.[7] The conclusions Lot reached (which did not altogether satisfy him) are less memorable than a subsidiary step in his argument: he felt compelled to provide very free interpretations of the key terms *terra* and *mancipium*.[8] He was right to decide that, in *LBurg* 54, these words cannot be treated as self-explanatory. Another aspect of the law is equally arresting: the fraction of *mancipia* that the Romans were allowed to keep was twice as large as the fraction of *terrae* that was

---

pedition"; thus, the *faramanni* were the original Burgundian settlers ("founding fathers") and their descendants. I am indebted to my former student, Dr. Alexander Murray, for assistance with these words. For further discussion, see Appendix E.

[7] "Hospitalité," p. 979 with n. 5. This approach had been anticipated by Delbrück, *Kriegskunst*, vol. 2, pp. 341-343, and Ernst Mayer, review of Hartmann, pp. 204-205; it is still taken by Musset, *Vagues germaniques*, p. 286. On the current reluctance to transport ninth-century conditions into Roman times, Goffart, "Three Notes," pp. 167 with n. 9, 386 with n. 179, 388-389.

[8] "Hospitalité," pp. 984-985. On the premise of a bipartite estate, Lot took *terra* to signify only the tributary tenancies and *mancipia* to mean both the slave laborers of the seigneurial demesne (*indominicatum*) and the demesne lands themselves. These definitions are demonstrably mistaken: *LBurgExtrav* 21. 12 (next note) shows that the term *terrae* includes the land occupied by *mancipia*.

However dissatisfied Lot may have been with his results, an excellent local scholar believed that Burgundian toponymy yielded positive verifications of Lot's results: Maurice Chaume, communication to the Dijon Academy, reported in *NRHD* 4th ser., 12 (1933): 821-823. Yet the opinion of Wallace-Hadrill, "Gothia," p. 30 n. 2, on the advice of J. N. L. Myres, was "that a genuine *tertiatio*, settling Goths within the framework of the old estates, might leave few place-name traces. . . ."

left to them, and yet no overcrowding or other negative consequence was expected to ensue; in just the same way, *LBurgExtrav* 21. 12 (524) states that the Romans, by retaining half the *terrae*, would also be keeping all the *mancipia*.[9] In other words, Burgundian legislators presupposed that the total of *terrae* was invariably in a ratio of two to one to the total of *mancipia*. Since it is almost inconceivable that a regularity of this kind could apply to every individual Roman estate and proprietor, the legislators appear to have used *terra* and *mancipium* to signify something other than ordinary private land and slaves. What did these terms mean?

In the later Visigothic codes, *terra* is an all-purpose word, often having the indefinite sense of real estate as well as that of cultivated land.[10] Such is not the case in the Burgundian legislation of a century earlier. Where worked land is meant, we always hear of fields (*agri*) or, more rarely, tenancies (*colonicae*). Partners share a common field; the boundaries of fields are subject to dispute; holders of a field or tenancy have a pro rata claim to woods; a field cannot be sold apart from its tax liability; the king's lands are fields, some of which he gives away *ex integro* complete with bondsmen. "Land" seems to be deliberately avoided in all these contexts.[11] On the occasions when *terra*

[9] *LBurgExtrav* 21. 12: "De Romanis vero hoc ordinavimus, ut non amplius a Burgundionibus, qui infra venerunt, requiratur, quam ad praesens necessitas fuerit: medietas terrae. Alia vero medietas cum integritate mancipiorum a Romanis teneatur. . . ." Godomar was making provision for Burgundians withdrawing into the kingdom from territory that had come under Ostrogothic rule: Binding, *König-reich*, pp. 260-262; Schmidt, *Ostgermanen*, pp. 163-164.

[10] E.g., *CE* 320, *LVisig* 5. 3. 4, 5. 7. 16 (real estate), *LVisig* 4. 5. 3, 5. 4. 19, 8. 4. 23, 31, 12. 2. 18 (arable).

[11] The references are, respectively: *LRB* 17. 4; *LBurg* 55. 2; *LBurg* 67, cf. *LRB* 17. 5; *LRB* 40; *LBurg* 38. 8, 89. 1, and 54. 1-2, 55. 5. Another term in this class is *possessio*: *LRB* 17. 5, *LBurg* 67, 84. 1, and 89. 1 (*possessorum agri*). Mayer, Lot, Schmidt (*Ostgermanen*, p. 171 n. 3), and others identified *ager* with seigneurial demesne (*Herrenland*) in contrast to *colonicae* as tributary tenancies. Although

133

occurs, it is almost invariably associated with the process of allotment. Typically, *terra* is synonymous with *sors* in *LBurg* 84 and contrasted to something different that Burgundians might have, namely, a *possessio*—land by private ownership.[12] We seem to be dealing with an abstract and technical usage.

Historians differ over the sense of *mancipium* in *LBurg* 54. Some have believed that the term embraces *coloni* as well as slaves, others, that only slaves are meant. Lot went so far as to specify that these *mancipia* were the slave cultivators of the seigneurial demesne (*indominicatum*) of a bipartite estate.[13] Like many texts of the age, the Burgundian laws are less precise than one would like in their references to bondsmen. There were reasons for uncertainty. The category of fugitives, about whose pursuit important laws were framed, included technically free men (*ingenui*) as well as slaves (*servi*); strangers who turned up at one's door were presumed to belong to someone, even if *ingenui*, and had to be treated accordingly; one legal rule applied to a slave "in the [domestic] service of a master" (*in obsequio domini constitutus*), as distinct, it would seem, from slaves established in the countryside and almost never

---

agri are occasionally contrasted to *colonicae* (*LBurg* 38. 8, 67), the instances are neither numerous nor explicit enough to justify our concluding that a manorial structure was present or that *ager* signifies one of its parts; e.g., *agri* in *LRB* 40 cannot possibly mean only *Herrenland*. As for *colonica* (*LBurg* 38. 8, 67), it should not be summarily equated to the Frankish *mansus*; see the texts listed in Ducange, *Glossarium*, s.v. "colonus," and J. F. Niermeyer, *Mediae Latinitatis lexicon minus* (Leiden, 1976), ss.vv. "colonia, colonica."

[12] In addition to *LBurg* 54 and *LBurgExtrav* 21. 12: *LBurg* 1. 1 (*terra sortis titulo adquisita*), 14. 5 (*terra sortis iure*), 67 (*terrarum modus* distinguished from *possessio*), 84 (*terra = sors*). In *LBurg* 79, no technical sense of *terra* can be meant, but the subject is title to land rather than the soil itself.

[13] Delbrück, *Kriegskunst*, vol. 2, p. 348; Mayer, review, pp. 203-204 (important); Seeck, *Untergang*, vol. 6, p. 424 (note to p. 129). Slaves only: Brunner, *DRG*, vol. 1, p. 75 n. 10; Lot, "Hospitalité," p. 981.

seen by their owners.[14] The vocabulary of the laws reflects these difficulties. *Colonus* definitely means a tenant farmer, usually, but not necessarily, a bound one; *originarius* more categorically signifies a hereditarily bound *colonus; servus* is the preferred term for slave. As for *mancipium*, it retains the basic sense of "slave" and can mean only this in several passages. Yet there are also contexts in which it is a blanket designation for bondsmen of several kinds. This wider meaning is clear in *LBurg* 7, "regarding *servi* and *originarii* who are accused of crime": every sentence of the law applies to both categories, but the writer, in varying his forms, occasionally omits *originarius* or *colonus* and uses *mancipium* or *servus* as a collective term. Thus, when we find a law authorizing a freeman returned from captivity to recover those *mancipia* of his whom his relatives have seized, it seems reasonable to infer that the word denotes *coloni* as well as slaves.[15] The same consideration applies

---

[14] *LBurg* 6. 4, "ingenuo aut servo fugienti." Presentation of strangers, *LRB* 6 and *LBurg* 39. 1-3. Pursuit of slaves, *LBurg* 20. 2. See also the discussion above, Chapter IV n. 28.

[15] In *LBurg* 38. 8-10, owing to the mention of a *conductor, colonus* might be meant in the ordinary sense of "tenant farmer." *Originarius* (as in *LBurg* 17. 5) is more categorical than *colonus* because, by the fifth century, *origo* was equated to "birth status": *Interpretatio* to *CTh* 5. 17. 1. Recovery of *mancipia* (an application of the Roman law of *postliminium*): *LBurgExtrav* 21. 2. Cf. the general discussion by Lot, "Hospitalité," p. 981 with n. 4, who maintained that "les deux conditions sont toujours nettement distinguées"; this is correct as far as it goes, but the pertinent issue is whether *mancipium* (or *servus*) was sometimes used as a blanket term (*pars pro toto*). For a particularly clear instance where it is, see Leo I *Epistolae* 4. 1, ed. Hubert Wurm, *Apollinaris* 12 (1939), 85-86, whose early sixth-century rubric forbids the ordination of any *servus alterius*, but whose text refers both to *servilis vilitas* and to "[illi] qui origini aut alicui conditioni obligati sunt." The "servile" conditions are defined in *NValent III* 35. 1. 3 as being those of *originarii, inquilini, servi,* and *coloni*. Later illustrations include "liberum vel servum mancipium" in *LVisig* 12. 2. 14, and Hincmar's treatment of *ecclesiastica mancipia* as a higher category than *servi* and *ancillae* (MGH *Epistolae*, vol. 8, p. 35, no. 63).

to establishing the meaning of *mancipia* in *LBurg* 54. The word is not associated with servile tasks or constraints of such a kind as to suggest that it signifies slaves exclusively; on the contrary, the context calls for *mancipia* to mean any persons obligated to cultivate the soil, exactly the same categories as the potential fugitives of *CE* 277. 2. The agrarian *mancipia* whom the provisions of *LBurg* 54 firmly attach to half the *terrae* of the kingdom, as well as to the *agri* given by the king, can hardly be thought not to have numbered a sizable proportion of *coloni*.

In the Visigothic laws, the fiscal dimension of barbarian allotments is suggested by the extravagant prescription of *CE* 277. 1-2; in *LBurg* 54, the salient oddity is the even ratio of *terrae* with and without *mancipia* upon them. The artificiality of this proportion has already been pointed out. In the real countryside, the spectrum of conditions may have ranged from major landlords whose properties were fully tenanted by bondsmen, all the way down to small farmers working their acres with slaves whom they fed and housed. Only a handful of proprietors, if that, could have had estates of which precisely half was in the hands of *mancipia* and half not.[16] What could have led the Burgundian legislator to believe that the amount of plain *terrae* was equal to that of *terrae* occupied by bondsmen? It is at least conceivable that this assumption stemmed from the Roman registers of tax assessment, the only public records that both conveyed a collective image of the countryside and documented a distinction in *terrae*: it was an elementary principle of assessment registry that *terrae* with *mancipia* attached to them bore a higher tax rating than those declared only in their owner's name.[17] These registers of tax

---

[16] Cf. Lot, "Hospitalité," pp. 979, 984-985. Lot's bipartite model does not apply; in the ninth-century polyptychs, which he considered relevant, seigneurial demesnes attain half the total acreage only by including the woods and wastes, but, in the Burgundian laws, the woods and wastes are a separate item from *terra*.

[17] In Gallic assessment registration, declarations of land (*agrorum*

liability could just possibly have embodied a half-and-half proportion of tenanted to untenanted land that, without having to be true for any given proprietor declaring his taxable assets, was nevertheless accurate for the territory as a whole.

On this hypothesis, the words *terra* and *mancipium* take on the character of technical terms with precise meanings. The *terrae* of *LBurg* 54 were specifically "arable lands declared for taxation," and the accompanying *mancipia* were "publicly registered cultivators, slave or *coloni*."[18] If Gundobad had spoken of a grant to his people of two-thirds of the "fields," the idea that Roman *possessores*

---

modus) and persons (*hominum numerus*) were converted by a schedule (*Gallicani census formula*) into a homogeneous assessment unit, the *caput*, such that the total assessment of a district—lands and men—was expressed in multiple *capita* (*Panegyrici Latini* 5. 5. 5, 6. 1, 11; Goffart, *Caput*, pp. 49-52). These *capita* were still in use in the days of Sidonius (*Carmen* 13) and Caesarius of Arles (*Opera*, ed. G. Morin, vol. 2, p. 289). Further on the distinction of land declared with and without persons upon it, *CTh* 11. 1. 26 (399). In such a system, the rating of *agri* with *homines*, both converted to the same assessment unit, was necessarily higher than the rating of *agri* without *homines*. See also *CTh* 11. 3. 2 (327), buyers of slaves-*adscripti censibus* were subject to *inspectio*, i.e., having their assessment raised; *CTh* 7. 20. 8 (364), as an inducement to veterans to appropriate vacant lands, they were assured the privilege of not incurring tax liability for the slaves they introduced into the property; *CTh* 5. 13. 4 (368), a similar case.

[18] Interesting evidence for the continuity of this distinction in the specific context of tax assessment occurs in Gregory of Tours *Historiae* 5. 28 (the Merovingian king Chilperic imposed new taxes on landowners, first, *de propria terra*, then also, *tam de reliquis terris quam de mancipiis*), and in the *Annales Bertiniani* a. 877, ed. F. Grat et al. (Paris, 1964), pp. 212-213, together with MGH *Capitularia*, vol. 2, p. 354 (a Danegeld was levied from *mansi indominicati* and from *mansi ingenuiles* and *serviles*, with the latter contributing from both *census dominicus* and *facultas sua*). These texts establish a remarkable link between Roman taxation and Carolingian estates (without necessarily implying that *terrae* with *mancipia* in *LBurg* exactly anticipated ninth-century tributary *mansi*).

were expropriated would have a secure basis. As it is, the abstract "lands" of *LBurg* 54, and the artificial ratio of occupancy by *mancipia,* justify our supposing that here too, as with the Goths, the tax resources of the district allowed the barbarians to obtain allotments at public expense.

LBurg 54 is a document whose complexities are not rapidly exhausted. Once the fiscal aspect of *terrae* and *mancipia* is discerned, the next step in analysis is to examine how these resources were apportioned. We saw that the earliest layer of *LBurg* 54 implies an "original" partition of houses, woods, and lands on a fifty-fifty basis between Burgundians and Romans. This ratio tallies very well with the chronicler's statement that, in 443, the Burgundians "divided" Sapaudia with the *indigenae,* and even with Marius's tale of a division in 457 with certain Gallic *senatores.*[19] As earlier commentators have observed, a partition of this kind would be identical to the one spelled out in a Burgundian law of 524: "Let no more be claimed by the Burgundians . . . than . . . half the *terrae.* Let the other half, together with the totality of *mancipia,* be held by the Romans. . . ." Another point to recall is that a division of public resources operated at two levels. The Burgundian laws, like the Visigothic, mention a division only between barbarians and Romans, but the same division had a direct bearing on the barbarian king and his troops: since the latter were tax exempt, the "Roman" quota denoted the royal share of public assessments and revenues.[20] If, therefore, the "original" Burgundian apportionment was on the basis just described, then a remarkable qualitative distinction occurs between the troops' share and that of the king. One full category of tax assessments—plain *terrae*—was awarded to the Burgundian *faramanni,* and the other category—*terrae* occupied by

[19] Above, Chapter IV nn. 7-8.
[20] On the division between king and followers, above, Chapter IV at n. 22 and below, Chapter VIII at n. 15.

mancipia—was reserved by the king for himself. This correlation calls for a few comments.

What lends credence to the idea that the initial Burgundian division was of this kind is its administrative simplicity. Lot went to great pains in an effort to fit various fractions of arable, slaves, and waste into a rational unit of Burgundian tenure, but he felt defeated by the attempt.[21] The arrangement proposed instead has a simplicity that stemmed from its following the lines of a preexisting distinction in assessment registry. All plain *terrae* went to the Burgundians. In other words, the totality of Roman properties whose owners personally paid taxes to the state —a total that probably included every poor or marginal farm—became subject to barbarian allotment. Out of this pool, each *faramannus* was granted one or several taxpayers of his own.[22] (It is worth mentioning, in connection with such a grant, that the assignment of military persons to civilian ones was the process of *hospitalitas*.)[23] As for the Burgundian king, he got the *terrae* with *mancipia*; that is to say, his share of Roman taxpayers embraced all the landlords whose wide holdings had to be worked and managed by registered bondsmen.[24] Even a Roman as-

---

[21] "Hospitalité," pp. 984-986: the one point that seemed certain to him was that the initial partition had been complicated. Cf. Mayer, review, pp. 203-205 (rather tangled).

[22] That *terrae* were registered without *mancipia* did not mean that they were necessarily cultivated by the owners, but only that the labor force was not bound to the land by public registry; the owner answered in person for the taxes and public charges on the assessment. *CTh* 11. 1. 26 (399), addressed to the praetorian prefect of Gaul, clearly implies that the registry of bondsmen on the land had not been mandatory.

Without explicit evidence but by analogy with Italy, I suggest that the plain *terrae* formed a total allocation, out of which *sortes* of uniform size (or as uniform as possible) were awarded to each qualified Burgundian; below, at nn. 32-33.

[23] Below, Chapter VI.

[24] The landlord was ultimately responsible, but the registered

sessed in both categories could be in no doubt about which part of his property owed its tax to the barbarian king and which was subject to allotment. The social aspect of the settlement, discernible among the Goths in Italy and Gaul, has somewhat sharper outlines in the Burgundian scheme: the poorer Romans were mediatized by barbarian "superiors," whereas the richer Romans—regional aristocrats—were reserved the honor of coming into contact with the king. A trace of "hospitality" on this side of the arrangements may be discerned in the official designation of important Romans as "table companions of the king" (*convivae regis*).[25]

As regards the *faramanni*, what has been charted up to now is the award to them of tax revenues with their accompanying property assessments—the *terrae* of Burgundian law as equivalent to the *millenae* of the *Variae* and the *sortes* of *CE*. But other types of assets are also mentioned in the Burgundian code and have to be accounted for, notably houses and gardens (*LBurg* 54. 3), woods (*LBurg* 13 and 54. 2), and wastes (*LBurg* 31). Gundobad treated the quota governing such assets as a long established rule that his new ordinance did not permit the Burgundians to alter.[26] In other words, the *faramanni* had shared in such wealth for quite a few years. The modern interpretation of these texts has been guided by the idea that *hospitalitas* entitled the barbarian beneficiary to a fraction of every part of a Roman farm (*fundus*): as the

---

tenant answered directly to the collectors and was entered in the assessment books as being responsible for public charges in the owner's behalf.

[25] *LBurg* 38. 2; the title would be taken into Frankish law: *Pactus legis Salicae* 41. 8 (ed. K. A. Eckhardt, MGH *Leges*, vol. 4). One is reminded that, under the Visigoth Athaulf, a rich reluctant Gallo-Roman had been named *comes largitionum privatarum* to the usurper Attalus: Paulinus *Eucharisticus* lines 293-296.

[26] *LBurg* 54. 3, "sicut iam dudum statutum est." Also "novam nunc . . . faramannorum conpetitionem." For a discussion, below, n. 46.

host yielded half the arable (*terra*), so did he have to relinquish half of everything else. Each Burgundian allotment would thus have been a package ceded by one and the same host.[27] This interpretation has been inferred from *LBurg* 13, 31, and 54 as well as the equivalent Visigothic laws, and it provides the traditional account of *hospitalitas* with its most impressive basis.[28] The proof, however, is hardly conclusive. It must be kept in mind that military quartering applied only to houses, as we have seen, and that no source explicitly illustrates the award of an allotment package to a barbarian.[29] If the laws are read in the fiscal perspective that has been adopted here, the salient difference between the various assets listed in *LBurg* 54 is that one lot—the *terrae* and *mancipia*—had once been

[27] Gaupp, *Ansiedlungen*, pp. 339-351, 394, 397; Saleilles, "Établissement," pp. 72-73; Schmidt, *Ostgermanen*, pp. 173, 327, 362, 505; Jones, *LRE*, p. 252; Musset, *Vagues germaniques*, p. 286 and next note. The idea of a package is rooted in two misconceptions: that Roman billeting involved the partition of the host's "estate," and that *LBurg* 54 edicts a partition and spells out what each individual share will consist of.

[28] The most challenging recent interpretation along these lines is by *Levy, Law of Property*, p. 84.

Of the Visigothic texts, *LVisig* 10. 1. 6-7, 9, are quoted or discussed below, n. 32. Though inclined to be more cautious than Garcia Gallo, "Notas," pp. 47-48, 54-60, in inferring that *LVisig* 8. 5. 2 and 5 are relevant to the allotments, I think a good case can be made that they are. The sense of the badly garbled 8. 5. 2 appears to be that, where partners receive unequal numbers of pigs (implicitly belonging to others) to fatten in the undivided woods they share, the pigs will be treated as a single herd, and the total *decimae* paid by the pig-owners will be apportioned among the partners in proportion to their share of arable land (*pro rata terrae*). In addition to extending the same rule to *pascua*, 8. 5. 5 specifies that "pasture fee" (*pascuarium*) will not be charged among partners, except to one who has completely enclosed his allotment. Little may be drawn from these rules to document relations with Roman hosts.

[29] The lack of proof for an allotment package deserves to be stressed, since many authors have read *LBurg* 54 as though it were precisely this and have extended it by analogy to Gothic settlements (as, e.g., Schmidt as above, Chapter III n. 23).

141

enrolled in the registers of tax assessment, whereas the other lot was not. The alternative to the idea of a package is that the regulations concerning unassessed items—houses, woods, and wastes—were a needed complement to the grant of registered assets.[30]

A preliminary issue in this regard is the distinction between an individual award and a total allocation: do the assets and fractions listed in the Burgundian code refer to the allotment of a single *faramannus* or do they itemize a total fund out of which allotments were dispensed? The same question was encountered and answered when the Italian evidence was examined in Chapter III.[31] The Burgundian laws lend support to either possibility. *LBurg* 13 and 31 are so phrased as to portray one Roman together with one Burgundian in joint tenure of woods and wastes;[32] on the other hand, Gundobad's wording in *LBurg* 54 implies an allocation: "We order in general that half the

---

[30] The standing of these items vis-à-vis assessment is discussed in Appendix C.

[31] Above, Chapter III at nn. 29-31, 42.

[32] *LBurg* 13: "De exartis. Si quis, tam Burgundio quam Romanus, in silva communi exartum fecerit, aliud tantum spatii de silva hospiti suo consignet et exartum, quem fecit, remota hospitis commotione [i.e., communione] possideat." Cf. *LVisig* 10. 1. 9, "De silvis inter Gotum et Romanum indivisis relictis. De silvis, que indivise forsitan residerunt, sive Gotus sive Romanus sibi eas adsumserit, fecerit fortasse culturas, statuimus, ut, si adhuc silva superest, unde paris meriti terra eius, cui debetur, portioni debeat conpensari, silvam accipere non recuset. Si autem paris meriti, que conpensetur, silva non fuerit, quod ad culturam excisum est dividatur."

LBurg 31. 1: "Inter Burgundiones et Romanos id censuimus observandum: ut quicumque in communi campo nullo contradicente vineam fortasse plantaverit, similem campum illi restituat, in cuius campo vineam posuit." (31. 2 spells out what happens *post interdictum.*) The parallel Gothic texts are *LVisig* 10. 1. 6-7, but, perhaps owing to revision, they are concerned with planting in other people's property, rather than "in communi campo"—the interesting trait of *LBurg* 31. In this context, *campus* almost certainly means waste land (French, "terrain vague"); cf. Niermeyer, *Lexicon minus*, s.v. "campus, 10."

woods pertain to the Romans . . . [As regards houses and gardens,] the Romans may have possession of one-half." What permits a choice between these ostensibly contradictory forms is that only Gundobad's regulation is directly concerned with barbarian allotments. The object of *LBurg* 13 and 31 (as well as of the corresponding *LVisig* 10. 1. 9) is not to award shares but to formulate a method of compensation between equal partners. In speaking in the singular about host and guest, or Roman and Burgundian, they propose a model exemplifying the same general rule as *LBurg* 54 and establish a way to implement it: any Roman or Burgundian who appropriates woods or wastes must compensate his opposite number with an equal quantity. There is a relationship here of host to guest and vice versa, and concrete cases would, no doubt, involve proper names. It need not follow, however, that the physical setting for any such relationship was one Roman *fundus* partitioned between its native owner and a barbarian guest.[33] What we have, in the case of woods and wastes, is an allocation to be administered in such a way that, when a Burgundian dealt with one or several Roman hosts, neither he nor they were entitled to appropriate and develop more than half the (unassessed) lands that went with the (assessed) *terrae* to form the unit of private ownership. We will return to this rule presently to study its implications and purpose.

Houses and gardens were also among the items of property that were not declared for taxation, but, otherwise, they bore little resemblance to woods and waste.[34] In view of all that has been written about *hospitalitas*, it is sur-

---

[33] The text coming closest to this is *LVisig* 10. 1. 7, which decrees the loss of vines planted within "alieni fundi territorio, in quo ipse [= the planter] consors non est." It might possibly be inferred that, just as some *fundi* were *alieni* to Goths, so did each one have a *fundus sui iuris, in quo ipse consors est,* but this would be stretching the text beyond its self-evident point: that one's allotment had physical limits beyond which one was in a *fundus alienus*.

[34] For the tax status of houses, see Appendix C.

143

prising to observe that *LBurg* 54. 3 is the unique evidence documenting the distribution to barbarians of house property in either Gaul or Italy (the passages of Paulinus of Pella and Sidonius about "guests" in their houses illustrate only military billeting of the conventional, transitory kind).[35] Another noteworthy point is that no source portrays Burgundians or Goths permanently occupying part of a house in company with the Roman proprietor; the one pertinent text—*LBurg* 38. 7— shows Burgundians and Romans living in the same *villa* but in separate dwellings (*domus*).[36] Therefore, when Gundobad contrasted the inviolable "Roman half" of houses and gardens to the Burgundian share, he was very likely referring to a total fund, and not to the partition of single Roman houses. The applicable rule would have been that Romans could safeguard up to half their house property; the balance was

[35] For Paulinus, above, Chapter III n. 3; Sidonius, below, Appendix D.

[36] *LBurg* 38: (5) ". . . a consistentibus intra terminum villae ipsius, tam Burgundionibus quam Romanis"; (7) ". . . iter agens ad Burgundionis domum venerit, et hospitium petierit, et ille domum Romani ostenderit. . . ."

In order to offset Ennodius's rosy portrayal of Ostrogothic settlement, Courcelle, *Hist. litt.*, p. 205 n. 2, cited a passage from what he took to be an African sermon collection, Pseudo-Fulgentius *Sermo* 19, in *Patrologia Latina* 65: 884C: "Durum est ut communes nobiscum mansionis habeat parietes, cum quo non habemus similes mores." If this were taken in the sense Courcelle intended (Romans having a hard time with an uncouth barbarian sharing their "walls"), it would be the unique, and invaluable, text documenting house sharing after settlement. But Courcelle left out the context. In a free exposition of 1 (3) Kings 17:17-24, the homilist evokes the lady who sheltered Elijah the prophet and has her tell her husband that it is hard for a celestial man of God to share the same walls with terrestrial sinners like themselves; and thus she talks him into building Elijah an upstairs apartment. Injecting barbarians into this seems impossible. Even the *amara captivitas* that the homilist ascribes to his congregation in the opening sentence cannot be interpreted as anything more specific than the human condition. For a genuinely topical extract from the same collection (which is more likely to be Gallican than African), see below, Chapter VI n. 7.

subject to being requisitioned and awarded to Burgundians for permanent occupancy.

This category of assets calls for a few more comments. If the requisitioning of houses conformed to established precedent, rather than being an emergency measure, its legal basis had to be the *munus hospitalitatis* traditionally weighing upon Roman citizens. At the same time, it is worth noting that this *munus* was responsible for the only outright, uncompensated expropriations of Roman property that the settlements entailed. The relative legality of the operation may have stifled complaints. Nevertheless, when *hospitalitas* of the traditional kind entered into the arrangements, as a conceivable extension of the rules set out by Arcadius in 398, it was anything but a gentle imposition. As far as we may tell, all other Roman losses were offset by adjustments in taxation. That of houses, however, did not even eliminate the *munus hospitalitatis*. The obligation continued under the new regime, tempered only by its being borne jointly by both nationalities.[37]

Precisely how, and in what quantity, houses and gardens were given to individual Burgundians is a matter for conjecture. Whatever the details, the need for shelter makes it a near certainty that physical conveyance of such property took place. A different approach was taken to woods and wastes. Instead of their being requisitioned from Roman landowners and given to Burgundian *faramanni*, a rule was instituted that, first, authorized the *faramanni* to participate alongside their hosts in the development, or private appropriation, of such lands and, second, assured both nationalities that neither one could bring uncultivated ground into productive use without simultaneously surrendering to the other its proprietary interest in an equal amount of land of equivalent quality.[38]

The implication of this rule for Roman landowners was

[37] As specified in *LBurg* 38 (above, Chapter II n. 10).

[38] See the texts in n. 32 and *LBurg* 54 at the beginning of this chapter.

145

the opposite of that for Burgundian guests. For the latter, the positive incentive was obvious: by clearance or improvement, they could take private possession of land that would be theirs on a more certain basis than their award of *terrae*.[39] The obligation to abandon an equal amount of woods or wastes hardly mattered to them, since the undeveloped land they had to relinquish had never been theirs anyway. Presumably, the small number of Burgundians, the abundance of uncultivated land, and the limited energies the newcomers could bring to land clearance as long as they were active soldiers acted together to set a tolerable limit upon Roman losses at the hands of Burgundian developers. On the Roman side, however, the rule allocating a share of woods and wastes to Burgundians made land clearance a thoroughly distasteful enterprise. Appropriation by one's Burgundian guest was a possibility; the one certainty of loss to a barbarian occurred whenever the Roman host took the lead in developing his own uncultivated land. A *possessor* who appropriated such lands necessarily stripped himself of an equal amount of his property in favor of his guest. The best way, therefore, to maintain the proprietary integrity of one's holdings was to leave the existing limits of cultivated to uncultivated lands intact.

Such a rule makes better sense in a fiscal than in an economic perspective. In its absence, the distribution of barbarian *sortes* would have given Roman proprietors a powerful impetus to appropriate and bring into production those lands that had not hitherto been classified as taxable arable, that is, *terrae*. In the days when the Roman government had been securely in place, it had intermittently sent out official inspectors, revised assessment declarations, and thus kept its eye on the shifting limits between cultivated and undeveloped soil. Obviously, all owned land

---

[39] On the understanding that *terrae* entitled the recipients to tax payments by the Roman host, whereas appropriated (and enclosed) woods or wastes became enclaves of private ownership.

could not be taxed as though equally productive, but neither could the taxpayers be allowed to allege that their registered arable had gone "desert" while they secretly pocketed the full profits of bringing unassessed land into production.[40] Once barbarians arrived and were awarded allotments of *terrae*—tax assessments and their proceeds— what was to become of these restraints on cheating by the taxpayers? Just as the officials of the barbarian kings did not dispense stipends to the troops, so were they not about to assume a supervisory function prolonging that of the Roman state; the fisc in its new guise confined itself to administering the king's own resources.[41] But, if the award of *terrae* to barbarians meant that fiscal supervision was abolished, something had to be done to prevent Roman landowners from receiving tacit permission to neglect their assessed *terrae* and to rush into development of their woods and wastes, whose returns hereafter would entail no payments to the allotment holder, let alone to the state.

One possible remedy would have been a directive to the effect that barbarian guests were authorized to defend their revenues by seeing to it that the *terrae* were properly cultivated. Such a rule, however, would hardly have been

[40] The best illustration of these procedures is provided by the laws specifying that persons and collectivities petitioning for tax relief on the grounds that land had become "desert" must undergo inspection of their total property or territory: *CTh* 13. 10. 8 (383), 11. 4 (393), 15-17 (417); for the third-century rules, with which the later ones are consistent, *Dig.* 50. 15. 4. 1. *CTh* 13. 11. 1 (381) threatens the death sentence for deliberately inducing sterility (e.g., by tearing out vines or cutting olive trees). *Dig.* 50. 15. 4. 9 suggests that, between one assessment and the next, proprietors would spontaneously declare increases in their wealth; this is rather difficult to believe. We know too little about revisions or renewals of assessment (cf. Jones, *LRE*, pp. 454-455; Goffart, *Caput*, pp. 108-109, 143 n. 16). As far as one may tell from the laws, no interest was taken in having the state share in the profits of an expansion in cultivable area; the main concern was to keep the total assessment at its original level or at least to restrain it from shrinking.

[41] Below, Chapter VIII.

compatible with the amiable fiction of "hospitality." The alternative was the rule whose details we have examined: Romans were free to develop the woods and wastes they owned (and to retain the full returns) but only at the cost of making a gift to their guests of an equivalent extent of their lands.[42] Whatever legitimate grievance they had over barbarians' taking private possession of undeveloped soil belonging to Romans was nullified by the elimination of fiscal inspection and taxation of the parts that the owners appropriated or merely retained. A realistic balance was struck between gain and loss.

If fiscal considerations were paramount in the effect of this rule upon Romans, it served also to safeguard a variety of Burgundian economic interests. In addition to the two we have seen—a right to appropriate woods and wastes, and protection against Roman neglect of allotted *terrae*— another is suggested by the following article of *Lex Romana Burgundionum*: "There is a common right to woods, mountain grazing, and pastures, as available to each [landowner] in proportion to [the extent of his] property."[43] Where did a Burgundian stand in relation to this law? His *sors* embraced a quantity of Roman *terrae*, not one-half or two-thirds of a *fundus* or other unit of ownership, but, instead, anything from the full assessment of several small owners to a fraction of the assessment of a large one. Did these *terrae* entitle the Burgundian to share in the common privilege (*ius*) assured to landowners by *LRB* 17. 5? The most explicit answer occurs in *LBurg* 67, a law en-

---

[42] "Making a gift" is not meant literally. The procedure, clearly implied by *LBurg* 54. 3 (*faramannorum conpetitio et calumnia*), was for the Burgundians to sue for compensation.

[43] *LRB* 17. 5: "Silvarum, montium et pascui ius, ut unicuique pro rata possessionis subpetit, esse commune." The phraseology of this law is rather obscure. A possible reading is that the lands in question were "common" because belonging to no one. The preferable alternative is that "common" means the opposite of "appropriated, delimited, fenced off," as in *LRB* 17. 4, *LBurg* 1. 1 and 13, and, by extension, in *LBurg* 31.

tered later, and presumably also issued later, than Gundobad's *LBurg* 54. By its terms, the limitation of one-half
remained operative; thus, for example, a Burgundian could
not appropriate more than half the woods even if his allotment were composed of the totality of his host's assessed
arable. Otherwise, however, the text specifies that a Burgundian would share in common woods not only, like
Romans, in proportion to "ownership," but also "according to the amount of *terrae*"—the abstract "lands" of which
the original *sortes* were composed.[44] By the time *LBurg*
67 was formulated, the Burgundians, in addition to being
allotment-holding guests, were beginning to fit into the
countryside as owners.

We are now in a position to understand why *LBurg* 54
devotes separate clauses to distinct elements of allotment:
first, *terrae* and *mancipia*; second, woods; third, houses
and gardens. These clauses do not list the components of a
package awarded to each *faramannus* from the belongings
of one Roman host; rather, they itemize the three separate
allocations out of which Burgundian allotments had been
distributed. The *terrae* and *mancipia* came first because
they were clearly most important; in the law of 524, they
would be entered without reference to anything else.[45] The
other items were mentioned only because Gundobad's
ordinance *de terris et mancipiis* had given rise to abusive
Burgundian claims in their regard that *LBurg* 54 was
meant to stop by confirming the existing rules.[46]

[44] *LBurg* 67: "De silvis hoc observandum est. Quicumque agrum
aut colonicas tenent, secundum terrarum modum vel possessionis suae
ratam sic silvam inter se noverint dividendam; Romano tamen de silvis
medietate in exartis servata." As will be argued shortly, Burgundians
prior to Gundobad's *ordinatio* had only abstract allotments unless
they had also received royal gifts of *agri cum mancipiis*; afterwards,
they obtained a share of concrete ownership. As a result, *LBurg* 67
refers to both *possessio* and *modus terrae* (for a parallel, see *LBurg*
84: *sors* and *possessio*).

[45] Above, n. 9.

[46] *LBurg* 54. 3-4: "novam nunc et superfluam faramannorum con-

We cannot tell how soon after 443 the first Burgundian allotments took place or what officials were involved in carrying them out; *LBurg* 54 allows us only to discern what, in Gundobad's day, was recognized as the original award. To begin with, each *faramannus* had a "place where hospitality had been assigned to him." The choice of the vague word *locus*, not "house" or "estate," is indicative of the broad sense of *hospitalitas* itself in the context of barbarian settlement.[47] The legislator's meaning was not that the *locus* provided hospitality but that the *faramannus'* grant was circumscribed by some definite locality where he resided when not at war. In that "place," the Burgundian obtained a roof of some kind and the cultivable enclosure that went with it. We should probably not imagine that this involved cohabitation with a Roman host; if necessary, Burgundian housing could have been provided by collectively regrouping Romans into the half of house property reserved to them. Next, the Burgundian obtained a grant of *terrae* or, as one might say, the legally enforceable commitment that a Roman landowner, or several, would deliver to him, as the designated barbarian guest, the due tax payments of the Roman's *professio*. This arrangement did not require the Burgundian to re-

---

petitionem et calumniam." These parts of Gundobad's law pose no problem of interpretation: on the strength of the new award (i.e., an additional one-sixth of the *terrae*, increasing the total from one-half to two-thirds), the Burgundians were abusively claiming a corresponding increase in compensation for *exartae* (i.e., woodland appropriated by Romans) and in house property. It appears, therefore, that Gundobad's ordinance *de terris et mancipiis* had addressed itself only to *terrae et mancipia* (just like *LBurgExtrav* 21. 12), implicitly leaving the status of other assets unchanged. This silent implication, however, did not prevent the Burgundians from assuming that suits over *exartae* and houses (or even seizures) were justified. Hence the need for Gundobad to dot the i's in *LBurg* 54. 3-4.

[47] Cf. the equally broad and indefinite usage of *locus* in *CTh*. It seems clear that the word was deliberately chosen to cover a variety of individual situations. Note also *locus hospitum* in *CE* 276. 3.

side on the Roman's estate, let alone to participate in its management. The final element entering into the *sors* was that the *faramannus* could make legal claims upon the uncultivated and unassessed lands of the proprietor(s) whose *professio* he held; he could either appropriate some of these, subject to compensating his host, or require compensation from the Roman for the latter's appropriations. The terms of allotment were comprehensive and well designed to satisfy the needs of the barbarian troops, to restrain Romans from evading their payments, and to safeguard established rights of property. The provisions about woods and waste even gave the Burgundians scope, if they wished, to apply such personal resources as captured slaves to the task of developing land. On the other hand, *sortes* of this initial kind fell considerably short of turning soldiers into settled landowners.

Legal sources are perhaps most frustrating when asked to answer questions of chronological history. Something we might very much like to know is how the extensions of Visigothic or Burgundian territory affected the terms of allotment. The modest districts that Constantius and Aëtius granted to the newcomers underwent successive expansions; by the opening of the sixth century, the two kingdoms included the whole of Gaul from the Mediterranean north to the Loire and the Langres plateau. Yet the codes are innocent of any clauses suggestive of territorial growth or of the extension of allotments to new districts.[48] Their reticence, along with much else, assures us of the hypothetical nature of any attempt to reconstruct the details of settlement.

[48] For the expansion of the kingdoms, Schmidt, *Ostgermanen*, pp. 140-146, 462-495. I do not know where in *LBurg* 54 Thompson found evidence for an extension of territory ("Settlement," p. 66). The attempts by several scholars to correlate the conditions of settlement with successive expansions are necessarily arbitrary since the sources offer no guidance. The passage of Marius of Avenches comes closest, but it is hardly trustworthy (above, Chapter iv nn. 8-9).

Only two changes in the circumstances of the Burgundians after the "original" allotments are attested to by *LBurg* 54. First, it is stated that some *faramanni* were singled out by the kings for gifts of "fields with bondsmen." There was no one moment for these expressions of royal generosity; the number of beneficiaries had accumulated over the years since the arrival of the Burgundians.[49] As shown with some emphasis by *LBurg* 55. 2, such gifts were a type of property different from *sortes* or *terrae*. Because bondsmen occupied these *agri*, ownership by private law came with their acquisition.[50] Since the royal share of the original division included the totality of Roman *terrae* with *mancipia* registered upon them, the Burgundian kings were well placed to make gifts of this kind to a select few among their followers.[51] The second change recorded by *LBurg* 54 is Gundobad's issuance of an ordinance *de terris et mancipiis* intended exclusively for those *faramanni* who had not received royal gifts. Only after this measure came into effect do we encounter Burgundians with "fields by right of hospitality" (*LBurg* 55. 2) and holding "fields and tenancies" (*LBurg* 67).[52] The social implications of Gundobad's ordinance are plain: its purpose was to narrow the disparity in fortunes between those *faramanni* with extra grants and those having only their original, and presumably diminished, allotments. Gregory of Tours offers a comment that may be pertinent: "Gundobad gave milder laws to the Burgundians, so that they might stop

---

[49] *LBurg* 1. 3, 38. 6, illustrate the normality of royal gifts.

[50] *LBurg* 55. 5: "ex eiusdem agri finibus, quem barbarus ex integro cum mancipiis publica largitione perceperit." These *agri* are sharply contrasted to those held by Burgundians *hospitalitatis iure* (*LBurg* 55. 2).

[51] Cf. the reference in *LVisig* 10. 1. 8 to royal gifts of *tertia Romani* to Goths, with the comments above, Chapter iv at nn. 31-33.

[52] Cf. in the earlier parts of *LBurg*, *sortis titulum* (1. 1), *terra sortis iure* (14. 5), *sors parentum* (47. 3), common *silva* and *campus* (13 and 31).

oppressing the Romans."[53] We know what manner of oppression barbarians were able to exercise vis-à-vis their Roman hosts.[54] Gundobad's award to the ordinary Burgundians might have been one of these "milder laws," intended to stem the abusive conduct of his people toward the Romans by wholesale redress of a legitimate grievance. But the premise of such a scenario is that *LBurg* 54 simply documents an evolutionary step in the development of Burgundian allotments. The greater likelihood, as we shall see, is that the distribution of *mancipia* came in the wake of a political crisis: Gundobad had incurred debts of gratitude toward the *faramanni* who had helped him recover his kingdom, and he had also acquired the wherewithal to pay them off.

Before turning to these matters, it is important to observe what Gundobad allocated to the Burgundians whom he rewarded, and why *LBurg* 54 makes his ordinance sound as though, in spite of its late date, it had been the first grant of *terrae* and *mancipia* to its beneficiaries. The composition of Gundobad's award is implicit in the statement that royal gifts had consisted of *agri cum mancipiis*; if there was something for the ordinary *faramanni* to envy, it was the type of property that the kings' favorites had obtained. Its desirability surely resided in the fact that a holding of *agri cum mancipiis* was not only additional to, but also qualitatively different from, the original *sors*; it meant crossing the threshold from collecting revenue to controlling a landed establishment, or (in a somewhat more hazardous formulation) from occupying the status of a beneficed soldier to attaining that of a lord with tributary subjects of one's own. The vital component, therefore, of Gundobad's grant consisted of the *tertia mancipiorum* and the one-sixth of the *terrae* that they occupied.

[53] *Historiae* 2. 33: "Burgundionibus leges mitiores instituit, ne Romanos obpraemerent."

[54] The incidents documented above, Chapter III at nn. 70-77.

153

By entering into possession of these bondsmen, the Burgundians became the unquestioned possessors of the *agri* that the bondsmen cultivated, as well as of their persons.[55] That such possession was "by right of hospitality" was a minor qualification by comparison with its being of concrete assets rather than of abstract *terrae*.[56] To be sure, the original allotments, dispensed from the old allocation of half the *terrae*, remained in force, but the new allocation, which enlarged one-half to two-thirds, was important because it qualitatively transformed Burgundian settlement. As such, it was novel and original.

The dramatic circumstances occasioning Gundobad's award of *terrae* occupied by *mancipia* are best introduced by asking whether such a grant implied the expropriation of Roman property. Little hesitation is possible. The authorization for Burgundians to claim bondsmen meant that they became the immediate and direct masters of these *mancipia* and the lands they cultivated, at the expense of the previous, and presumably Roman, owners. That this property was qualified as being "by right of hospitality" detracted only in a limited (and, one expects, short-lived) way from the Burgundians' title.[57] A clear expropriation

---

[55] Burgundians could hold *terrae*—i.e., the *professio* of land and its tax yield—without affecting the *possessio* of free Roman owners, but the same distinction could not hold where *mancipia* were concerned, for their bondage and the revenues they yielded by public law were indistinguishable from their condition by private law; even a bound *colonus*, though technically free and immovable from the land he cultivated, was *alieno iuri subiectus* (*LRB* 14. 6) and necessarily pertained to a *possessor* or *dominus*.

[56] The phrase "de agrorum finibus, qui hospitalitatis iure a barbaris possidentur" occurs in *LBurg* 55. 2; for the context, below, n. 63.

[57] See above, n. 55; inanimate *terrae* could render payments to Burgundians via their Roman *possessores*, but *mancipia* (with the *terrae* they were settled on) could only pass from master to master. The phrase *hospitalitatis ius* occurs only once (*LBurg* 55. 2), in the context of forbidding allotment holders to participate in lawsuits over the boundaries of their *agri* (below, n. 63). The qualification was a necessary safeguard in the period after Gundobad's award, when

would seem to have taken place. This damaging measure, however, had little in common with an act of arbitrary royal oppression, despoiling Romans for the sake of the Burgundian minority. The proprietors whose *mancipia* were given away were singled out by a political process. They were those men, Burgundian as well as Roman, who had had the bad judgment to choose the losing side in a contest between royal brothers.

Historians have already proposed that Gundobad's enlargement of the *sortes* was related to the outcome of a civil war in 500, an episode whose circumstances were sufficiently gripping that, many decades later, they were commemorated in some detail by the chronicler Marius of Avenches, as well as by Gregory of Tours. The less powerful Burgundian king, Godegisel, secretly obtained Frankish help, trapped his brother Gundobad in a battle at Dijon, and sent him fleeing for his life to Avignon. Safe within this impregnable fortress, Gundobad used the stalemate to wean the Frank Clovis back to neutrality. Godegisel was soon besieged in Vienne and, this time, the fortifications were penetrated. Not only was Godegisel executed, but also, in Marius's words, Gundobad "condemned to death, by a variety of choice tortures many seigneurs (*seniores*) and Burgundians who had sided with [Godegisel], and he recovered the kingdom he had lost, along with that which Godegisel had had." The *seniores*, whom Gregory calls "senators," were obviously Romans.[58]

---

faramanni were both *hospites* in respect to their original award of *terrae* and owners in respect to their *mancipia* and to whatever woods and wastes had passed out of *communio* and into their possession. Presumably, however, the tendency thereafter among Burgundians was toward the liquidation of mere *terrae* (as suggested by *LBurg* 84) and the enhancement of *possessio*—in short, a more or less rapid dismantling of the *hospitalitas* relationship and, with it, the qualified tenure *hospitalitatis iure*.

[58] Marius *Chron.* a. 500 (MGH *AA*, vol. 11, p. 234; perhaps Marius's fullest treatment of any incident): ". . . captaque civitate [= Vienne] fratrem suum interfecit pluresque seniores ac Burgun-

155

The domain lands of Godegisel fell to Gundobad as a part of the districts over which he had ruled, and, although no one affirms that Gundobad combined confiscations with the other executions, the victims are virtually certain to have been regarded as traitors and to have forfeited their property along with their lives. All those executed were landowners rich in *agri cum mancipiis* rather than in mere allotments: the domain of the luckless Godegisel, like royal property in general, fell uniformly in this preferred category, the Burgundians worth executing are likely to have belonged to the minority enriched with gifts of royal land, and the Romans were specifically *seniores* or *senatores*, rather than proprietors of the poorer kind to whom (as suggested above) Burgundian guests had been attributed. Regardless of whether Gundobad was ready to part with Godegisel's domain or not, the forfeitures from lesser traitors supplied him with a large fund of "fields with slaves" for distribution among the Burgundians whose support had restored his fortunes.

Although the terms of *LBurg* 54 do not suggest that it, or Gundobad's previous ordinance, distributes properties confiscated for political reasons, the chronological proximity of the civil war to the issuance of these laws favors the idea of a connection. So does the unavoidable conclusion that the award of *mancipia*, unlike the original grant of allotments, necessarily entailed the conveyance of private property. It would be odd if the only evidence for a generalized expropriation were uncovered among the Burgundians, who are reputed to have been considerably

---

diones, qui cum ipso senserant, multis exquisitisque tormentis morte damnavit, regnumque, quem perdiderat, cum id quod Godegeselus habuerat, receptum usque in diem mortis suae feliciter gubernavit." Gregory of Tours *Historiae* 2. 32-33: offers circumstantial details on how the alliances were made and broken and on the progress of the war; mentions Clovis (whom Marius omits); says nothing about tortures, and concludes with Gundobad's *leges mitiores* (above, n. 53). Other authors connecting this war and *LBurg* 54: e.g., Schmidt, *Ostgermanen*, p. 172.

more docile than the Goths vis-à-vis the Roman government. Besides, as Gregory of Tours shows, Gundobad's
memory was associated rather with defending Romans
from oppression than with subjecting them to sacrifices of
property.[59] However clearly, therefore, *LBurg* 54 implies
that Roman owners were dispossessed, we are well advised to explain this spoliation otherwise than by arbitrary
seizures from innocent proprietors.

The civil war of 500, though not even hinted at in *LBurg*
54, has many features that an acceptable explanation would
need. In the original partition of Roman public resources
among the Burgundians, the totality of *mancipia* was in the
king's share, rather than in that allotted to the *faramanni*.
The Burgundian kings had drawn upon their share over the
years to reward selected followers with *agri cum mancipiis*.
As a result, the general distribution of *mancipia* referred to
by *LBurg* 54, if carried out as an ordinary expression of
royal generosity, would have damaged not just Roman
proprietors but also the benevolent monarch, to whose
domain all the owners of registered *mancipia* were attributed. Even if no Romans were involved, it would be
paradoxical, or at least odd, to find a Burgundian king
impoverishing himself in this way. On the other hand, the
bloodbath that closed Godegisel's abortive undertaking
placed at Gundobad's disposal a large pool of *agri cum
mancipiis* that had not formerly been in his possession. To
judge from the account of Gregory of Tours, there was
little sympathy for the losers, their dispossession was not
a matter of nationality, and the cruel deaths inflicted upon
them were not deemed excessive punishment for siding
with the fomentor of a treacherous war between brothers.[60]

[59] Burgundian docility: Coville, *Recherches*, pp. 174-177; Musset,
Vagues germaniques, p. 113.

On Gregory, above, nn. 53, 58. It is hard to tell whether, in *Historiae* 3. 34, he praises Gundobad for having realized the superiority
of Catholicism to Arianism or blames him for refusing to profess
his change of faith in public.

[60] As above, n. 58. Gregory is manifestly hostile to Godegisel and

On the strength of his victory, Gundobad had the theoretical choice of permanently enlarging his own domain or of enriching the poorer *faramanni*, to whom he may now have owed a political debt. The circumstances gave him a positive incentive for distributing *mancipia* among the Burgundians.

Precisely how the resources that Gundobad awarded by his ordinance *de mancipiis et terris* were related to the property seized from his dead foes seems fated to remain as obscure as the other details of the implementation of his law. Some instruction has been drawn already from the statement that Burgundians were to "claim" their appointed shares from the "place" where *hospitalitas* had been assigned to them, but the phrase is no help in determining how each *faramannus* obtained his quota of "third bondsmen" and their fields. The one rather astonishing, but invaluable, detail available to us is that the term *tertium mancipium* had a definite, technical sense in Gundobad's reign; in the context of the law of fugitives, *LBurg* 39. 4 sets out a special, gentler procedure for occasions when an unknown "third bondsman" came knocking at one's door.[61] Whatever the means were for apportioning *mancipia* among the *faramanni*, the effects of the award are compara-

---

sympathetic to Gundobad in *Historiae* 3. 32; the account of the execution of senators is shortly followed by Gundobad's protection of Romans from oppression.

[61] Unlike other *homines extranei* coming to one's door, a "third bondsman" was to be treated in the same way as a captive returning from abroad (39.2): he need not be presented to the *iudex*, but must be sent back to his owner and not be hidden, on pain of penalty. The clause may have been drafted with a view to bondsmen fleeing from their new (Burgundian) masters to their old ones. Seeck, *Untergang*, vol. 6, p. 424 (note to p. 129), recognized the relevance of 39. 4 to 54. 1. Drew, *Burgundian Code*, p. 49, rendered *tertium* in 39. 4 as "thirdly," i.e., in the third place; since there are no first and second, however, this translation seems impossible. For another kind of "third bondsman," see *Interpretatio* to *CTh* 5. 18. 1, but the rapprochement is improbable.

tively well attested: all the passages documenting Burgundians with *agri, colonicae,* and *possessiones* occur only after *LBurg* 54. Whereas the core of the Burgundian code illustrates a concern for the inheritance of *sortes,* the late additions give prominence for the first time to the sale, lease, and regrouping of property.[62] These activities also made it necessary to formulate rules for safeguarding Roman interests against encroachments by the newly enterprising guests.[63] Posterity preferred to remember Gundobad for laws of this kind than for the refined tortures that had finished off the partisans of Godegisel.

Gaupp's theory about the role of Roman military quartering was developed in conscious reaction against the notion, forcefully stated by Savigny, that "immediately after the Conquest [sic], the land was partitioned between the Burgundians and the Romans." To this, Gaupp rightly objected that the Germans should not be thought to have arrived one day and to have partitioned the land on the morrow; a period during which they were accommodated

[62] The earlier laws are listed in n. 52; the later ones are *LBurg* 55. 2, 67, 79, 84. 1. The last of these is concerned with sales and regroupments, 67 and 79 with leases.

[63] *LBurg* 55. 2: whenever a suit arises over the boundaries of *agri* possessed by Burgundians by right of hospitality, only the Romans are to go to court. This is an updated version of *LBurg* 22 (cf. *CE* 312), which forbade Romans to avail themselves of Burgundian *patrocinium* by entrusting their *causae* to them. *LBurg* 67, reaffirmation of the Roman *medietas de silvis et in exartis. LBurg* 84. 2-3, a Roman host has a right of preemption to his guest's *terra* but may buy from him only if it is certain that the guest has *terrae* elsewhere (84. 1, a *sors* or a *possessio* in another *locus*). Thompson, "Barbarian Kingdoms," p. 8, was probably on the wrong track when he took *LBurg* 84. 2-3 to be a special favor to Roman landowners. The stated intent of the law, which is altogether plausible, was to restrain Burgundians from rashly selling away their *terrae* (one reason to sell them was that they had lost value ever since Gundobad had provided the Burgundians with *mancipia* of their own); the host's right of preemption was a way to enforce the king's order that Burgundians might sell only if they had *terrae* or a *possessio* elsewhere.

in accordance with the rules of *hospitalitas* helped to explain what happened to them between the moment of arrival and their definitive settlement.[64] It is no accident that Gaupp's narrative of the *Ansiedlungen* began, out of chronological order, with the Burgundians, or that Lot set forth from the same point; the order of their discussions tacitly acknowledged the importance of *LBurg* 54. Even for the very different argument of the present study, *LBurg* 54 remains a crucial text, invaluable not just for mentioning *hospitalitas* but much more for documenting the two widely separated steps in Burgundian settlement.

The *Landnahme* was even more gradual and qualified than Gaupp imagined. First, there was the moment of allotment. The barbarians assigned to some definite locality and given shelter might indeed have been provisioned for a while by an appointed *annonarius*, as envisaged by *LVisig* 9. 2. 6, but the commutation of such rations to allotments cannot have been long delayed.[65] There is no need to repeat the components that entered into a *sors*. Suffice it to say that, though based on landed security and involving a relationship to one or more Roman landowners, the allotment consisted primarily of a revenue; as "property," it was highly abstract. For all one knows, the Gothic *sortes* in Gaul and Italy never assumed a more concrete form than this.[66] The second step, attested only for the Burgundians,

[64] Friedrich Carl Savigny, *Geschichte des römischen Rechts im Mittelalter*, vol. 1 (Heidelberg, 1815), p. 254 (2d ed., 1834, vol. 1, p. 296), trans. E. Cathcart (Edinburgh, 1829), vol. 1, p. 279. Gaupp, *Ansiedlungen*, pp. 197-198, 317-318.

[65] Above, Chapter II n. 24 and Chapter IV at n. 34.

[66] As seen above, Chapter III at nn. 68-69, some Ostrogoths bought property and thus became taxpayers, but this affected individuals only, not the general condition of allotments. From the parallelism of *CE* 277. 2 with 277. 1 (above Chapter IV n. 25), Dopsch, *Grundlagen*, vol. 1, pp. 213-214, inferred that *mancipia* had also entered into the Visigothic allotments; the observation is shrewd, but better evidence is needed to establish that such was the case. A notable oddity of the later Visigothic kingdom in regard to agricultural bondsmen is its total lack of documented *coloni* and large category of fiscal

had been anticipated on an individual basis by royal gifts over the years of "fields with bondsmen." The favor was generalized as the sixth century began, when the outcome of a civil war suddenly enlarged the resources available to King Gundobad and gave him reason to be generous: every former *sors* that had not yet been combined with *agri cum mancipiis* by royal gift now obtained a quota of *mancipia* together with the lands they cultivated. This second award transformed the nature of settlement by turning the Burgundians into landowners. Through their tributary bondsmen, they acquired a title to property, a nucleus of ownership around which the older, abstract elements of their *sortes* could eventually be grouped by arranging with the Roman *possessores* to commute their obligatory payments for appropriate fractions of their lands. So conceived, Gundobad's ordinance *de mancipiis et terris* might be said to have brought about a Germanic "taking possession of the soil" (*Landnahme*). A preferable formulation might be that, in its wake, a new, Romano-Burgundian amalgam of landlords came into existence.

---

slaves: Goffart, "Three Notes," p. 183 n. 88; cf. above, Chapter IV n. 28.

VI

****

HOSPITALITAS AND THE
FIFTH-CENTURY SETTLEMENTS

THE argument of this study has been that Roman military *hospitalitas*, as set out in Arcadius's law of 398, is of very limited help in explaining the distribution of allotments to the barbarians in Gaul and Italy. The *sortes* stemmed from Roman public resources, notably the assessments of landed property and the tax payments they occasioned, which the Roman government could give to whomever it chose. The capital costs of barbarian settlement were borne, not by private hosts, but by the Roman state. Nevertheless, as observed before, the terms *hospitalitas* and *hospes* have a place in the sources; it cannot be doubted that "hospitality" of some kind played a part in the transactions we have been discussing. What that part was has been intimated in passing with reference to the Visigoths and Burgundians. A fuller discussion is in order.

In total, the words "guest," "host," and "hospitality" occur in five Burgundian laws and one Visigothic, as well as in seven pieces of literature. Among the latter, Paulinus of Pella and Sidonius attest to quartering in the strict sense of the Theodosian Code: the provision of temporary lodging to soldiers and government officials. Neither author permits us to infer that the host was also required to feed his guests.[1] The value of these passages is to establish that the authorities availed themselves of the *munus hospitalitatis* in fifth-century Gaul, a point that is further illustrated by the prolongation of the scheme under Burgundian and

[1] Paulinus, above Chapter IV n. 3; Sidonius, below, Appendix D at nn. 3-4.

162

Frankish auspices, as documented by *LBurg* 38 and later laws.[2] None of these texts, however, has any more bearing upon land grants than do the entries under the title *de metatis* of Roman law. There surely was a deliberate link between *hospitalitas* of this official kind and that encountered in the other sources, but it cannot be thought to be obvious, literal, or direct.

The relevance of *hospitalitas* to the award of permanent housing to the barbarians is almost equally tenuous. As observed before, only *LBurg* 54. 3 makes any reference to this subject; we have no information for Visigothic territory or for Italy. What is more, *LBurg* 54. 3 eschews the terminology of hospitality. Although not improbable, the idea that the expropriation and redistribution of "houses and gardens" was based on the old *munus* is only a guess.[3]

For some reason, the fraction two-thirds that enters into the Visigothic and Burgundian allotment schemes has been thought to bear a characteristic resemblance to the one-third of Arcadius's law on quartering; the Italian *tertia* has been observed to correspond with precision to the Roman billeting rule; and even the one-half discernible in Burgundian law might be said to tally with the quota of a traveling *vir illustris* in *CTh* 7. 8. 5.[4] The trouble with all these observations is that thirds and halves are common fractions; they no more bear the signature of military billeting than of, for example, the law of inheritance or any other law that they enter into.[5]

[2] *LBurg* 38 and its descendants, above, Chapter II nn. 10, 11, 26.

[3] Above, Chapter V at nn. 34-37.

[4] Not surprisingly, Gaupp, *Ansiedlungen*, p. 201, first made this point: *hospitalitas* explained the "Drittelteilungen." No one, I believe, has, in fact, argued a connection between *CTh* 7. 8. 5 and the Burgundian *medietas*, although it would be no less plausible than the link that Gaupp discerned.

[5] For the law of inheritance, in the specific context of a passage of Sidonius that has been thought to relate to allotments, below, Appendix D nn. 22-23. Other contexts: *CTh* 7. 4. 15 (369), frontier soldiers transport one-third of their rations and collect two-thirds

163

Except for the few instances in which traditional temporary quartering is meant, the sources unanimously associate *hospitalitas* and *hospes* with barbarian allotments. Special attention has already been drawn to the ironical reference of the *Passio s. Vincentii Aginensis* to a *sors hostilitatis* on whose pretext certain Visigoths engaged in plunder; Sidonius speaks—figuratively—of an official's "filling villas with guests"; and *LBurg* 55. 2 sets out a rule affecting fields held by *ius hospitalitatis*—a qualified title to land.[6] Perhaps the salient feature of all the other passages is that they involve a face-to-face relationship between barbarian(s) and Roman(s) in respect to material interests; wherever specified, these interests center upon land. There are no discernible precedents in Roman law for a *hospitalitas* of the kind found in any of these sources. As a result, we are left to conclude that whoever was responsible for linking allotments with *hospitalitas* devised a legal novelty, and that he did so with the circumstances of fifth-century

from camp storehouses; *CTh* 12. 1. 84, 142 (381, 395), reminders that there is a quorum of two-thirds in a city council when nominations are made; *CTh* 15. 1. 20 (380), provincial governors are to exert their zeal for building in a proportion of one-third for new construction and two-thirds for repairs and restoration of older public edifices; *Edictum Theodorici* 104, loss of a *tertia* of one's property is the penalty for illegally moving field boundaries; see also *Edictum Theodorici* 59, 67, 75, and 83, and *CE* 321. 4 (half-and-half). These laws are merely a selection.

6 *Passio s. Vincentii*, above, Chapter II n. 3; Sidonius, below, Appendix D at nn. 5-10; *LBurg* 55. 2, above, Chapter V nn. 56, 63.

The phrase "terra hospitibus deputata" in a context of barbarian invasion occurs in Ennodius of Pavia *De vita beati Antonii monachi*, ed. Hartel, p. 386. The sense, however, seems to be that the exemplary Bishop Constantius, "lest he should have any assistance in this world," distributed his possessions among "guests." Rather than being barbarians, the *hospites* are "strangers," implicitly contrasted to relatives, such as the hero of the *Vita*, Constantius's nephew Antony. It is noteworthy that Ennodius, whose familiarity with Ostrogothic allotments was observed in Chapter III, had no inkling that the terminology he used in this passage of the *Vita Antonii* might be ambiguous.

barbarian settlement specifically in view. Precisely who the innovator was is a less important question than what he invented.

After all that has already been said about the composition and award of barbarian allotments, it is almost superfluous to note that the novel sense of *hospitalitas* was not intended to legitimize massive expropriations of Roman property. Even those contemporary authors who set "hospitality" in a dim and negative context suggest complaints of a different order. Thus, what the hagiographer regarded as sinister about the *sors hostilitatis* was not the *sors* itself but its serving as the pretext for plunder. In other texts, a greedy Roman courtier was told to fear lest his ill-gotten gains should fall prey to an equally greedy "new guest," and a preacher contrasted God, the joy-bringing guest, to the thieving bullies actually being endured by his congregation.[7] The passages are valuable evocations of the condi-

[7] *Passio s. Vincentii*, ed. de Gaiffier, p. 180: "Nam veteres illius loci incolas gentis goticae et generationis unus precipue dominatus sub hostilitatis sorte omnis proprietatis iure privaverat. Diu generationis illius rapacitas, huc illucque baccata et repleta diversorum facultatibus nec expleta, tandem ad hunc presumptionis instinctum superbia et nimiis rapinarum divitiis elata et arriane haeresis venenis interius penetrata pervenit, ut diruere martyris basilicam . . . presumeret." *Vita patrum Iurensium* 94, ed. Martine (cited, Chapter III n. 78), p. 340 (direct discourse): "Tandem resipisce paulisper et vide utrum rura ac iugera tua [acquired by oppression, see above, Chapter III n. 78] novus hospes inexpectata iuris dispectione sibi non vindicet ac praesumat." The reference to *iuris dispectio* establishes that the *novus hospes* would not be seizing by virtue of a legitimate award. Pseudo-Fulgentius *Sermo* 80, in *Patrologia Latina* 65: 952-954: "Utinam ipse [= Dominus] sit hospes nobis superveniens benedictus, et iam non sit nobis hospes Gothus et Barbarus. Nam illis hospitibus arma et sagittae, at cum isto hospite pax cum iocunditate: qui venit hospitem non torquere, sed parcere; non exspoliare, sed vestire; non percutere, sed sanare. Ipsum hospitem apertis cordis nostri ianuis suscipiamus, et nunquam in nobis dominabitur inimicus." Courcelle, *Hist. litt.*, p. 144 n. 2, has placed us in his debt by contributing this new text to the file on *hospitalitas* (cf. above, Chapter V n. 36). G. Morin, "Notes sur un manuscrit des homélies du pseudo-Fulgence," *Revue béné-*

tions of the age, but they are not complaints that the institution of *hospitalitas* had stripped landlords of their patrimonies. The authors assumed that hospitality was neutral and confined themselves to affirming the misconduct of guests. As we now have seen, the lucrative grants made by the Roman authorities to the barbarians (or, if applicable, seized by the latter) were based on, and justified by, the various mechanisms of taxation and military expenditure. Since the association of these allotments with *hospitalitas* was not meant to specify their origin or composition, a different and more subtle basis for the connection has to be found.

Whereas military billeting had supplied quarters in a house, the new *hospitalitas* was loosely associated with an allotment of revenue. Another contrasting trait of the new institution was its duration: the traveling soldier was a passerby, expected to vacate the host's premises after a short stay; the Visigothic guests, however—the earliest in the sources—had already sojourned for over sixty years when we hear of them.[8] Yet the terminology did not weaken or acquire euphemistic overtones. Gundobad's usage, many decades after 443, is as firm and straightforward as Euric's, and (as will shortly be seen) so is that of Paul the Deacon, or of his early seventh-century informant, Secundus of Trent.[9] They and the other authors knew that they were

---

dictine 26 (1909): 223-228, offered two indications (pp. 224-225, 227 n. 3) of a Gallican provenance, which the allusion to Gothic guests forcibly implies.

[8] *CE* 276. 3; the *hospites* of this passage appear to be the Roman hosts rather than the Visigoths (see Appendix B), but the relationship was necessarily reciprocal. Sixty years is a conservative estimate of the interval between two moments whose precise dates are equally unknown: the original distribution of Visigothic *sortes* and the drafting of Euric's Code.

[9] On Paul and Secundus, see Chapter VII. Modern commentators have sometimes intimated that, owing to the application of *hospitalitas*, the Romans expected their guests to leave after a while (e.g., Coville, *Recherches*, p. 188). There is no evidence of such

166

referring to an institution that, unlike the billeting of the Theodosian Code, had no time limit. No one in our small sample had been disillusioned by the realization that the barbarians had come for an indefinite term.

The enduring quality of barbarian *hospitalitas* reminds us of a point that appears to have been overlooked in earlier discussions, or perhaps merely taken for granted; namely, that a variety of practices called "hospitality" coexisted with military quartering. In late antiquity, the latest to gain currency were those arising from the dictates of Christian charity. *Hospes* is the word that the Vulgate uses for the "stranger" whom the Christian is called on to take in for the Lord's sake (Matt. 25:35, 18:5). Clergymen and monks were specially obliged to receive all comers under their roofs, as well as to minister to their needs. A suitably edifying illustration occurs in the Life of St. Germanus of Auxerre: "He was especially punctilious in hospitality. His house was open to all comers without exception and he entertained them at his table without breaking his own fast. He washed the feet of all his guests with his own hands, following the example of the Lord whose servant he was."[10] Written into monastic rules, sometimes assigned a fixed share of church revenues, and institutionalized in endowed guest houses, Christian hospitality had an assured future. Yet its charitable dimension was a new and unfamiliar emphasis. The provision for religious pilgrims, the accent on the stranger's poverty, and the consequent association of food with shelter tended to tie Christian hospitality as specifically to ecclesiastical custom as soldiers' quarters were tied to state prerogative.[11]

---

expectations; the chroniclers (Chapter IV nn. 1, 7, 14, 16) indicate only settlements without time limit.

[10] Constantius of Lyons *Vita s. Germani Autissiodorensis*, ed. W. Levison, MGH *Script. rer. Merov.*, vol. 7, p. 253; trans. F. R. Hoare, *The Western Fathers* (New York, 1965), p. 290. The date of composition is ca. 480.

[11] D. Gorce, "Gastfreundschaft," in *Reallexicon für Antike und*

More traditional models had been and still were available. As the "barbarian," by definition, was one type of stranger, kept as far as possible from one's door, so the *hospes* was an acceptable stranger, privileged to be received under one's roof even though alien to one's family. *Hospitium* was, at all times, an established expression of friendship among private individuals. It had once been a mode of relationship between Roman and foreign communities, and, as late as the fourth century, it denoted the lasting bond entered into by a client collectivity and an influential patron.[12] There is reason to wonder whether the inventor or inventors of the fifth-century scheme, as well as

---

Christentum, vol. 8 (Stuttgart, 1972), cols. 1103-1120. The associations of *hospes* and cognate words in the seven volumes of the MGH *Script. rer. Merov.* are overwhelmingly monastic. Only one entry in the Carolingian capitularies—in a notably religious ordinance of 802 —orders that everyone must grant a roof, fire, and water to all those "traveling for the love of God and the salvation of [their souls]"; giving pilgrims more than this minimum is recommended as a charitable act: MGH *Capitularia*, vol. 1, p. 96 (cf. above, Chapter II nn. 11, 26). Unrestrained by official tradition, the ecclesiastical form letters for pilgrims ask for food as well as shelter: MGH *Formulae*, pp. 234, 278-279, 440. But there is an obvious link between such letters and the unique royal order of 802.

[12] R. Leonhard, "Hospitium," in *PW* 8 (1913): 2493-2498 (has the rare virtue of recognizing a connection between fifth-century *hospitalitas* and older Roman practices); Louis Harmand, *Le patronat sur les collectivités publiques des origines au Bas-Empire* (Paris, 1957), pp. 50-55, 336-337, 343-344 (fourth-century inscription, on an old pattern, documenting the institution of an enduring relationship of hospitality); E. Badian, *Foreign Clientelae (264-70 B.C.)* (Oxford, 1968), pp. 11-12, 154-155; Gaudemet, *Institutions*, pp. 278, 367-369, 519; O. Hiltbrunner, "Gastfreundschaft," in *Reallexicon für Antike und Christentum*, 8:1061-1103; Francesco de Martino, *Storia della costituzione romana*, 2d ed., vol. 2 (Naples, 1972), pp. 23-29; Karl-Heinz Ziegler, "Das Völkerrecht der römischen Republik," in H. Temporini, ed., *Aufstieg und Niedergang der römischen Welt*, vol. 1, pt. 2 (Berlin-New York, 1972), pp. 85-87.

For a Carolingian (ecclesiastical) document reminiscent of classical forms of hospitality, see *Collectio Sangallensis* 33, MGH *Formulae*, p. 417.

those who lived with it after implementation, might not have had in mind some of the other established meanings of "hospitality." Outside the military or Christian context, enduring and hereditary relationships of *hospitium* had been the rule; the *hospitalitas* in which the Goths, Burgundians, and Lombards were involved was of the same kind.

Practices of hospitality, of one sort or another, were common to all peoples, and notably to the Germanic barbarians. It is curious to observe, and perhaps highly relevant to our subject, that the only chapter of Tacitus's *Germania* (other than the one on amber) that we know to have been read with interest during the era of the invasions was concerned with hospitality.[13] In the text of the *Germania* transmitted to us, the chapter ends with four extraneous words transferred from a marginal gloss: *victus inter hospites comis*, "host and guest live together amicably." In his authoritative commentary, Norden gave probable grounds for dating this interpolation to "the age of Germanic *Einquartierung*."[14] He also believed he could reconstruct the thoughts that had been in the glossator's mind: ". . . a reader or copyist of the *Germania* appears to have vented his feelings by summarizing the contents of

---

[13] F. Haverfield, "Tacitus during the Late Roman Period and the Middle Ages," *JRS* 6 (1916): 196-200; Tacitus on amber (*Germania* 45) was cited by Cassiodorus *Variae* 5. 2.

[14] *Germania* 21; Eduard Norden, *Germanische Urgeschichte*, Appendix I, 2, "Eine Interpolation der germanischen Einquartierungszeit (saec. v)," pp. 454-457. It does not seem possible to extract specifically Germanic notions of hospitality from the *leges barbarorum*. See Chapter II nn. 11 and 17. *Lex Salica* 18, 91. 2 (cf. *Pactus legis Salicae* 55. 4, 56. 6, 73. 6), ed. K. A. Eckhardt, MGH *Leges*, vol. 4, pt. 2, prescribe fines for whoever gives hospitality to those guilty of various transgressions. The hospitality in question probably had the sense of patronage (as had sometimes been the case in private Roman practice), rather than of generosity to the needy. In the procedure laid down by *Lex Salica* 81. 1-2 (*Pactus* 46. 2, 5), the stress appears to be on the *hospites'* being "strangers," and therefore not relatives; their reception is incidental.

the chapter in this wise: 'so it was in the good old Germanic age, "host and guest live together amicably"; but now—oh, how matters have changed!' "[15] In other words, Norden attributed the gloss to a Roman "who had had an altogether different experience with the Germanic *hospites* of the raw present" and who "expressed his feelings in a kind of groan that the old Germans had surely been better men."[16] Though picturesque, and appealing to those inclined to stress the rigors of fifth-century conditions,[17] Norden's reconstruction of the circumstances tells us less about the glossator than about Norden himself: these were the editorial comments evoked from him by a perusal of Gaupp's monograph and of the Theodosian title *de metatis*. Even in the unlikely event that a Roman reader may reasonably be credited with the wish to celebrate the "guten alten Germanenzeit," it is far from being an established fact that the Goths and Burgundians were such habitually deplorable guests as to inspire rueful musings of this kind. The gloss itself is altogether colorless. As Norden observed, "the words are nothing but a weak summary of the contents of the chapter."[18] The circumstances inspiring someone to write them are beyond reconstruction. Only one thing seems certain: a late Roman reader paid such special attention to this chapter, and to none other, as to make a marginal jotting. He had learned from Tacitus that, among Germans (as among Romans), hospitality was a relationship in which the parties stood on an equal and amicable footing. Such information, whether derived from Tacitus or from more direct experience, could hardly fail to have been reassuring to those who organized the settlement of the Visigoths and Burgundians in Gaul.

[15] Norden, *Germanische Urgeschichte*, p. 455.
[16] Ibid., p. 135.
[17] Courcelle, *Hist. litt.*, p. 144 n. 2; Arnaldo Momigliano, "L'età del trapasso fra storiografia antica e storiografia medievale," Centro Italiano di studi sull'alto medioevo, Spoleto, *Settimane di studio*, 17 (1970): 115.
[18] Norden, p. 454.

Hospitality has a limited place in the evidence we have been examining. Contrary to what Gaupp and many others believed, the Roman *metatorum praebendorum onus* is not the key to the award of allotments in Gaul and Italy, but it was, demonstrably, a practice that the state resorted to in order to provide shelter for barbarian as well as native troops. In addition, there were nonmilitary aspects of hospitality that made the institution highly appropriate to the circumstances of the time. The Germanic barbarians were— or were thought by Romans to be—familiar with the roles of host and guest as amicable equals; enduring bonds of hospitality were an established custom in Roman relations with foreigners. Although the precise reasoning that entered into the invention of fifth-century *hospitalitas* is beyond our grasp, an awareness of what the institution was, and was not, permits us to conceive of it as an original synthesis of the available influences. The positive content of the new *hospitalitas* appears to have consisted of two things: an administrative process borrowed from military quartering, and a definable social relationship between the affected parties based on the accepted roles of host and guest.

Hospitalitas as an administrative device is easy to understand once it is realized that the old *munus* could apply to the barbarian case for reasons other than the shelter for which its terms provided. Billeting had called for some definite soldier to be matched to his equally definite host. In a similar way, the award to a barbarian of one or several Roman taxpayers required a process by which two identified parties, singular or plural, were placed in communication with one another. Organized troops were normally formed into units that depended on their officers or paymasters for rations.[19] Unlike them, the barbarians with

---

[19] During a truce between a Roman and a Gothic army in the Balkans, ca. 470, Gothic units were matched to Roman ones for purposes of supply: Priscus, fragm. 39, in K. Müller, *Fragmenta historicorum Graecorum*, vol. 4.

VI. HOSPITALITAS

allotments were detached from their units, at least for purposes of supply, and assigned to a special kind of paymaster—civilians who were themselves detached from the normal apparatus of tax collection and given new duties. What this procedure had in common with billeting was the indispensable pairing of soldiers and civilians, names to names.[20]

Perhaps the most intriguing, and obscure, question raised by the pairing of barbarians with Romans is what criteria were applied in the selection of the "basic" barbarian *hospes*, entitled to a single unit of allotment. The sources provide two special terms, *faramannus* among the Burgundians and *millenarius* among the Ostrogoths. The latter is possibly meaningful, inasmuch as the name signifies a military rank as well as a tax unit, but one is hard put to decide whether the double sense was intentional or not.[21] Many historians have believed that a *sors* went to each able-bodied barbarian warrior—an idea inspired by the theory of primitive democracy among the Germanic peoples.[22] Nothing in the evidence examined here contradicts such a principle, but nothing confirms it either. Besides, the expression "able-bodied warrior" is not self-explanatory; an interpreter is needed to decide whether it designates a supernumerary archer or a heavily armed soldier of the front rank or some intermediate category.[23] *Hospi-*

[20] On the application of the same administrative process to a variety of needs, cf. Goffart, *Caput*, pp. 144-145. For the procedure of billeting, Procopius *Bell. Vandal.* 1. 21. 10: "the clerks drew up their lists of the men and conducted the soldiers to their lodgings, just as usual." Procopius also mentions ordinary muster rolls, ibid., 2. 16. 3.

[21] Cf. above, Chapter III at nn. 48, 52-53. *CE* 322. 2 proves that Visigothic *millenarii* occupied an official rank and were not identical to ordinary holders of *sortes* (not surprisingly, since the tax *millena* was alien to Gaul). The lack of evidence for officer-*millenarii* in the Ostrogothic kingdom (above, Chapter III n. 52) makes me doubt that those of *Variae* 5. 27 were anything but holders of *millenae*.

[22] Typically, Schmidt, *Ostgermanen*, p. 362, "every independent free man."

[23] For further discussion, see Appendix E.

172

talitas was a procedure; it was up to those administering the scheme to determine who the "guest" was and whether to divide the Roman taxpayers among few guests or many. As a result, the circumstances of fifth-century settlement are compatible with a variety of views concerning Germanic social organization.

Hospitalitas was no less important in defining the relations of the two parties to each other. The facts of the situation were that the Romans were "givers" and the barbarians "receivers." How were these circumstances to be portrayed to the participants?[24] As pointed out in Chapter IV, a variety of identities were available: payer to collector, victim to thief, patron to client, employer to employee, dependent to lord. Excluding these and all other possibilities, the invocation of hospitality affirmed that the relationship would be of host to guest. The rich and subtle idea of hospitality, common to both cultures, established a principle of equality and a model of civil conduct between barbarian soldiers and defenseless Roman *possessores*.

Whatever the new *hospitalitas* was in origin, the two aspects just discussed are those that proved enduring and are attested by the sources. Yet one may wonder whether, in addition, the inventor or inventors of the institution may not have had something loftier in mind. Elevating the humdrum rules of military quartering to an abstract level, they may have chosen to extend the concept of the soldier's *hospitium* to the total territory ceded to the barbarians. Significantly, the word *sors*, "allotment," was long used to denote, not just the individual awards to barbarians, but also the Visigothic and Burgundian kingdoms.[25] The main

[24] The likelihood that *hospitalitas* was meant to affect social behavior is suggested by the well-known evidence from Ostrogothic Italy, where *hospitalitas* was eschewed but where a great deal of attention was paid—notably in the *Variae*—to lecturing Romans and Ostrogoths on the *civilitas* they should manifest to one another; cf. Ensslin, *Theodorich*, pp. 223-226.

[25] Sidonius *Epistolae* 7. 6. 10, 8. 3. 3; *LBurg* 6. 1, 20. 2. For other names, see Schmidt, *Ostgermanen*, pp. 169, 503. *Sors* was also used

173

implication of this nomenclature might then be that the *hospitium,* rather than being a private house, was equivalent to the whole province or combination of public districts assigned to each barbarian people. As a further consequence, the share or *sors* that the soldier-guests were entitled to would consist of "lands" whose public character paralleled the public character of the *hospitium* itself; *terrae* of this kind were the assessments booked in state records rather than the *possessiones* in private hands. As for the "host," his identity in such a scheme would be a matter of political choice. The part could potentially have been taken by the Roman emperor or given to the barbarian king, but it was "the Romans"—the landlords cum taxpayers of the district—who, as it seems, obtained the role of collective hosts vis-à-vis the Visigoths and Burgundians.[26]

An organizing abstraction of the kind outlined may have inspired the early barbarian settlements, but the idea remains a mere possibility, inferred only from the application of the term *sors* to the Visigothic and Burgundian realms. We are on more solid ground in concluding that *hospitalitas* was experienced as administrative process and social definition. It is no wonder that, in Leovigild's *Codex revisus,* the term *hospes* is normally replaced by *consors,* "partner."[27] The fifth-century relationship was bound to

---

to denote a Merovingian *Teilreich*: Council of Clermont, 535, in MGH *Concilia,* vol. 1, p. 71.

[26] It is curious to note, in this connection, that Claudian *De bello Gothico* line 536 puts words into Alaric's mouth suggesting that the Romans of Illyricum had made him their *dux.*

[27] E.g., *LVisig* 5. 7. 2, 8. 5. 2, 5 (*consortes vel ospites*), 10. 1. 6, 7, 14, 10. 3. 5. As early as the mid-fifth century, Paulinus *Eucharisticus* line 502, refers to his sons' making their fortunes "Burdigalae, Gothico quamquam consorte colono," but the correct sense of the line appears to be "at Bordeaux even though in cooperation with the Gothic settler," with neither *consors* nor *colonus* having any precise reference to land allotments (cf. the version of Claude Moussy, Sources chrétiennes 209 [Paris, 1974], p. 92, which is even less technical than mine).

vanish; it was designed as a buffer, to absorb some of the tensions of a difficult encounter. That its terminology was still vigorous in the sixth century, and never acquired pejorative connotations, speaks well for the statecraft of its inventors.[28]

This redefinition of the sense of *hospitalitas* brings to an end our examination of the evidence documenting the terms of fifth-century settlement. There is one more kingdom, however, in which barbarian *hospites* appear, namely, Lombard Italy. Their existence is attested by Paul the Deacon's *History of the Lombards* and a set of equally late Italian sources. A recent commentator thought it proper to warn against our "exaggerat[ing] the importance of the *hospitalitas* agreements. They affected only the barbarian states of the first generation, born before the end of the fifth century in the Mediterranean basin. It was during the second generation, and in the north of Merovingian Gaul, that the more durable syntheses took place."[29] It is true that a positive link between fifth-century *hospitalitas* and the Merovingian Franks has yet to be discerned. But this is not to say that the older arrangements were a forgotten antiquity to all the "second generation" kingdoms. The Lombard evidence to whose examination we now turn establishes that the *hospitalitas* experienced by the Goths and Burgundians set an example that even Justinian's reconquest was unable to blot out.

[28] Niermeyer, *Lexicon minus* s.v. "hospes, 3.," specifies: "inhabitant of an estate who is not personally subservient to the lord." Since this definition is quite possibly compatible with the terms of barbarian allotment, the *hospites* of this kind who occur in ninth-century and later evidence may exemplify what ultimately became of the circumstances we are studying. But, on verification, the passages cited by Niermeyer do not necessarily substantiate his definition. The question is better left to future investigation.

[29] Musset, *Vagues germaniques*, p. 288.

VII

****

THE LOMBARDS AS LATECOMING
"GUESTS"

Nowhere has the idea of a connection between the billeting
of Roman soldiers and the settlement of a barbarian people
caused more intense discomfort than among the historians
of Lombard Italy. Here it is out of the question to suppose
that Roman officials comparable to Constantius, Aëtius, or
Liberius presided over a peaceful and harmonious accommodation between barbarians and provincials: the Lombards imposed themselves by force, in considerable confusion, and with brutality.[1] Yet the institution of an
ordered arrangement between the Italians and their conquerors is attested by an excellent source in two passages
mentioning *hospites*. Lucien Musset, evidently embarrassed
by a word that seems so inappropriate to the factual circumstances, has called the Lombard regulation "a mechanism that may have been inspired by the memory of the
regime of *hospitalitas*."[2] But Paul the Deacon conveys
something quite different from a fuzzy memory: his deliberate use of the term *hospites* is borne out by evident familiarity with the mechanism being described. The source
itself presents no insuperable problem of interpretation.
What difficulties there are arise principally from the modern notion that the fifth-century barbarians had benefited
from the military *hospitalitas* prescribed by Arcadius's law
of 398. That law, however, was irrelevant to Lombard history. What the Lombards remembered, and instituted with

[1] Hartmann, *Geschichte*, vol. 2, pt. 1 (Gotha, 1900), pp. 34-55;
Thomas Hodgkin, *Italy and Her Invaders*, vol. 5, 2d ed. (Oxford,
1916), pp. 150-173.
[2] Lucien Musset, in Folz, *De l'Antiquité au monde médiéval*, p. 121.

176

great clarity, was the distinct and novel *hospitalitas* that had entered into the earlier barbarian settlements.

Our information appears in chapters of Paul the Deacon's *Historia Langobardorum* that a recent author has rightly said to be among the "most tortured"—by modern commentators—in Paul's work, and that another author has called "incomprehensible."[3] Paul wrote at the close of the eighth century, but he had an excellent informant on early Lombard affairs, namely, the *Historiola de gestis Langobardorum* by Secundus of Trent, who died in 612. Although the contribution of Secundus to Paul's *Historia* is of debatable extent, it is generally agreed that the sentences mentioning *hospites* stem from him. Secundus's testimony is that of a contemporary who stood close to the court of the Lombard kings, well placed to know what was going on.[4]

The references to *hospites* occur in closely linked chapters narrating events ten years apart. The contents of each chapter parallel one another in three clearly articulated segments.

2. 32 (a. 573)	3. 16 (a. 584)
1. The monarchy. After Cleph's death, no successor was elected; the Lombards were split among more than thirty dukes, each in his own city (six dukes and their cities are named).	The monarchy. Restoration of the monarchy by the election of Cleph's son Authari.

[3] Ernesto Pontieri, *Invasioni barbariche*, p. 244; Amelio Tagliaferri, *I Longobardi nella civiltà e nell'economia italiana del primo Medioevo* (Milan, 1969), p. 59.

[4] Paul and Secundus: Thomas Hodgkin, *Italy and Her Invaders*, vol. 5, pp. 69-80; Heinz Löwe in Wattenbach-Levison, *Vorzeit und Karolinger*, fasc. 2 (Weimar, 1953), pp. 205-206, 221-224. Since Paul qualifies his own work, as well as Secundus's, as *historiola*, it is doubtful that the title was Secundus's choice.

2. Financial arrangements affecting the Italians and Lombards, including the first reference to *hospites*.

Financial arrangements affecting the king and dukes, as well as the Italians and Lombards. Second reference to *hospites*.

3. Editorial comments. Conditions were terrible—massacres, spoliations, burning, and so forth; most of Italy was subjected to the Lombards.

Editorial comments. All was now well; safety, prosperity and justice.[5]

The lines of editorial comment (3) are Paul's own, obviously intended to celebrate the blessings of monarchy by comparison with any other regime. Paul borrows words from the *Dialogues* of Gregory the Great to describe the miseries of Italy under the dukes, and his celebration of the reign of Authari—reminiscent of Bede's praise of King Edwin—is believed to be greatly exaggerated.[6] The opening segments (1 and 2), however, are drily factual, and, if Paul intervened at all to alter Secundus's phrasing, the changes seem to have been made in the sentences on the ducal and royal regimes rather than in those where *hospites* are mentioned.[7]

Just before the first chapter that interests us, we are told that Cleph, in his short reign, "put to death many powerful Romans and drove many others from Italy."[8] The report is

[5] Paul the Deacon, *Historia Langobardorum*, ed. L. Bethmann and G. Waitz, MGH, *Script. rer. Lang.*, pp. 90-91, 100-101.

[6] Gregory the Great *Dialogi* 3. 38; the same passage also contains a misunderstood borrowing from Gregory of Tours *Historiae* 4. 41; Bede *Historia ecclesiastica* 2. 16 (ed. C. Plummer [Oxford, 1896]); for Paul's role in these passages, Hartmann, *Geschichte*, vol. 2, pt. 1, p. 82 n. 8.

[7] In 3. 16, the sentence beginning "Quo praenomine" is definitely Paul's; in 2. 32, the identification and number of dukes may not be from a contemporary source.

[8] *Historia Langobardorum* 2. 31, p. 90: "Hic multos Romanorum viros potentes, alios gladiis extinxit, alios ab Italia exturbavit."

confirmed by Marius of Avenches: "He killed many [persons of] high and middling rank."[9] Marius, whom we have encountered as a historian of the Burgundian settlement, is, in this case, a contemporary, whose account is so close in form to what we find in Paul as to suggest that Secundus, too, wrote in the compressed sentences of a chronicler, and that Paul quotes him verbatim, or just about. The *Historia Langobardorum* goes on to relate Cleph's assassination and the institution of the rule by dukes. It continues with a statement on how this change affected the native population:

His diebus multi nobilium Romanorum ob cupiditatem interfecti sunt. Reliqui vero per hospites divisi, ut terciam partem suarum frugum Langobardis persolverent, tributarii efficiuntur.[10]

In these days, many of the Roman nobles were killed out of greed; the rest were apportioned among "guests" and turned into tributaries, paying the third part of their harvests to the Lombards.

Paul then launches into mournful comments, in which, besides noting widespread death and destruction, he appears to be saying that the Lombards under the dukes remained on a footing of active warfare, extending the ambit of their rule beyond the regions of Italy originally seized under Alboin's leadership.[11] He does not suggest that the Lombards settled down.

Ten years passed. Great dangers threatened the Lombards as a result of an alliance between the Byzantines

[9] Marius *Chron.* a. 573 (MGH *AA*, vol. 11, p. 238): "plures seniores et mediocres ab ipso interfecti sunt." On Marius, above, Chapter IV n. 9.

[10] *Historia Langobardorum* 2. 32, p. 90.

[11] Ibid., p. 91: "Per hos Langobardorum duces . . . exceptis his regionibus quas Alboin ceperat, Italia ex maxima parte capta et a Langobardis subiugata est." Besides, Paul's next book opens with accounts of Lombard incursions into Gaul (3. 1-10). Cf. Musset, *Vagues germaniques*, p. 142.

179

and the Franks. In the emergency, the monarchy was restored in the person of Authari. The text continues:

Huius in diebus ob restaurationem regni duces qui tunc erant omnem substantiarum suarum medietatem regalibus usibus tribuunt, ut esse possit, unde rex ipse sive qui ei adhaererent eiusque obsequiis per diversa officia dediti alerentur. Populi tamen adgravati per Langobardos hospites partiuntur.[12]

In his days, for the sake of restoring the kingship, the dukes of the time granted a full half of their resources to royal uses, so that there might be the wherewithal to nourish the king himself, his adherents, and his servants. The "burdened people," however, were apportioned among Lombard "guests."

The enthusiastic comments that directly follow assure us that "burdened people" (whatever its precise meaning) is a neutral term; it does not describe the sad "burden" that now fell upon the Italians in general but merely identifies a category of persons familiar to the reader. Moreover, Paul's lyrical lines indicate the belief, however erroneous, that peaceful and orderly conditions now descended upon the Lombard realm.

Scholars have spent more than two centuries inconclusively debating over these passages and have had good reason to do so: they are our principal information for, among other things, the fate of the Romano-Italians under Lombard rule. In general, two widely divergent interpretations have been developed. One of them, advocated by Muratori and Giannone, but almost never encountered in recent times, holds that Paul's text means what it says: a considerable element among the Roman population retained its standing though subjected to a sacrifice of property to the Lombards.[13] The alternative interpretation is that what-

---

[12] *Historia Langobardorum* 3. 16, p. 101.
[13] Pontieri, *Invasioni barbariche*, pp. 237-243, contains a valuable

ever Italians were not killed or expelled were reduced to serfdom, compelled to a uniform render of one-third of their harvests, and apportioned among the Lombards. With small, individual modifications, this version has been adopted by Gaupp, Hodgkin, Hartmann, Lot, Bognetti, and many others.[14] Yet it is an uncomfortable interpretation in the light of Paul's wording: it requires that *reliqui* (in 2. 32) should mean "the remaining Italians," contrary to its obvious grammatical sense, "the remaining *nobiles*"; the words *tributarii efficiuntur* are construed as "to turn into bondsmen," which is neither mandatory nor probable; and the two arrangements involving *hospites* are treated as identical or synonymous (this is usually done by ignoring one entry or the other).[15] However agreed historians

historiographical sketch of the subject, to which I owe the references to Muratori and Giannone. See also Carl Hegel, *Geschichte der Städteverfassung von Italien* (Leipzig, 1847), vol. 1, pp. 336-348.

[14] Gaupp, *Ansiedlungen*, pp. 503-515; Hegel, *Städteverfassung*, vol. 1, pp. 349-407; Hodgkin, vol. 5, pp. 188-189, 232, vol. 6, pp. 580-586; Hartmann, *Geschichte*, vol. 2, pt. 1, pp. 40-42, 63-65; Lot, "Hospitalité," p. 1005 n. 4; Gian Piero Bognetti, "Appunti per una storia dei Longobardi in Italia," in Bognetti, *L'età longobarda*, vol. 4 (Milan, 1968), pp. 644-648, 651-652, also ibid., pp. 76-78. A valuable collection of earlier critical opinions was provided by W. D. Foulke in his translation of Paul: *History of the Langobards* (Philadelphia, 1907), pp. 91-93, 114-116.

[15] Bognetti, *Età longobarda*, vol. 4, pp. 76-77, believed that evidence was continually mounting in favor of identifying *reliqui* with the Italians in general, not the *nobiles*, but it is hard to see how accumulating evidence (of archaeology or whatever) can affect a point of grammar. According to Pontieri, *Invasioni barbariche*, p. 231, Manzoni (1842) was responsible for the once popular identification of *tributarii* with the category of *aldii* found in Lombard law. Hegel, *Städteverfassung*, vol. 1, p. 353, concluded that, in the second reference to *hospites*, Paul "nur dasselbe habe sagen wollen, was in der ersten," and this provided a basis for making *populi adgravati* equivalent to *reliqui*, and vice versa. Hartmann, *Geschichte*, vol. 2, pt. 1, p. 42, supposed a gradual settlement extending over ten years, and paid no special attention to the *populi adgravati* sentence. Mitteis, *Staat*, p. 31, relegated Lombard *hospitalitas* to the period after the restoration of the monarchy.

have long been in reading Paul along these lines, they have not been happy to do so. The very occurrence of "hospitality" in something so forcible as the Lombard invasion has appeared to be a contradiction in terms: what business did Paul have—let alone the eyewitness Secundus— to portray these ferocious conquerors as "guests"?

The first step in a reappraisal of these events must be to discard the normal modern presuppositions with regard to *hospitalitas*—that it entailed one barbarian's coming, with his dependents, to take up residence under the roof of a Roman host and to live off his substance. This is the scenario suggested (in part) by Arcadius's law of 398, but, as we have seen, there is no reason to think that such a procedure was ever involved in the settlement of barbarians anywhere. In Paul's *Historia,* the operative concept is expressed by the formula "aliquos per hospites dividere, *al.* partire," that is to say, to set a certain group of persons in relation to another group as "hosts" to "guests," the ones giving, the others receiving. The apportionment applied, not to houses, lands, or livestock, but to persons, in the event, to persons who, in 2. 32, would pay a tax of one-third their harvests, and who, in 3. 16, were simply *adgravati,* "burdened" with obligations vis-à-vis their possessors. In Paul's sentences, the "givers" are identified, first, as *reliqui* (*nobiles*) and, second, as *populi adgravati*—but not as "hosts"; the *hospites* were exclusively the Lombard "receivers." The assignment of persons to persons had long constituted the essence of *hospitalitas* in its application to barbarian settlement. The process has been described several times in this study as consisting in the award of one or more personal taxpayers to a barbarian, and something of this kind is evidently what Paul reports.

Before developing these observations, several subsidiary matters must be dealt with. According to Paul, Cleph killed or expelled *viri potentes,* and, after his death, many *nobiles* were killed. It is not quite clear whether *potentes* and *nobiles*—words that probably stem from Secundus—

are meant as synonyms or as descending categories.[16] If the *viri potentes* were a distinct, uppermost category, then they were indeed swept from the scene. As for the *nobiles*, regardless of where they may have stood in a sophisticated scale of social standing, they were nevertheless the major remaining landlords of northern Italy. Paul says unmistakably that, although many among them were killed, some —the *reliqui*—survived and were suffered to live: they became *tributarii*. This word too is controversial. *Tributarius* can have the sense of *colonus*, as it does in the Gaudenzian Fragment and perhaps in the expression *Romani tributarii* of *Lex Salica*, but these instances hardly prove that being a tributary—that is to say, a taxpayer— was synonymous with being a *colonus* or bondsman.[17] Paul's phrase *tributarii efficiuntur* tells us that the *nobiles* were turned into taxpayers, that they were subjugated and suffered a loss of dignity. It does not mean, however, that they were bound to the soil or deprived of personal freedom. The historians of the age often relate occurrences in which tribute was imposed. For example, the Merovingian kings subjected the rebellious Gascons "and made them tributaries" (602) and the emperor Constans, in dire straits, "became a tributary to the Saracens" (654), although he re-

[16] It seems difficult at present to speak with confidence about the social structure of sixth-century Italy. E.g., in the title of *Regula s. Benedicti* 59 (ed. E. Wölfflin [Leipzig, 1895]), the two terms *nobiles* and *pauperi* are sufficient to classify all those who might offer their children as oblates. What does *nobilis* mean? Does it refer to a small or large body of people? The term certainly does not look as though it had remained stable since the fourth century. In the ninth-century Frankish kingdom, a social category superior to *nobiles* was recognized to exist: Jean Devisse, *Hincmar, archévêque de Reims, 845-882* (Geneva, 1975), pp. 490-491.

[17] *Fragmenta Gaudenziana* 16, 19-20 (MGH *Leges*, vol. 1, pp. 471-472); *Lex Salica* 69. 7-8, MGH *Leges*, vol. 4, pt. 2, p. 116 (*tributarius* contrasted to *possessor*). *Tributarius* expressed the fact that colonary status was imposed by the state, rather than (as slavery) by private subjection; but it did not follow that any obligation to render payments or service to public authority made one a *colonus*.

covered his strength and finally "refused to pay tribute" (658).[18] The Gascons and the Byzantine emperor did not become peasant bondsmen, and neither did the many others whom the historians show us being forced to make tributary payments. Being free of such a humiliation was preferable, of course, to enduring it, but the fact of paying a tax did not, by itself, transform a landowner into a serf. In sum, the *nobiles* of northern Italy were neither wiped out nor reduced to servitude. Only their tax exemption, if present before, was terminated.

We may now attempt to interpret the first of the two passages (2. 32). After the initial shocks of a conquest that was severe but comparatively rapid, tensions began to enter into the relations of the Lombards with the social leaders of northern Italy. Many of the latter were killed or driven out, and their possessions may have come into the hands of Cleph and other Lombard chiefs. A more orderly arrangement was indispensable if a measure of legality was to replace the haphazard and violent requisitions that were taking place, and its institution coincided with the temporary lapse of the monarchy (573). Some, perhaps even many, of the Italian *nobiles* had survived the Lombard depredations. Far from being turned into bondsmen, they retained their properties and continued to manage them; the Lombards simply imposed a heavy but not intolerable tax-in-kind upon them, consisting of one-third of their harvests. A certain number of Lombards—as few, conceivably, as the thirty dukes—were designated as "guests," entitled by this token to collect and exact the payments of their Roman tributaries. The intent of these terms was not to spare

[18] Fredegar *Chron.* 4. 21, 81, MGH *Script. rer. Merov.*, vol. 2, pp. 129, 162; cf. also Fredegar 3. 11, 4. 45, ibid., pp. 95-97, 143-144. Along the same lines, Victor Vitensis *Historia persecutionis Vandalicae* 1. (4.) 14, ed. C. Halm, MGH *AA*, vol. 3, p. 4 (where *eis* should most likely be understood to mean "to the Vandals"); Gregory of Tours *Historiae* 2. 32 (line 10 and end of the chapter), 3. 32 (last sentence), ed. Krusch-Levison, pp. 78, 80, 128; and Gregory *In gloria confessorum* 101.

the Italo-Romans, who had no reason to rejoice, but to avoid further disruption of economic life. The Lombards had more urgent business to attend to than land management. No provision appears to have been made for allotments to the Lombard lower ranks; as the events of the next years suggest, the dukes and their followers engaged in continuous campaigning in a variety of directions. The flow of tribute from the Italian landowners to their "guests" was probably redistributed among the Lombards in whatever way the leaders chose.[19]

Ten years later, the Lombard monarchy was restored, and with it came a reordering of tributary relationships. It is doubtful, in fact, whether here, any more than in Gaul and Ostrogothic Italy, ten years would have gone by without some modifications of the initial arrangements. However that may be, the only information we have is provided by Paul's second chapter (3. 16), which must be analyzed without undue speculation about intervening changes. In view of what has been established about earlier settlements, notably that of the Burgundians, Paul's report contains two arresting details: the equal division between king and dukes, and the award to "guests" of the *populi adgravati*. To the first, there corresponds the important, but usually unnoticed—because undocumented—division of Roman public resources between the barbarian kings and their people, which we have already observed in fifth-century Italy and Gaul.[20] In Lombard Italy, that division of resources took place in 584 and is explicitly reported. Its difference from the divisions made by earlier barbarians, namely, the role of the dukes, was due to the peculiar event of 573, whose result was that the Lombards had designated leaders to stand in their stead in the division with the king. As for the *populi adgravati*, they bring to mind the *tertium mancipium* of Gundobad's ordinance, whose distribution to those Burgundians hitherto lacking *agri cum mancipiis*

[19] On redistribution, Appendix E.
[20] Above, Chapter v at n. 20.

185

marked the moment when they first obtained a landed allotment.[21] In the light of this parallel, it hardly seems likely that the Lombard *hospites* of 584 (3. 16) were identical to those of 573 (2. 32); in using the word, the historian intended, not to identify a special group of men, but to evoke the administrative process of "apportioning among guests."

Some terms in Paul's second chapter require closer examination. First, what were the *substantiae* that the dukes shared with the new king? Bognetti ventured that a cash payment was meant: the *substantiae* were not real estate but "the reserves accumulated in the interregnum."[22] Such an interpretation is almost certainly mistaken. The word for liquid assets would have been "treasure," as in the story of Rosamund's flight to Ravenna, taking with her "omnem Langobardorum thesaurum."[23] Unlike precious metal, the *substantiae* that the dukes divided with Authari had the capacity to bring annual returns: the king's half was to "feed" him and his court. Aurelius Victor had used exactly the same verb in reference to the tax-in-kind levied in northern Italy to support "the army and emperor who were always or almost always in residence."[24] Paul or Secundus deliberately chose the general term *substantiae*, whose meaning it would probably be wrong to confine even to something like "estates" or "lands." What was shared were productive "resources" from which public revenues flowed, in whatever form they had in 584.

One element, however, was excepted from this division, namely, the *populi adgravati*. Many scholars have been troubled by Paul's conjunction *tamen*: does it denote a contrast to the foregoing sentence or a worsening of the

[21] Above, Chapter v at n. 61.

[22] *Età longobarda*, vol. 4, pp. 651-652.

[23] *Historia Langobardorum* 2. 29.

[24] Aurelius Victor *De Caesaribus* 39. 31: "omnis eadem functione moderateque ageret, quo exercitus atque imperator, qui semper aut maxima parte aderant, ali possent" (ed. Dufraigne, p. 52).

condition of the *populi*, or is it merely a weak copulative, meaning "and"?[25] Once it is clear that the public resources of the Lombards were apportioned, and that Paul applauded the arrangements he described, it necessarily follows that the first of these possibilities applies: the function of *tamen* can only be to introduce an exception to the division of *substantiae* between king and dukes. Their shares did not include the *populi adgravati*, in whom the leaders divested themselves of an interest and whom they awarded to the Lombards. In such a context, identifying the *populi adgravati* is a simple matter. They were the same category of the population referred to as potential "fugitives" in *CE* 277. 2, as *mancipia* in *LBurg* 54, and as *servi*, or *condumae, cum cespitibus suis* in eighth-century Lombard charters[26]—the settled, hereditarily burdened slaves and *coloni* of the late Roman world.

In sum, the revival of Lombard kingship was accompanied by a major modification of the settlement of 573, a modification that affected every element residing in the kingdom. Ten years before, the surviving Roman landowners had been left in full charge of their lands and dependents but were subjected to a sizable tax-in-kind on their harvests. Shared out among an unknown number of "receivers," the Roman owner-taxpayers had been the main public resource of the Lombard conquerors. In 584, these assets were divided both vertically and horizontally. The taxpayers relinquished their settled bondsmen—the *agri cum mancipiis* of *LBurg* 54—whom the barbarian leaders apportioned among Lombard *hospites* wholly different, presumably, from those of 573 and less prominent than they. As for the balance of public resources, whatever its composition, it was shared evenly between the dukes

[25] Debate summarized by Foulke, notes to Paul the Deacon, *History of the Langobards*, p. 116.

[26] For the third of these categories, a representative collection of instances is provided in Goffart, "Three Notes," pp. 178-179 nn. 68, 70.

and the king. As Paul rightly, though rather too lyrically, observed, the foundations of an ordered polity had been laid. What remains somewhat obscure is the fate of the onetime Italian *nobiles*. In strict logic, the settlement of 584 imposed a large capital levy upon their fortunes—the (total ?) loss of the bound cultivators subject to them, complete with lands—and otherwise did not alter their liability to the king or dukes for an annual tax of one-third upon the balance of their wealth, consisting of the properties they directly managed (the *mansi indominicati* of later Gallo-Frankish terminology). One hesitates to affirm that this deduction precisely describes what happened to the *nobiles*, but it may serve in lieu of more complex speculations. Even though left with enough land and dignity to retain a respectable status, the Italo-Romans had good reason to be aware that they had indeed been conquered.

The Lombard settlement was not an application of "the regime of hospitality"; rather, it illustrates the utilization of an administrative process of "dividing among guests" as part of an ordered regulation of public resources. The Roman origin of these concepts and methods is unmistakable, but, by the second half of the sixth century, no Roman official was needed to implement them: they were part of the intellectual baggage of barbarian government, tried, tested, and absorbed by several earlier peoples in Gaul and Italy. Within a wider study of barbarian land grants, the case documented by Paul makes several contributions. It confirms the division of revenues between king and people that is only faintly discernible among the Goths and Burgundians, and it reflects the distinct categories of *terrae* with and without *mancipia* that is so important in the analysis of *LBurg* 54—a distinction, moreover, that is valuable for understanding the mode of land management at the junction point between late Rome and the early Middle Ages. Not least, the occurrence of *hospites* in Paul's *Historia* establishes a clear instance where an institution

188

devised with a view to fifth-century barbarian settlement was directly borrowed by such a latecoming people as the Lombards. Since a continuity of this kind from first to second "generation" of settlers can be more often imagined than proved, it is useful to be able to document an unambiguous example.

A final group of texts, from the periphery of Lombard Italy in the eighth and ninth centuries, may help to explain why Paul—no stranger to this region—was able to write about Lombard "hospitality" in the sixth century as though the subject were not an obscure antiquity. These documents are all concerned with the condominium that the Lombards of Capua, in the Duchy of Benevento, and the "soldiers" (*milites*) of the Byzantine duchy of Naples exercised over Liburia, the modern Terra di Lavoro, a rich agricultural district lying between Capua and Naples. The condominium had complex ramifications, and it endured long enough to leave traces in charters dating from as late as the Norman period.[27] The discussion undertaken here is not meant to clarify its every detail but will focus only on the early documents that contain two words, *tertiator* and *hospitatica*, that are evidently related to barbarian allotments.

The "thirders" (*tertiatores*) of Liburia are central to these texts: a charter of 703 or 748 portrays a Lombard widow selling her half of a *tertiator* couple to a Neapolitan church, which presumably owned the other half already; a treaty with Naples by the Beneventan duke Arechis (ca. 780), regulating the condominum over Liburia, is often concerned with the jointly owned *tertiatores*; and a capit-

[27] The wider setting is stressed by Giovanni Cassandro, "La Liburia e i suoi *tertiatores*," *Archivio storico per le provincie Napolitane* 65 (1940): 197-268, an inconclusive treatment of the subject, though long (I am deeply grateful to Professor E. A. R. Brown, of Brooklyn College, for providing me with a copy of this article). See also Ferdinand Hirsch in Nicola Acocella, ed., *La Longobardia meridionale* (570-1077) (Rome, 1968), p. 25 with n. 57.

ulary of Prince Sicard of Benevento (836) devotes eleven of forty-nine entries to *tertiatores*, "those who divide themselves," with nine of the entries, unfortunately, surviving only as rubrics.[28] Despite these comparatively rich sources, the status of *tertiatores* remains an unsettled topic. One scholar went so far as to associate them with the *tertia* of Ostrogothic times. A more common opinion, still voiced in 1966, derives their name from "the third part of the harvests" (*tercia pars frugum*) mentioned by Paul.[29] A minority of historians, however, has long pointed out that the latter derivation is virtually impossible: no *tertiatores* are attested outside this small region of Italy, and the *milites* of Byzantine Naples benefited just as much from their payments as did the Lombards of Benevento-Capua.[30] The connection to Paul is also undermined by the

[28] The charter: *Regii Neapolitani archivi monumenta*, vol. 1 (Naples, 1845), pp. 1-5. The Arechis treaty and Sicard capitulary (clauses 4, 14; rubrics: 20, 21, 25, 26, 29, 30, 32, 47): ed. F. Bluhme, MGH *Leges* (*in folio*), vol. 4, pp. 213-215, 216-221 (the gloss for *tertiatores*, "eos qui se dividunt," occurs in Sicard clause 14). The latter documents were published twice more in the nineteenth century: *Codex diplomaticus Cavensis*, ed. M. Morcaldi, M. Schiani, and S. de Stefano, vol. 3 (Milan, 1876), pp. 244ff., and B. Capasso, ed., *Monumenta ad Neapolitani ducatus historiam pertinentia*, vol. 2, pt. 2 (Naples, 1892), pp. 135-156 (with annotations and emendations). I have not seen these editions.

[29] Ostrogothic *tertia*: Fabien Thibault, "L'impôt direct et la propriété foncière dans le royaume des Lombards," *NRHD*, 3d ser., 28 (1904): 192. The common opinion: survey by Paul Fabre, "Une hypothèse sur les *tertiatores* de la Terre de Labour," *NRHD*, 3d ser., 17 (1893): 701-702; bibliographic essay by Cassandro, "La Liburia," pp. 264-268, also 202-207; lately, Nicola Cilento, *Le origini della signoria Capuana nella Longobardia minore*, Istituto storico Italiano per il Medio Evo, Studi storici, fasc. 69-70 (Rome, 1966), p. 66.

[30] Cassandro, "La Liburia," pp. 206-207, agreeing with Hartmann (1900) and E. Besta (1927), as well as Fabre, "Une hypothèse." See also G. Cassandro, "Il ducato bizantino," in *Storia di Napoli*, vol. 2, pt. 1 (Naples, 1969), p. 131, insisting that the passages of Paul stem from Secundus and apply only to the part of Italy that Secundus was familiar with. This filiation is likely (above, n. 4), but it is not so firm as to disprove the connection of Paul's *tercia* to Liburia. On

observation that the "third" applicable in Liburia was almost certainly different from a rent. None of the Beneventan texts associates the *tertia* with a contribution of this proportion; on the contrary, several articles of the Arechis treaty justify an alternative interpretation, based on an alienable fraction of the ownership unit, rather than on a payment.[31] We will return to the meaning of *tertiator* as soon as certain preliminary aspects are examined.

However defined, the *tertiatores* were closely involved, whether as managers or as cultivators, with the agriculture of Liburia, and they were distinct from "slave men and women" (*servi et ancillae*), to whom separate rules applied.[32] The memorable oddity affecting the *tertiatores* was that, over their heads, as it were, much of Liburia was shared equally, but without partition, by two collectivities, the Lombards and the Neapolitans. In the 880s, the Lombard historian Erchempert expressed the belief that this arrangement came about in the days of Charlemagne, when Duke Arechis of Benevento, under the threat of a major Frankish attack, bought off the enmity of the Neapolitans by assigning "stipends" (*diaria*) to them in this frontier zone.[33] Despite its plausibility, Erchempert's al-

---

the contrary, owing to Paul's familiarity with Beneventan conditions, the Liburian arrangements might argue against Secundus as source, though I doubt that they do.

[31] Cassandro, "Ducato bizantino," p. 149, recognized the lack of evidence for a rent. The alternative interpretation is given below.

[32] The distinction is obvious from the opening of the Arechis treaty: "Incipit pactum . . . de servis et ancillis et de terris et de Legurias et de tertiatoribus, quae communes est inter partes" (ed. Bluhme, p. 213); it is most fully illustrated by the two chapters dealing with the abandonment of farms: clause 12 by *tertiatores*, clause 14 by *servi communes* (clauses 7 and 13 set down additional rules applicable to slaves but not to *tertiatores*).

[33] Erchempert *Historia Langobardorum Beneventanorum* 2, "Neapolitibus, qui a Langobardis diutina oppressione fatigati erant, pacem cessit eisque diaria in Liguria et Cimiterio per incolas sancita dispensione misericordiae vice distribuit, titubans, ut conici valet, ne ab eorum versutiis Franci aditum introeundi Beneventum repperirent"

legation seems untrue.[34] The rules laid down by Arechis and Sicard faintly suggest that Liburia, though jointly owned, was basically a dependency of the duchy of Naples, and not of Benevento. Besides, the condominium necessarily antedated 748 (the later of two possible dates for the charter, noted above, that presupposes its existence) and might easily go back to the seventh century.[35] Although the attribution of a half interest to the Lombards resembles the settlements examined in the previous chap-

---

(ed. G. Waitz, MGH *Script. rer. Lang.*, p. 235). I have not seen the edition of Erchempert by N. Cilento, Istituto storico Italiano per il Medio Evo, Fonti (Rome, 1967).

For the definition of *diaria*, a term of Byzantine fiscality, see *CJ* 1. 2. 17 (Anastasius); Justinian *Novel.* 123. 16 (546); Franz Dölger, *Beiträge zur Geschichte der byzantinischen Finanzverwaltung besonders des 10. und 11. Jahrhunderts* (Leipzig, 1927), pp. 126-127; A. Andréades, "Deux livres récents sur les finances byzantines," *Byzantinische Zeitschrift* 28 (1928): 301; Nicolas Svoronos, "Recherches sur le cadastre byzantin et la fiscalité aux XIe et XIIe siècles: le cadastre de Thèbes," *Bulletin de correspondance hellénique* 83 (1959): 24 n. 3, 27, 114, 117, 120-123. Whereas the tax units, like *millena*, touched on in Chapters II-III, first referred to assessed property and then to the revenue it yielded, the meaning of *diarion* took the opposite course, from a revenue (originally, a day's ration) to a unit of tax assessment. Its most general Western counterpart is "benefice." The word occurs in the seventh-century Gallo-Frankish *Testamentum s. Leodegarii* (*Corpus Christianorum*, ser. Lat. 117: 514) in the simple sense of a daily issue of food ("quotidiana diaria et stipendia").

[34] Explicitly discounted by F. Bluhme, "Das *pactum de leburiis* und die beneventanischen Tertiatoren," *Historische Zeitschrift* 24 (1870): 126 n. 3, and Cassandro, "Ducato bizantino," pp. 132-134. According to Waitz, in MGH *Script. rer. Lang.*, p. 232, Erchempert is rather inaccurate before about 850.

[35] Arechis clause 12 envisages the possibility that *tertiatores* might suffer "oppressiones a parte de Neapolim," but not from the Lombard *pars*; and Sicard clause 14 twice insists "ut nulla nova eis [= tertiatoribus] a parte rei publicae imponatur," with penalties for (*ali*)*quis rei puplice* who might do so. Cf., in the same sense, Fabre, "Une hypothèse," p. 704 n. 1. The mere rubrics, Sicard clauses 26, 30, 32, might arguably support the same conclusion.

192

ters, the case of Liburia is also evocative of the agreement concluded by the Byzantines with the Arabs in 688
to share Cyprus between them rather than continue fighting for its exclusive possession. Naples may have made a
similar peace treaty with the Lombards of Benevento in
order to stop the latter's depredations.[36]

The parallel case of Cyprus helps to counteract the modern opinion that, prior to being shared, the lands of
Liburia had been publicly owned.[37] As in seventh-century
Cyprus, the resource that was awarded to the two parties
belonged to the state but was not the land itself. The
landowners of Liburia were taxpayers, as they had been
for many centuries, and the assets divided half-and-half
between the *milites* of Naples and the Lombards of Benevento-Capua consisted of the public payments of the Li-
burians, as distinct from the private revenues that accrued
to the landowners by virtue of their unimpaired proprietorship.[38] With a characteristically medieval reluctance to dis-

---

[36] On the division of Cyprus, Romilly Jenkins, "Cyprus between
Byzantium and Islam, A.D. 688-965," *Studies Presented to D. M. Rob-
inson*, vol. 2 (St. Louis, Mo., 1953), pp. 1006-1014. Further bibliography in Franz Dölger, *Regesten der Kaiserurkunden des oströmi-
schen Reiches von 565-1453*, pt. 1, *Regesten von 565-1025* (Munich,
1924), p. 31 no. 257; the tax revenues of Armenia and Iberia were
also shared equally between Byzantium and the Caliphate. Cassandro,
"Ducato bizantino," p. 130, noted this parallel.

[37] Fabre, "Une hypothèse," p. 703; Cassandro, "La Liburia,"
pp. 210-216.

[38] Arechis clauses 3, 9, 10, establish conditions by which each
Lombard and Neapolitan overlord might renounce the payment he received and exchange it for either one-half or one-third of the property
from which his payment came (the details presently). The variable
fraction implies that the payment was not an economic rent or a price
paid by the *tertiator* for a precise proportion of the lands he occupied.
A reasonable alternative is that the payment was, in origin, half the tax
that the Roman or Byzantine state had fixed upon the assessed value
of the property. The total tax had been equally divided between the
two groups of overlords, and, as long as there was no increase, it did
not matter whether the share of lands on whose account an individual payment was made was one-half or one-third.

tinguish public from private law, the documents issued by
Arechis and Sicard permit as many as four levels of "ownership" to be discerned in Liburia: the *res publica* of
Naples and the duke of Benevento each exacted a modest
tax from the *tertiatores*;[39] the absentee Neapolitan and
Lombard overlords (*domini*) shared equally in the possession of rents and other services from the *tertiatores* and
settled slaves;[40] the *tertiatores* were entitled to sell their
farms to whoever paid the price, provided the buyer duly
undertook the seller's obligations toward his superiors; and
the slaves, although hereditarily bound to the farms they
had to cultivate, were also irremovable from them.[41] The

[39] The confusion of public and private law was Byzantine as well
as Western: Dölger, *Beiträge*, p. 140. According to Sicard clause 14,
the *tertiatores* owed Naples "the ancient custom, that is *responsaticum
solum, et angaris et calcarias.*" The latter two are familiar survivals
from the extraordinary burdens of late Roman times; for a parallel
survival, see *Lex Baiuuariorum* 1. 13 (*angariae, calcefurnum*), MGH
Leges, vol. 5, pt. 1, pp. 286-290. The only clues to the size of the
responsaticum (not a well-attested levy) are that Sicard treats it
limitatively and that it amounts to a hog and four pigs in the impressive rental list affixed to the charter of 703/748. (Cassandro,
"La Liburia," pp. 250-251, went quite astray on the *responsaticum*
and *calcariae.*)

The payment to the duke of Benevento is described as a gift,
again limitatively, "unum semel in annum." Cassandro, "La Liburia,"
p. 249, followed Capasso in emending *ad ducem* to *adducere*. This
is scarcely defensible, since the infinitive is not called for by the
sense, and *nec non et* parallels *simul et* in introducing a third class of
payments. The *exenium* to the duke echoes the *responsaticum* to the
Neapolitan state, both of them largely symbolic payments acknowledging the joint ownership of Liburia at its highest level.

[40] Sicard clause 14 describes these as "ad domin[o]s su[o]s angarias
et pensiones secundum antiquam consuetudinem" (which suitably
complements the considerations above, n. 38). Arechis clause 7 speaks
of written agreements between Lombards and Neapolitans regulating
the service of their jointly owned slaves.

[41] The sales by the *tertiatores* will be discussed presently. On the
immobility of slaves, Arechis clause 14 (special pains to defend the
slave from being taken from his farm by the Lombard party); Sicard
clause 6, mutual restitution of fugitive *servi et ancillae*, with a cus-

most intriguing of these rights, as we shall shortly see, was the *tertiator*'s prerogative to divest himself of the land he occupied by legal sale.

Once Liburia is recognized to have been unaffected by Paul's *tercia frugum*, it can be connected to the forms of barbarian settlement that we have been examining only through the word *hospitatica*, which occurs twice in the Arechis treaty. On its first appearance, *hospitatica* lends itself easily to being translated as "allotment," that which gave an overlord certain proprietary rights vis-à-vis the *tertiatores*, but the initial context seems to limit this allotment to the Neapolitans.[42] The restriction is eliminated by the second entry mentioning *hospitaticae*: they had been given to Lombards as well as Neapolitans. Four clauses of the treaty are concerned with farms that could not be sold; they were shared equally by the overlords, they were cultivated by slaves, and they could become vacant, perhaps by the flight of the occupants.[43] The entry that clarifies the meaning of *hospitatica* deals with property of this kind: "If a suit arises over vacant farms, and one party says 'that those farms belonged to *tertiatores* so-and-so,' and the other party says 'that they did not belong to those *tertiatores* whom you say, but belonged to such-and-such whom we say'—in such a suit, let there not be an oath, lest one or the other side should lapse into perjury on this account. [Instead] let there be a careful inquiry about what allotment [the disputed farms] pertained to of old, and then there can be an end to the matter without oath

---

tomary premium to the official bringing them back to their owners. Cf. *Chronicon Beneventani monasterii S. Sophiae*, ed. F. Ughelli, *Italia sacra*, vol. 8 (Rome, 1662), cols. 576, 580, where manumission is used as a device for evicting slaves and seizing their farms.

[42] The passage is quoted below at n. 55.

[43] Arechis clauses 2, 7, 13, 14; the basic contrast is between lands "in which shillings are not given" and those where they are, i.e., respectively, the lands occupied by slaves (forbidden to alienate their holdings) and the lands of *tertiatores* (with rights of sale).

and perjury."[44] The passage implies that, on a day to day basis, farms and men were what mattered in Liburia; the unit called *hospitatica* was both ignored by the residents and invisible to the eye. Yet the *hospitaticae* came to life whenever Lombards and Neapolitans sued each other over the ownership of an abandoned farm (the departed occupant probably was a slave, and not a *tertiator*). The inquest that the court conducted was expected to reveal what *hospitatica* the disputed farm was anciently attributed to, that is to say, the allotment in which it had been originally comprised; and, since this same *hospitatica* was expected to have passed by descent to one of the litigants, the inquest would yield positive proof of ownership.

So interpreted, the term is invaluable for establishing that, at some time in the past (*antiquitus*), a unit composed of specifically designated farms, perhaps even a unit of homogeneous size, was assigned to individual Lombards and Neapolitan *milites*. Rather than there having been only a sharing of the revenues of Liburia by the two governing authorities, allotments of concrete farms and live tributaries had been conferred upon individual beneficiaries, and a special word, drawn from the vocabulary we are familiar with, was coined to express them. However little account was subsequently taken of these *hospitaticae*, the memory they left—we are not told whether orally or in writing—was sufficiently firm and enduring to

[44] Arechis clause 11 (ed. Bluhme, p. 214): "Si horta fuerit intentio de fundis exfundanis, et dixerit una pars: 'quia ista fundora de talibus tertiatoribus fuerunt,' et alia pars dixerit: 'quia non fuerunt de his tertiatoriis, quos dicitis, sed de istis fuerunt, quos nos dicimus,' non sit inde sacramentum, ut una quaelibet pars in periurium exinde incurrat; inquiratur diligenter ad qualia hospitatica fuerunt pertinentia antiquitus, et tunc sine sacramentum et periurio poterit inde esse finis." I tend to think that the *tertiatores* were not only tributaries obligated to the overlords on their own account but also middlemen between the overlords and their slaves; hence the vacated *fundora* pertained to some *tertiator* or another.

be accessible for legal purposes for a long time.[45] This was not *hospitalitas* as defined within the title *de metatis* of the Theodosian Code, but it was virtually identical to the awards made to Goths, Burgundians, and other "guests" in the provinces of the Roman West.

If the *hospitaticae* of the Lombards and Neapolitans were individual shares of a revenue that, prior to the division, had been the Roman or Byzantine land tax, the logical consequence seems to be that the persons called *tertiatores* descended from the taxpaying landowners (*possessores*) of the past. This conclusion is not beyond dispute.[46] The earliest reference to *tertiatores* features the sale of some of them as though they were chattels; besides, Sicard's capitulary permits Lombards to sell *tertiatores*, on the strict condition that they may not be shipped abroad except as punishment for proved homicide. The sale of human beings, even outside a marketplace, tends to give them a servile coloring.[47] Yet the same capitulary shows that the condition of the *tertiatores* was hardly humble:

[45] The charter recording a sale of *tertiatores* (n. 27 above) may help to explain why *hospitaticae* are so rarely mentioned: if a Lombard or Neapolitan wished to alienate his allotment, or a part of it, he sold or donated the *censiles homines* (Arechis clause 12), alias *tertiatores*; the *hospitatica* itself, however, was not an object that could be sold: it was merely a record.

[46] Cassandro, "La Liburia," pp. 255-263, was more qualified than in "Ducato Bizantino," p. 149, where he equated their condition to that of slaves. He insisted especially on one feature of the charter of 703/738: the buyer agreed that, when children were born to the sold *tertiator* couple, the seller would be owed half their estimated value (the main sale was of half the potential parents). One would have to know what this meant before attributing undue weight to it in an evaluation of *tertiator* status.

[47] The charter, above, n. 27; Sicard clause 4 (cf. clause 3, prohibiting Neapolitan purchases of Lombards). My reading is that a 'real" slave, i.e., one compatible with classical doctrines of slavery, was the kind that might be freely set aboard ship and sold abroad. Not only *tertiatores* but also the settled *servi et ancillae* mentioned in the Arechis treaty probably fell outside this category (Arechis clause 14 is suggestive).

they were exempt from a levy collected from other subjects of Naples for payment to the Lombards; they were protected from the forced sale of their produce to the state at fixed prices; and they were allowed to fatten their pigs in the local forests without payment, as though a right of free pannage went with their lands.[48] Even more eloquent are the special pains taken to prevent them from being elevated into the military elite, as either Lombard *exercitales* or Neapolitan *milites*.[49] The *tertiatores* would not have enjoyed such privileges, or been singled out for special attention, if they had been mere chattels subject to casual sale. Even the word *colonus* that is coupled with *tertiator* in one of Sicard's rubrics is better interpreted in the general sense of "farmer, cultivator" than in parallel with the *coloni* of contemporary documents from the north.[50]

[48] These exemptions are known only from rubrics. Sicard clause 32, "Ut coloni terciatores non dent in collata nec in pactu"; the *collata* is described in Sicard clause 2 (*pactus* is probably a synonym, as *porci* in clause 29 below, rather than a separate levy). Clause 30, "Ut invitus non detur pretium at terciatores pro tritico aut vino"; Cassandro, "Ducato bizantino," p. 144, was mystified by this entry, which refers quite clearly to the levy known in the sixth century as *coemptio*. Clause 29, "Ut non tollatur a tertiatoribus excusaticum [= escaticum] et porcos" (the gloss is owed to Muratori, noted in ed. Bluhme, p. 217 n. 12); freedom from this due is important evidence of proprietorship, cf. LVisig 8. 5. 2 (above, Chapter v n. 28), LRB 17. 5 and LBurg 67 (above, Chapter v nn. 43-44).

[49] Rubrics again: Sicard clause 20, "Ut non praesumat aliquis terciatorem exercitalem aut militem facere"; clause 21, "Ut si terciator absconse exercitalis factus fuerit, aut miles." The mobility these rubrics attest to is reinforced by the *tertiator's* right to sell or abandon his lands (Arechis clauses 3, 9, 10, 12). As a result, I doubt the conviction of Cassandro, "La Liburia," pp. 252-253, after Hirsch (in Acocella, *Longobardia meridionale*), that the local *hospites* documented from the tenth century onward were *tertiatores* under a new name. They may well have been the successors of the *tertiatores* but need not be their descendants holding on precisely the same terms: the change of name needs explaining.

[50] Sicard clause 32 (quoted above, n. 48). The northern *coloni* I

The stature of the *tertiatores* is most precisely illustrated by the articles of the Arechis treaty that establish what the "third" was from which their name was derived. The treaty, in which a *tertiator* is once glossed as a "rent [or tax] paying man" (*censiles homo*), shows the Lombard and Neapolitan overlords exercising joint ownership over two categories of property in Liburia. In the first, "shillings are not given," and "the Lombards had divided the lands and slaves with the Neapolitans by written [charters] or had regulated (*definitum*) them between themselves in whatever way."[51] It was the second category, the one in which "shillings are given," that the *tertiatores* were involved with.

In the second category, as in the first, there was joint, undivided lordship, but the trait prominently featured in the three relevant clauses is that the lands of the *tertiatores* were bought and sold for shillings, *solidi*—Byzantine gold pieces in this region, rather than the northern units of account. The clauses emphasize what may happen when the *tertiator*-occupant of such a farm sold it either to a stranger able to pay the price or to one of the overlords. If the *tertiator* sold out to a stranger, the overlords might wish to "re-collect" (*recolligere*) the lands, that is to say, to terminate the community of lordship. Until a sale occurred, the community had safeguarded the occupancy of the *tertiator*, leaving him undisturbed as long as each overlord received his due payment (*census*). The passage of the property

---

have in mind are, typically, those of the famous St. Germain polyptych. Liburia, however, was Byzantine territory, where the meaning of *colonus* might tend to its Greek equivalent, *georgos*, the so-called "free peasant" of the Byzantine *Nomos georgikos*: Walter Ashburner, "The Farmer's Law," *Journal of Hellenic Studies* 30 (1910): 97-108. See also the comment on *LBurg* 38. 7, 9-10, above, Chapter v n. 15.

[51] The gloss, clause 12 (Bluhme's explanation, p. 214 n. 11 of his edition, should be disregarded); *census* is imprecise, either rent or tax. For the first category of property, clauses 2 and 7; the division is half-and-half without exception (as also in clause 14).

from the established occupant to his legal successor was the ideal moment for the Neapolitan and Lombard overlords to carry out a concrete division and consequently to assume outright possession of one-half each. Thus, if a sale took place, the overlords had the right to intervene and, by each refunding one-half of the sale price—in effect, a preemption—to stop the land from passing to the buyer. Instead of conveying the property to the latter, the *tertiator* pocketed his price and turned the lands over to the overlords, for eventual partition and individual assumption of possession.[52] Preemption, however, was not the only possible response to a sale.

The alternative course of action is even more interesting. If the two overlords would not each refund half the price, the lands were divided in three parts, one-third to be securely possessed by the Lombard party, another by the Neapolitan, and the last by "those men who have [given] those shillings," that is, the buyers.[53] In later

[52] The three clauses are nos. 3, 9, 10. Clause 3, "Terras autem, in quibus solidi dati sunt per scripta, firmantes ipsas cartas inter partes per sacramenta cum tribus personis intus domum suam, si voluerimus ipsas terras inter partes recolligere, licentiam habeant Neapolitani reddere med. ex ipsi solid. et Langobardi similiter, et dividere ipsas terras per medietatem." The balance of the passage is quoted in the next note. Bluhme placed the second comma after *dati sunt*, but I think a better sense is obtained by the placement adopted here. The opening—notably *suam*—is obscure. In view of the accent placed in clauses 9-10 on verifying whether sales are legal, I understand these sentences to specify the conditions for a valid sale, or "giving of shillings"; the *domus*, therefore, is that of a *tertiator* (as is the only other *domus* in the treaty, clause 12). For confirmation of the idea that the occupants are the sellers, see clause 4: Lombards or Neapolitans are forbidden to acquire Liburian lands wholly owned by the opposite *pars*; any sales or mortgages of such land by "ipsi homines, qui habitant in ipsa fundora" are quashed with loss of *ipsos solidos* paid for them.

[53] "Sin autem, dividantur in tres partes: unam partem tollant Langobardi, aliam Neapolitani et aliam qui ipsos solidos datos habent; facientes inter utrasque partes talem firmatione in scriptis, ut a tunc securiter Langobardi tertiam partem, et Neapolitani tertiam, et ipsi

clauses, basically the same transaction is portrayed except that the formerly indeterminate purchaser is replaced by one or the other of the joint overlords.[54] Accordingly, we find a Neapolitan who has bought out a *tertiator* being called to account by a "Capuan party," that is, a Lombard: "And if the Capuan party wishes to refund half the shillings set down in the charters, let the lands be divided in half; and if he refuses to refund half the shillings, let the lands themselves be divided into three parts. Let the Neapolitan party take one part of them by virtue of the allotment and another for the shillings, [and] the Capuan party takes the third part."[55] Since the overlords are potential buyers, it is apparent that they were not ordinarily entitled to take physical possession of either one-half or one-third of the property; the indispensable condition for their doing so was that the *tertiator* should be alienating his occupancy to a buyer.[56] The same point is confirmed by a clause showing the overlords partitioning the lands vacated by a *tertiator* who had formally abandoned his homestead without a sale.[57] Yet it is also apparent that, when a legal contract

---

homines, qui ipsos solidos [datos] habent, tertiam partem securiter possideant."

[54] Arechis clauses 9 (a Lombard buys land in Liburia and a Neapolitan contests the sale), 10 (the same in reverse, see next note). The entries are particularly concerned with the procedure for verifying whether or not the sale is valid.

[55] Arechis clause 10, "Et si voluerit pars de Capua reddere med. de ipsi solidi, quas ipsae cartulae continunt, dividantur ipsae terrae per med.; et si noluerit reddere med. de ipsi sol., dividantur ipsae terrae in tertiam partem: unam partem tollat exinde pars de Neapolim pro ipsa hospitatica, et aliam pro ipsi solidi, tertiam partem tollat exinde pars de Capua." For the beginning of the quotation, see Bluhme, "Das *pactum*," p. 142, altering his edition (p. 214).

[56] Cf. the comparable instances in fifth-century North Africa: Christian Courtois, in *Tablettes Albertini. Actes privés de l'époque vandale*, ed. C. Courtois, L. Leschi, C. Perrat, and C. Saumagne (Paris, 1952), pp. 208-211 (Courtois' invocations of a "social drama" or "crisis" seem exaggerated).

[57] Arechis clause 12: if the *tertiator* feels forced to vacate ("ex-

to sell was entered into by the *tertiator* with a buyer, each overlord had the right to intervene and take possession of one-third of the property without paying anything for it, merely "by virtue of the allotment." That is curious enough, but, one might add, why a share of only one-third when, in every other respect, the share of each overlord is clearly one-half? The only satisfactory explanation for both anomalies seems to be that, whenever "shillings [were] given," in other words, whenever a sale and purchase took place, the rentpayer (*censiles homo*) obligated to overlords in Naples and Capua was recognized to be the full-fledged owner of a *tertia* of the lands he occupied, with the unimpaired right to alienate this fraction for a price. The half that each overlord had the right to preempt was a half of this third, namely, one sixth, and either overlord could acquire this same third in full by paying the *tertiator*'s price, thus doubling the share he could claim "by virtue of the allotment." The onetime owner of the entire property (*possessor*) derived his new name from the *tertia* that he continued to possess fully enough to dispose of it by sale.

These clauses of Arechis's treaty presuppose that the overlords were actively interested in substituting themselves for the *tertiatores* and undertaking the direct management of the shares allotted to them. The chances are that this assumption is mainly a legal fiction, and that the procedure of tripartition called for in case the sale price was not refunded was basically a formality rather than a concrete division of lands. By dramatizing the three shares, the one or two overlords who had not participated in the sale were able to assert their right to the payments and services that the *tertiator*-seller had customarily rendered;

---

fundare se"), "ponit post regiam [= main door] domus suae ipsum fustem, sicut antiqua fuit consuetudo, et vadit ubi voluerit." The overlords can try to convince him to return and resume his service, or they may install a man "from elsewhere," or if they cannot or do not want to, "dividant inter se fundum et terris ipsius."

the buyer was obliged to assume them as the condition for peaceful enjoyment of the two-thirds that he could not buy from the *tertiator* but nevertheless expected to enjoy (and had probably paid for).[58] The eventuality of a joint pre-emption by the overlords, with each one refunding half the sale price, looks even more fictional than the triparti-tion. Their ostensible desire to take personal possession furnished a plausible pretext for intervention in a contract to which they were otherwise alien; it was their first step toward vindicating the revenues they were owed by the lands being sold and ensuring that they were perpetu-ated.[59]

In addition to documenting the *tertiator's* residuary own-ership and dramatizing the overlord's prerogatives "by vir-tue of the allotment," the procedure of tripartition also implied a form of commutation for the payments to the Lombards and Neapolitans, a commutation so disadvan-tageous to the *tertiator* as to encourage him either to con-tinue paying or to sell out to someone who would. Com-mutation was not expected to appeal to the overlords either: the portion that each one might appropriate by re-nouncing the *census* owed to him by the *tertiator* was one-third less than the full half share that he was theoretically entitled to. From the standpoint of the *tertiator*, the sur-render of two-thirds of the property he occupied and man-

[58] It seems reasonable to assume that the object for which the *solidi* were paid was the entire unit occupied by the *tertiator*; what went with the latter's third was the occupancy (or *dominium utile*) of the whole. Note that, in Arechis clauses 9-10, the uninvolved overlord has to sue his opposite number in order to avoid being deprived of his *census*.

[59] The rules instituted in Liburia solved the problem posed by the Roman law title "sine censu vel reliquis fundum conparari non posse" (*CTh* 11. 3; less illuminatingly, *CJ* 4. 47); cf. *LRB* 40, "Omnes agnuscant, agros se conparare non posse, si eorum censum non statim, cum possessionem ingressi fuerint, susceperint dissolven-dum" (also Chapter III n. 68 and Chapter VIII n. 42). The buyer who risked the summary loss of two-thirds of his purchase unless he under-took the *census* was unlikely to delay regularizing his position.

203

aged was an extravagant amount to exchange for liberation from a burden that outsiders were willing to buy for the sake of what went with it. Yet, despite the excessive cost to all concerned, the option of permanent commutation of rent for capital was built into the relations of the *tertiatores* to their Lombard and Neapolitan superiors. In areas where commutation was desired rather than discouraged, it cannot have been beyond the ingenuity of legislators to draft its terms in such a way as to make the option palatable and advantageous to the affected parties.

Although different from the arrangements reported by Paul the Deacon, the case of Liburia, with its curious provision for the *milites* of Naples as well as for the Lombards, explicitly documents several aspects of barbarian allotments that otherwise could be only suspected. Those who had given the name *hospitaticae* to these allotments were conscious that the Lombards and Neapolitans were "guests" of the peculiar type that (as we know) had been invented in the early fifth century. Predictably, the *hospitaticae* had no connection with housing; the overlords of Liburia had found lodgings elsewhere than with their agricultural slaves and *tertiatores*. They were city-dwelling absentees, whose *census* and *pensiones* for their shares were paid in nearby Capua and Naples by the obligated occupants of the land.[60] The overlords remained remote. The exploitation of Liburia was effectively managed by a group of resident proprietors whose position had not deteriorated from what it had been under exclusively Neapolitan, or Roman, rule. Their old taxes were divided into two shares remitted to individual beneficiaries rather than to a single government; their ownership of the ancestral property had dwindled to the right to alienate a one-third share of the whole; from *possessores*, they had become *tertiatores*. But, because the remittances were probably no greater than the former land tax, and because no one

---

[60] On the Neapolitan *milites* and their Lombard counterparts, Cassandro, "La Liburia," pp. 216-224.

wished to carry out effective divisions of the soil, the *tertiatores* are unlikely to have endured anything worse than
the redefinition of a basically unchanged status.[61]

If the Italy of Odoacer and Theodoric is crucial in documenting the nature of early barbarian allotments, that of
the Lombards has comparable value for establishing the
endurance and adaptability of the grants called "hospitality." The evidence from both periods brings before us
something considerably subtler than the expropriation and
enslavement of Italo-Roman landowners by supposedly
land-hungry Germanic invaders. The provinces that the
barbarians would enter contained public revenues as well
as private property; the operating farms and estates that
formed their principal economic resource were organized
in such a way as to provide sustenance for the cultivators,
the owners, and—through the taxation of agrarian property—the government. A long-standing body of law, and
the use of written records, permitted these separate
shares or interests in agricultural land to be kept distinct.
In a situation of this complexity, the need to accommodate
barbarian immigrants could be faced without undue alarm.
Provided that the newcomers were willing to abide by
rules of the same kind as everyone else, ample room could
be made for them at the expense of the party ultimately
responsible for their presence, namely, the Roman state.
The dispersal of public resources into the possession of individual barbarians even had a side effect that western
Romans might have found positively attractive: its consequence, in the long run, was to eliminate taxation as a
component of public service. The concluding chapter gives
special attention to this dimension of the subject.

[61] The assumption of modern commentators that the *tertiatores*
were cultivators (cf. above, n. 46) is perhaps too categorical. For
comparison, a Roman *possessor* might, among other things, cultivate
his own farm, but he would be wrongly described as merely a cultivator. The old *conductor* was also something more than a tiller of the
soil. Cultivation was only one of several possible roles for a resident
farmer.

VIII

****

CONCLUSION: THE DEVOLUTION
OF TAXATION

THE traditional account of the "regime of hospitality" has long occasioned unease among historians. Jones judged the system to have been just as inequitable to the barbarians as it was to the Romans.[1] Lot, Musset, Thompson, and others felt obliged to insist that the partition of lands affected only large landowners. "Simple good sense," Lot said, imposed this conclusion, even if the documents did not.[2] Lot was also disturbed by another problem: the barbarian armies would have lost all cohesion if their members had been dispersed as landowners throughout the countryside.[3] Perhaps the most provocative objection was voiced by Professor Wallace-Hadrill, in a study that accorded greater weight to the negligible archaeological and toponymic traces of Visigothic settlement in Gaul than to the written evidence on allotments. He concluded that the Visigoths, after almost a century of residence, continued to be a rootless army of occupation: "They had remained isolated in a Roman province indifferent to their fate; and, in the end, found it easier to pack their bags and go." The idea of their having been major landlords for many decades was hard to reconcile with the rapidity of their departure after a single military defeat.[4] In a con-

---

[1] *LRE*, p. 252.

[2] Lot, "Hospitalité," pp. 989-993, quote from p. 992; Thompson, "Settlement," p. 68 with n. 25; Musset, *Vagues germaniques*, p. 285.

[3] Lot "Hospitalité," pp. 994-995 with n. 3; also in Ferdinand Lot, Christian Pfister, and F. L. Ganshof, *Les destinées de l'Empire en Occident* (Paris, 1928), p. 102 n. 4.

[4] Wallace-Hadrill, "Gothia," p. 48. On archaeology and toponymy,

text in which difficulties like these had been discerned, it is small wonder that Musset should have warned that "*hospitalitas* agreements" were a transitory and less important type of settlement than the colonization of fiscal land organized by the Frankish kings.[5] Recent scholars have become increasingly fascinated by settlements of the latter type, whose traces are apparent in records of the eighth and later centuries.[6] The future seemed to belong to them, rather than to the adaptations of Roman law devised for the sake of the Goths and Burgundians.

There is a simple explanation for the low estate to which the "regime of hospitality" has descended. Gaupp's study, however admirable, was simply a first step away from the then prevailing view that the fifth-century settlements had been conquests.[7] The attention he drew to the chronology of land allotments and to their precedents in Roman law was a salutary corrective to previous oversimplifications; he inaugurated detailed and critical study of the subject. As it happened, however, the excellent beginning Gaupp had made was mistaken for a final solution. His central finding—the link between military

M. Broens, "Le peuplement germanique de la Gaule entre la Méditerranée et l'Océan," *Annales du Midi* 68 (1956): 17-37.

[5] Musset, *Vagues germaniques*, p. 288.

[6] For an introduction to, and bibliography of, this subject, Anne K. G. Kristensen, "Danelaw Institutions and Danish Society in the Viking Age," *Mediaeval Scandinavia* 8 (1975): 33-42. A starting point in this line of investigation was Heinrich Dannenbauer, "Hundertschaft, Centena und Huntari," *Historisches Jahrbuch* 63-69 (1949): 155-219 (repr. in Dannenbauer, *Grundlagen der mittelalterlichen Welt* [Stuttgart, 1958], pp. 179-239). Musset's implication that colonization of fiscal land (which is guessed at rather than proved) stands in contrast to "*hospitalitas* agreements" is unfortunate and should not be perpetuated. The details of any kind of early barbarian settlement are still too obscure to be firmly classified into types. Dannenbauer and others have stressed the Roman institutional background to settlement, but there is room for making this background more precise.

[7] Above, Chapter v n. 64.

quartering and barbarian land grants—was never again scrutinized; it turned into an unquestioned fact, sometimes narrated by later historians in ludicrously distorted form.[8] Gaupp had not departed from the belief of his predecessors that the allotments were composed of expropriated property. By his account, provincial landowners were stripped pursuant to Roman law, rather than by barbarian seizure as formerly believed, but they were stripped all the same.[9] Delbrück realized the magnitude of the problem that dispossessions on a scale of one-third or two-thirds implied, but only Fustel de Coulanges had the boldness to venture an explanation of how the barbarians might have been provided for without expropriating Romans. His theory was deeply flawed and inspired no imitators.[10] By default, the traditional premise of expropriation also became an unquestioned aspect of the story.

Perhaps the best measure of how little Gaupp's findings were developed in the century following their publication is that the stock of evidence and observations he had put into circulation was augmented by only one novel idea: the intelligent but problematic hypothesis that the Roman lands to be partitioned consisted of bipartite estates on the Carolingian model. Delbrück and Mayer were its initiators, and Lot set the matter at the center of his discussion.[11] Their idea had the merit of drawing at-

[8] Yet Binding, *Königreich*, p. 16 n. 45, believed that Gaupp had exaggerated the relevance of *hospitalitas*. For distorted summaries, above, Chapter II n. 6; the list might easily be lengthened.

[9] He came very close to being forced to question this premise. In discussing *LBurg* 55, he raised the question how two Romans who had lost two-thirds of their lands to Burgundian guests could still be contesting their boundaries, and he was unable to devise a satisfactory answer (*Ansiedlungen*, pp. 362-363).

[10] Above, Chapter III nn. 1, 8.

[11] Ernst Mayer in *Göttingische gelehrte Anziegen* 165 (1903): 203-205; Delbrück, *Kriegskunst*, vol. 2, pp. 338-343 (surely the direct inspiration for Lot's study); Lot, "Hospitalité," p. 979. Only Lot

tention to the terminology of *LBurg* 54 and to the contrasting treatment of *terrae* and *mancipia*. Like Gaupp's *hospitalitas*, however, it crystallized before being adequately explored and tested. The land tax context of the settlements (which Gaupp had dimly perceived) was prematurely superseded by a bipartite estate context, retrojected from the ninth century to the fifth.

The course taken by discussions of the "problem of hospitality" differs little from the treatment of other vexed subjects of late Roman research. A casual observer might be tempted to extend to it the words recently applied to another *quaestio disputata*: "Since [the documents] have been minutely examined by scholars over a century without consensus on many major and still more minor points of interpretation, there is small reason to hope for anything better now."[12] But such weary despair has no more relevance to fifth-century settlement than it does (one suspects) to any other problem. The length of time that documents have been in view matters little by comparison with how often, how comprehensively, and how accurately they have in fact been studied. The record of what has been done with *hospitalitas* suggests that the examination of the sources has been spotty, that consensus has been reached over the wrong points, and that many differences of interpretation have arisen from extraneous premises. Far from being old and played out, Gaupp's problem is much as it was left by its inventor—a promising idea in need of verification and development.[13]

---

thought it necessary to specify that the idea of bipartite estates was being applied to the Burgundian texts, but he presented the matter as an established fact: the barbarians were settled on estates whose structure was the same as the estates inventoried by ninth-century polyptychs.

[12] Ramsey MacMullen, *Roman Government's Response to Crisis, A.D. 235-337* (New Haven, Conn., 1976), p. 137, about late Roman taxation.

[13] Gaupp's *Ansiedlungen* was published in the same year as Ben-

The present study originated from two observations: that the military billeting prescribed by the Theodosian Code had to do with temporary shelter, not with permanent land grants, and that, in any case, massive, official expropriations of Roman property cannot be shown to have taken place in fifth-century Gaul and Italy. These negative points could be complemented by the finding that Cassiodorus's *Variae* illustrate a mode of barbarian allotment that asked no more of the Italians than what they already contributed in taxes. If such was the case in Theodoric's kingdom, might not the same have been true earlier in Gaul? In other words, it looked as though the fifth-century allotments to the Goths and Burgundians were based, not on an implementation of the billeting system, but on a distribution of the main asset of the Roman state, namely, the proceeds of taxation and the property assessments on which taxes were levied. This is the main hypothesis that the sources have been called upon to confirm or disprove. As for the "hospitality" synonymous with billeting whose traces occur in all but the Ostrogothic records, it seemed less likely to have been the mainspring for the allotments than a device or procedure facilitating the distribution of state resources. This complementary idea also needed testing. The relevant evidence has now been examined and discussed region by region. On the basis of these analyses, a comprehensive account may be attempted of how the allotments to barbarians took place and of the effects they had on the parties involved and the structures of taxation.

A few words of warning are in order before launching into this synthesis. The materials that we have studied were never meant to provide realistic portrayals of behavior by barbarians, Romans, or whoever; they come largely from law codes and other writings that deliberately

---

jamin Guérard's superb edition of the polyptych of St. Germain des Prés.

convey an abstract, ordered, and generalized image of society. We may rightly doubt that sources as distantly removed as these from the harsh realities of daily life accurately mirror the age they document. Yet, in the absence of other information, we are bound to pretend that they do and, accordingly, to recreate the historical circumstances and developments they imply, if only as a formal exercise. No claim is made that this will yield a precise account of fifth and sixth-century conditions—the past "as it really was." The most that is aspired to is formal correctness in the joining together of a few statements whose claim to prominence is that they are verifiable in contemporary documentation. These statements may differ from our impressions of the age, but they set a few hard limits on our imaginative evocations, and, because open to amendment and correction, they provide a focus for constructive argument.

If we may still use the phrase "regime of hospitality" to describe the conditions accorded to the fifth-century barbarians, it should be understood in a different sense from that accepted in the earlier literature. Within the districts awarded to federate Visigoths and Burgundians by Roman generals, *hospitalitas* defined the mutual relations of the resident provincials and the occupying barbarian army, and, in its technical guise as a system of military billeting, it supplied the model for pairing civilian taxpayers and salaried barbarian soldiers. No institution of this kind had ever before existed in the Roman state. Someone invented it, with a view to providing a gracious name, as well as an administrative technique, for a set of arrangements whose substantive content was rather masked than revealed by the term "hospitality." Those arrangements were basically fiscal—an adaptation of public income and outlays to new circumstances. The allotments to federate barbarians were not the end of Roman taxation in the West, but they marked an important stage in the devolution of the tax system from refined fourth-century complexities toward the simplifications of the Frankish period.

Even a *hospitalitas* requiring expropriation used to be portrayed as a gentle device because official and legal.[14] What made expropriation unnecessary was that, in every territory affected by barbarian settlement, there were public resources—state lands perhaps, but especially a population of regimented taxpayers whose property stood bond for annual contributions to the government. The surrender of these resources was unavoidable even in those instances when the initiative in setting the terms of settlement rested with Roman generals. As military allies of the empire, the barbarians were entitled to rations and pay, and, if they were to be allowed to garrison a territory under kings of their own, even the surplus of local revenues, if any, could hardly have been retained for the Gallic prefecture. The surviving evidence does not tell us what financial arrangements the generals Constantius and Aëtius made, but it does allow us to distinguish two steps in the transfer of public revenues: first, a division of the total into separate allocations, one for the barbarian leader, the other for his army, and, second, a distribution of the army's share in individual, heritable allotments. The latter step has monopolized the attention of earlier scholars, but the underlying partition between king and troops appears to have been at least as far-reaching in its consequences.

It must be admitted at the outset that we can only guess at why such a division was made, or at whose behest.[15] The

---

[14] This was easy to do when Roman *hospitalitas* was thought to require the host to share all his worldly goods with the official guest regardless of his nationality (above, Chapter II n. 6).

[15] A similar division occurred in the Vandal kingdom: Victor Vitensis *Historia persecutionis* 1. (4.) 13; Procopius *Bell. Vandal* 1. 5. 11-14; Courtois, *Vandales*, p. 279. A possibility that cannot be excluded is that the idea stemmed from the practice of dividing booty; but since the Vandals had been *foederati*, exposed to Roman ideas concerning the allocation of rations and pay, the existence of a

Visigothic and Burgundian settlements of 418 and 443 were on a moderate scale; Constantius and Aëtius could hardly have imagined that they were "founding the barbarian kingdoms," as we might be tempted to say. To convey all public resources exclusively to the barbarian kings would have been to treat them as though they were the heirs and assigns of the Roman state, rather than subsidized allies. If any model was in the generals' heads, it is likely to have been that for distributing a given revenue between one dignitary (the illustrious commanding officer) and the various units forming his army. Contemporary practice in Roman government was suggestive of such patterns, which in time would also impose themselves in the partition of episcopal revenues between a bishop and his clergy.[16] Certain items, such as imperial lands, went to the kings in their entirety, but the major asset—the roster of taxpayers, with their official declarations of taxable property (the

---

division among them does not have to be ascribed to barbarian custom.

[16] For divisions of revenues in Roman government, the most explicit text is Justinian's ordinance on the restored praetorian prefecture of Africa (*CJ* 1. 27. 1 [534]); its elaborate list specifies everyone's salary in food and fodder rations, as well as their money equivalent, such that the prefect himself received 100 lb. gold and everyone else (over 400 officials) shared a total of 7183 *solidi*, i.e., 100 lb. minus 17 *sol.* (99.7%). The division is almost precisely half and half. A similar list (*CJ* 1. 27. 2) illustrates a 70:30 division between each African *dux* "and his men" and the ducal *officium*. In Justinian *Novel.* 25 (535), the emoluments of the praetor of Pisidia, after deduction of fees to the palace, are virtually equal to those of his *officium* (224:216 *solidi*). For the division of church revenues, Jean Gaudemet, *L'Église dans l'Empire romain (IVe-Ve siècles)* (Paris, 1958), pp. 308-310; Jones, *LRE*, pp. 902-903, who called it the dividend system, pointed out that Cyprian attests to its existence in the West as early as the mid-third century.

It is particularly interesting to observe, in this connection, that the Burgundian kings prior to 476 are now argued, quite plausibly, to have derived their authority from Roman military offices: Ian Wood, "Kings, Kingdoms and Consent," in *Early Medieval Kingship*, ed. P. H. Sawyer and I. N. Wood (Leeds, 1977), pp. 20-21.

censuales paginae)—was split, in perpetuity, between the commanding officer and the rank and file. In a Roman context, a division of this kind, by whose terms the right of each subordinate to his stipend was as fully guaranteed as the right of his chief, presupposed the moderating role of a sovereign emperor, able to adjust or even to abolish the rules as public need dictated.[17] The unintended course taken by events in the West brought it about that this same division was integrated, without its moderator, into the fabric of barbarian government. The precedent once set had great appeal. Under Romulus Augustulus, the army of Italy insisted on being accorded the same conditions; conversely, the standard-bearer of a restored Lombard monarchy was able to secure for himself the supreme commander's rightful share of the conquered Italian tributaries.

On a practical plane, the division of taxpayers most directly affected the Roman bureaucracy. In fifth-century Italy, for example, the theoretical implication of allocating one-third of the land tax to the army was to withdraw the corresponding number of taxpayers from the existing machinery of collection and redistribution. It is believable that such a measure should have been so objectionable to the civil government in 476 that the army had to resort to mutiny in order to vindicate its demands.[18] If bureaucratic

[17] On guarantees in respect to salaries, a particularly impressive example occurs in the fifth-century (Eastern) laws ordering that the stipend and perquisites of those reaching a specified rank in their organization will be paid to their heirs if they die in their year of service: *CTh* 6. 24. 11 (432), *CJ* 2. 7. 15 (472), 12. 20. 3 (Leo I), 12. 19. 11 (Anastasius), 2. 7. 22. 6 (505), 12. 17. 4 (Justinian). The codes contain several statutes in which emperors reorganize *officia*; e.g., *CTh* 6. 27. 23 (430), *CJ* 12. 19. 10 (Leo I); for a known instance when this was painful, Procopius *Anecdota* 24. 19-20, 30-32.

[18] The resistance of bureaucrats (those of the Italian prefecture and the *magister militum*) is better suited than that of landowners to explaining why a mutiny (including the killing of Orestes, onetime *notarius* to Attila) was necessary to vindicate the soldiers' demands (above, Chapter III—provided, of course, that Procopius's report about this may be believed at all).

214

resistance arose at an earlier date in Gaul, no trace of it has reached us. The prefectoral and diocesan personnel were left with enough to do outside the modest districts assigned to the Visigoths and Burgundians, and the provincial *officiales* who remained behind would be sufficiently employed tending to the royal share of revenues without also acting as military paymasters. Under the circumstances, a division of public resources may have seemed a salutary and needed measure of administrative simplification. Over a longer term, however, bureaucrats were bound to be the main victims of a settlement that allocated a distinct slice of revenues directly to barbarian troops. The officials' livelihood dwindled with every step that narrowed the interval between taxpayers and those entitled to support from tax receipts. None but bureaucrats need have mourned the change, but, for them at least, it marked the turning point in the prosperity of their profession.[19]

In the Visigothic and Burgundian laws, the division of resources hides behind a distinction between Roman and barbarian shares, the latter being expressed as "two parts" in *LVisig* 10. 1. 8 and as "one-third of the bondsmen and two parts of the lands" in *LBurg* 54. Only by inference may we conclude that the balance, or "Roman share," represents those taxpayers who answered directly to the barbarian king for their assessments. The situation is clearer in Ostrogothic Italy, provided we listen to Cassiodorus rather than to Procopius. In letters dated within two decades of the time when the initial settlement took place, the *tertiae* are portrayed as a simple allocation of assessments, out of which each barbarian entitled to a *sors* received the quantity of tax proceeds that was his due. Cassiodorus's other

---

[19] De-bureaucratization (if I may be forgiven the word) is one of the major institutional phenomena in the passage from a late Roman to an early medieval West. A major step, earlier than the settlements in question here, was the withdrawal of the Gallic prefecture to Arles. For important aspects of this story, Matthews, *Aristocracy*, pp. 69-87, 346-351.

letters abundantly establish that the balance of public assets, including even those *tertiae* that were not distributed as allotments, remained at the disposal of the Ostrogothic king.[20] Once it is understood that, in both Gaul and Italy, state resources were the wherewithal that was subjected to partition, a pair of problems that bedeviled earlier scholars—how to chop up farms and farmhands into manageable bits and how to dispossess Roman landlords without their feeling it—is eliminated. Private farms had nothing to do with the matter. The terms of settlement addressed themselves to taxpayers and their assessments, assigning one pool to the barbarian king, the other to his troops, with the second to be shared out in individual portions.

The Ostrogothic and Lombard evidence, which provides the best basis for an informed judgment, suggests that the distribution of individual allotments was carried out as rapidly as circumstances allowed. Gaupp had thought otherwise. The principal advantage he attached to his version of *hospitalitas* was that it established an intermediary stage between the arrival of the barbarians in Aquitaine or Sapaudia and their definitive *Landnahme*. We need not share his concern about the chronology of "annexation," for the award of personal allotments to the barbarians had no necessary connection to their becoming direct possessors of the soil.[21] The Gothic or Burgundian

---

[20] Unallotted *tertiae* paid the *illatio tertiarum*, which the government collected for its own uses, with the option of either cancelling the separate account and having its proceeds amalgamated to the *tributaria summa* (*Variae* 1. 14), or converting the tax into new allotments (2. 17).

[21] The concept of *Landnahme*, which differs from mere "settlement," is made much of in German writings; its overtones are nationalistic (as in, annexation or making the soil Germanic), rather than legal or agrarian. I take the liberty in this paragraph of having it denote ownership of the soil as distinct from a right to agrarian revenues.

sors was primarily a claim to revenue, payable to the beneficiary by one or more Roman taxpayers and secured by their assessed property. A barbarian *Landnahme* might result from this, by open or covert harassment, legal foreclosure of debt, or amicable commutation of annual payment into capital, but it was not a condition of the relationship. Only a bureaucratic apparatus would have allowed the allocation to the troops to be administered en bloc, as a sort of military treasury. Although (Roman) personnel was probably available to man such an apparatus, the barbarian leaders, or their patrons, appear to have preferred to do without it. The alternative was immediate distribution of allotments to the beneficiaries.

To the extent that persons had to be matched to persons, the process of distributing *sortes* closely resembled that of assigning soldiers to billets in private houses—in short, *hospitalitas*. Whoever was charged with this weighty, but manageable, task needed two lists: one naming the barbarians to be provided for; the other composed of that fraction of the *censuales paginae* that was allocated to the troops. Because composed of tax assessments, allotments did not have to be made in haphazard quantities or at the sole expense of large Roman landlords. Tax proceeds could be apportioned in uniform slices, and they could be extracted from whatever leaves of the assessment books the distributing authorities chose. The case of the Alans who were awarded *deserta rura*—bad debts vis-à-vis the state—must surely have represented the ideal solution from the Roman standpoint. A second best would have been to form allotments from the declarations of small, marginal proprietors, the kind of problematic taxpayers whom the collectors would have been relieved to cross off their books. A barbarian warrior could be expected to have greater success than the normal officials in extracting the due payments from such landowners as these; even elsewhere in the Roman world, a dose of military force was sometimes

217

thought to be effective in encouraging the flow of revenue from land.[22] The barbarian settlements, in taking this form, need not have enlarged the working population, but the individualized pressure that the allotment holders might exert upon their personal taxpayers could conceivably have been more salutary for agricultural production than the normal tax system had been.[23] The assignment of allotments was completed when each beneficed barbarian received a document—his special "assignment of (public) debt" (*delegatio*)—naming the Romans who henceforth owed him their tax payments (*praestatio*) and inventorying the assets in whose behalf the payments were made (*professio*).

The Roman list, directly derived from the public assessment books, is easier to evoke than its barbarian counterpart, the list of "guests." It need no longer be thought that allotments varied widely in size or that the barbarians were treated very unequally among themselves. Exceptionally large grants could, of course, have gone to outstanding personalities, but *LBurg* 54 implies that equality was the original rule, and Cassiodorus's reference to a standard fiscal unit points in the same direction. The obscure question is by what criterion individual Goths, Burgundians, or Lombards were initially chosen to benefit from the award of a permanent stipend; our ignorance of the composition and organization of these peoples at the moment of settlement is complete. According to Vegetius, late Roman military custom was to channel rations to the troops through the *dignitates*.[24] If such a system had been

[22] *CTh* 1. 14. 1 (386), 11. 7. 16 (401), 7. 4. 27 (406); *NTheod* II 7. 1, 3 (439-440); *CJ* 12. 35. 15 (458), 12. 37. 17 (Anastasius), Justinian *Novel*. 17. 10, 25 (535), 30. 1. 1, 5-6, 7. 1 (536), 116 (542). We would hear more about such practices and their significance if as much emphasis were laid upon changes from fourth-century conditions as upon their continuity.

[23] On the tax system and agriculture, a suggestion is made in Goffart, *Caput*, p. 136 n. 50.

[24] Vegetius *Epitoma rei militaris* 3. 3 (quoted below, Appendix E).

extended to the award of allotments, it might have justified a distribution among a minority of "dignitaries," with the rest of the barbarian people being treated as their dependents.[25] The condition of the Lombards under the first dukes comes to mind as an extreme instance of matters taking this course. Another model—not necessarily contradictory if *dignitas* was modestly interpreted—can be detected in two letters of Theodoric: he used the "mess" (*condoma*), probably equivalent to Vegetius's ten-man "tentful" (*contubernium*), as the basis for issuing travel money to a detachment of Gepids. By analogy, the personage whom Vegetius called the *caput contubernii*, equivalent to the *decanus* of *LVisig* 9. 2. 4, would have been the "basic barbarian" for purposes of allotment.[26] The attractive feature of this model comes from the ease with which the military "tent" or "mess" lends itself to being converted into the civilian "household" or family—the social unit within which the *sors* was evidently meant to descend.[27] Although no connection between Roman ad-

[25] For officers dispensing rations to an Ostrogothic garrison in Italy, *Variae* 3. 42.

[26] The Gepids: *Variae* 5. 10-11; for commentary, Goffart, "Three Notes," pp. 175-187. *Caput contubernii*: Vegetius 2. 13. Contrary to the latter, however, the Visigothic *decanus* had officer status—he was a *praepositus exercitui* (*LVisig* 9. 2. 1); yet the fine he incurred for evasion or desertion was extravagantly small—ten or fifteen *solidi*—by comparison with the death penalty inflicted upon a *centenarius* for the same fault (9. 2. 3). Besides, there appear to have been "privates" without rank (latter part of 9. 2. 4). This exceptionally important set of laws eludes straightforward interpretation; what one would give for the *CE* versions!

For a study of the *contubernium* in Frankish sources (where it is once equated to *convivium*, i.e., "mess" in the military sense), see Heike Grahn-Hoeke, *Die fränkische Oberschicht im 6. Jahrhundert. Studien zu ihrer rechtlichen und politische Stellung* (*Vorträge und Forschungen*, Sonderband 21) (Sigmaringen, 1976), pp. 276-283. The Frankish instances ought now to be brought together with the late Roman and Gothic occurrences of the term.

[27] The familial dimension of *condoma* is discussed in Goffart,

219

ministrative patterns and the distribution of barbarian allotments can be proved, the idea that such patterns were applied has much to recommend it. Every group we have been concerned with must have had intermittent experience with them, as muster or ration rolls, in the years immediately preceding its settlement.

Once the distribution had taken place, how much difference did the institution of barbarian allotments make to the "delegated" Roman taxpayers, and how rapidly were changes in circumstances perceived? The questions are more easily asked than answered. The terminology of "hospitality," well entrenched in the records, implies that all parties concerned were exhorted to model their behavior toward each other on that of hosts and guests; the talk of *civilitas* in Ostrogothic Italy was presumably meant to produce the same effect. There is no reason to assume that the aspirations embodied by these gracious words were consistently disappointed or that the experience of being a Roman host was uniformly deplorable. Even though there are documented complaints against greedy and oppressive guests, the notion of hospitality does not appear to have been cast into disrepute as a result of fifth and sixth-century events. However that may be, these terms are a minor aspect of the matter; at best, they mirror human conduct within a situation, without telling us anything about the situation itself. One would like to grasp the relations of allotment holders to their hosts at a more concrete level.

The hitherto prevailing conception of these relations has presupposed that the allotments were fractions of working farms, conferred upon the barbarians at the expense of Roman owners. On this hypothesis, the barbarians either managed their own properties or acted as partners to their Roman hosts, taking an appropriate share of the harvest; in either eventuality, the two parties would have been

---

"Three Notes," pp. 175-187. For the descent of *sortes*, *LBurg* 1, 14, 24, 47, 51.

closely involved with each other. Much more remote and intermittent relations would have resulted from the conferral of allotments composed of tax assessments and their payments, as has been argued here. *Sortes* of this kind would have been compatible with the barbarians' remaining clustered in cities and taking delivery there of the payments made by their personal taxpayers. The host's contact with his guest need hardly have been much more intimate, or more frequent, than with the former tax collector, and the countryside would have been barely touched by the barbarian presence. The latter view has obvious attractions. In addition to the evidence and arguments already mustered in its favor, it would meet Lot's objection to the dispersal of barbarians, and it would complement Professor Wallace-Hadrill's idea of the Visigoths as a rootless army of occupation.[28] The difficulties arise when one tries to document the practical implications of either hypothesis. There is no doubt that several passages of the Visigothic and Burgundian codes evoke the image of barbarians residing in a rural setting and taking part in agricultural life,[29] but the laws do not confirm the equation of allotments with working farms, and their late date sharply limits their value as testimony to the circumstances prevailing in the decades immediately following the initial settlements. Documenting the contrary hypothesis is even harder. There are reasons for believing that the barbarians remained concentrated instead of spreading out thinly over the land, but we have no illustration of the *sors* as a simple salary; not even Italy provides a source portraying Roman landowner-taxpayers rendering dues to city-dwelling Ostro-

---

[28] Above nn. 3-4.

[29] E.g., *LBurg* 72 (setting animal traps outside *culturae*), 89 (animals wandering into vineyards), 92 (a woman leaving the farmstead to look after the livestock). But the attempts to reconstruct rural life in the barbarian kingdoms on the basis of these and the other laws of the same kind, as done by Binding, *Königreich*, pp. 36-37, and Dopsch, *Grundlagen*, vol. 1, p. 212, are hardly satisfactory.

goths, as though to a new breed of tax collectors.[30] Although late, the image of barbarians in direct contact with the soil enjoys the advantage of being verifiable.

Evidence on any subject is so rare in this epoch that arguments from silence have a more than ordinary reason for being resisted. Without reference to barbarians, a law of 440 lists a series of allotments pertaining to the public works of Rome; one letter of Cassiodorus records an increase in the allotment for heating the municipal baths of Spoleto, and a second concerns the allotment of an unnamed bishopric.[31] In none of these cases, or any others, do we possess complementary information telling us how the beneficiaries derived revenue from their grants and whether that revenue was in money or in kind. It does not follow that we should doubt the existence of these allotments or their profitability; the only lesson is that our ability to generate pertinent questions exceeds the capacity of the surviving debris to provide satisfactory answers.

One substitute for concrete evidence might come from considering the wider context of these transactions. Where Roman fiscality in the West is concerned, the long-term tendency may be said to have been for public revenues to take on the form of land rents.[32] As economic life was

[30] We come very close in Cassiodorus *Variae* 6. 22. 3: at royal cost, a unit of soldiers (*militum numerus*) serves the Gothic count of Syracuse, but does not endure the perils of war; the count is to prevent these *milites* from being arrogant toward the landowners, to limit them to the collection of their due taxes-in-kind (*annonae*), and to keep them from intervening in the lawsuits of strangers (*extranei*) (*LBurg* and *LVisig* also repress the third of these practices). The proof would be absolute if we could be sure that the royal outlays (*nostrae expensae*) had consisted in the award of a *sors* to each *miles* of this unit. It certainly does not look as though the count of Syracuse dispensed rations to his troops like the *dux* and *praepositi* of *Variae* 3. 42.

[31] *NValent III* 5. 1. 4 ("cespes formensis, arensis, calcarius et vecturarius"); *Variae* 2. 37, 4. 20. For commentary, Goffart, "Three Notes," pp. 165-175.

[32] In *Caput, passim,* I sought to clarify an aspect of this tendency by pointing out the passage from an actively "liturgical" context of

structured from the fourth to the sixth centuries, taxes occasioned by landed assessments existed side by side with, and alarmingly resembled, private incomes arising chiefly from the proceeds of agriculture. The logical direction for simplification to take in such a system was towards a merger, or simple confusion, of the public and private types of revenue. The only reliable "tax" income would eventually stem from the assessment that the authorized collector—be he king, church, dignitary, or whatever—also happened to own as private property. Similarly, "private" revenue from agrarian rentals would need to be obtained from bondsmen and lands that were not only owned but were also derived, by grant or exemption, from the public assessment books.[33]

Although the outlines and course of the evolution are plain, its chronology is not. The trappings of taxation are likely to have been most durable in Italy, but, even in Gaul, the apparatus of public revenues was tenacious, since traces of it survive well into the Merovingian kingdom.[34] What matters to the present study is simply this:

---

taxation (in which, as an aspect of citizenship, persons contributed service as well as money or goods) to a passive context (in which taxes were a mere *praestatio* for land, grudgingly paid by proprietors unlucky enough not to secure exemption).

[33] For some details, Goffart, "Three Notes," pp. 382-386.

[34] The persistence of fiscality in Italy may be traced beyond the *Variae* in Justinian's Pragmatic Sanction (554), the Ravenna papyri, the letters of Gregory the Great, and a variety of other documents. The works of Gregory of Tours yield a considerable harvest of passages evocative of late Roman taxation; e.g., *Historiae* 3. 36, 5. 26, 28, 7. 15, 23, 9. 30, 10. 7, and the *tribunus* in *In gloria confessorum* 40, whose activities on behalf of a Merovingian queen remind one of those of the *tribunus* in *PItal* 1 on behalf of the chamberlain Laurentius. But contrary to Musset, *Vagues germaniques*, p. 282, according to whom these texts (which are not cited) document a public institution taken over from the Roman state, I would suggest that the Merovingian fisc was a domainial, or "private," institution, narrowly focused on the royal family. (No trace was left of the prefectoral side of late Roman government, which furnished fiscality with

the landed appearance that barbarian allotments have in the Burgundian and Visigothic law codes is no argument against their having originally been awards of public salaries; the evolution that we may expect the allotments to have had runs parallel to the evolution of fiscality itself—tax yields from abstract assessments turning into (tax free) proceeds from physically owned property.

If this course of institutional and economic change is kept in mind, the gaps in the evidence may, to some extent, be filled. Although it continues to be impossible to document allotments in the guise of mere tax proceeds, there are sources that illustrate the passage of barbarian *sortes* from a configuration of tax revenue to one of lucrative property. The first of these texts is *LBurg* 54, as interpreted in Chapter v. Toward the close of the fifth century, Gundobad enlarged the allotments of a certain category of Burgundians with an award of "bondsmen," together with the lands that these bondsmen cultivated; in doing so, he provided the beneficiaries for the first time with concrete real estate. One infers from the nature of the transaction that the original *sors* was more abstract, or akin to a state salary, than it became after Gundobad's award. The instance is symptomatic of a public revenue taking on the more comforting, because more secure, contours of physically possessed property. The same story is told in different terms by the sources examined at the close of Chapter iii, which portray several barbarians in Gaul and Italy reducing free landowners to the status of servile dependents. The result of such oppression is plain: by the loss of their

---

its most "public" face.) For a stimulating (though often mistaken) theoretical context, Ludo Moritz Hartmann, *The Early Medieval State: Byzantium, Italy and the West*, trans. H. Liebeschütz, Historical Association Pamphlets (London, 1949), and the same author's "Grundherrschaft und Bureaucratie im Kirchenstaate von 8. bis zum 10. Jahrhundert," *Vierteljahrschrift für Sozial- und Wirtschaftsgeschichte* 7 (1909): 142-158.

personal freedom, the Romans relinquished to the barbarians harassing them the private proprietary title to their lands, slaves, and livestock (whether or not the dispossessed owners stayed on the farm as bound peasants is less certain). The presupposition of these incidents, though not spelled out, appears to be that the barbarians originally had a lucrative claim upon the Romans, based on their lands as security; by more or less legal means, the claimants were able to foreclose on their debtors and thus to turn what had been a revenue, perhaps not wholly reliable, into securely private ownership of productive real estate. Not the least interest of these texts is their illustration that the oppressors included Roman *potentes*, as well as barbarians.[35] In other words, the possibility of carrying out such raids upon economically feeble landowners arose from the tax system itself and preceded the institution of barbarian allotments. Neither *LBurg* 54 nor the other documents clearly spell out what the *sortes* amounted to in their original form, but all of them testify to change—allotments becoming what they had not originally been. By establishing that the real estate in barbarian hands was the end point of an evolution, they permit us to doubt that the allotments had always been as agrarian as they occasionally look in the Visigothic and Burgundian codes.

What concrete form did barbarian allotments originally have, and what were the initial relations between hosts as "givers" and guests as "receivers"? The surviving sources do not tell us; they support only the negative observation that the allotments did not, at first, call for the barbarians' to take physical possession of the soil and its cultivators. The Burgundians and Lombards eventually settled into the role of proprietors, and so did the Visigoths in Spain. Whether the same was true for considerable numbers of Visigoths in Gaul or of Ostrogoths in Italy is doubtful, and

[35] In Salvian and the *Vita patrum Iurensium*, above, Chapter III at nn. 78-80.

perhaps even unlikely. What form did the allotments have for them and for the Burgundians and Lombards prior to their actual *Landnahme*? There seems to be no discernible alternative to the answer that has been argued and partly documented in the present study: each receiver of a *sors* obtained the *professio* of one or more Roman landowners and was personally entitled to the annual tax payment arising from that assessment; the relations between guest and host were an individualized version of those between tax collector and taxpayer, and not very different, in practice, from those between an absentee landlord and his tenant(s). No doubt some change—for the better or the worse is hard to say—was felt by any Roman obligated to make payments to a guest, rather than to the barbarian king, but he retained ownership and management of his property, paid no more than he formerly had to the state, and could limit contacts with his guest to the indispensable minimum. The countryside was not abruptly penetrated by foreign masters of the soil. Schematic statements like these can hardly pretend to mirror the complexities of real life, but, for lack of better information, we must be content with them.

By being collectively endowed with a more than adequate slice of state revenue, the barbarians were given an excellent inducement for sustaining the existing order in public, as well as private, economic relations. Self-interest committed them to respect not only slavery and private land ownership but also the colonate and tributary obligations. Their own exemption from taxation, paralleling the standard exemption of Roman soldiers, need not have won them a higher standing than normally accorded to the somewhat disreputable military profession.[36] Religion and

[36] Soldiers' tax exemption: Goffart, *Caput*, pp. 53-60. A law for Africa, *CTh* 11. 1. 28 (400), illustrates a situation comparable to that of the Ostrogoths (above, Chapter III at nn. 67-69): tax-exempt veterans incurred tax liability by acquiring property burdened with a tax charge.

occupation cut them off from the Romans, and so did the bar on intermarriage.[37] Nevertheless, whoever might have been tempted, as we are, to define their place in a unified social scale would have been inclined, on balance, to set them on a par with the advantaged elements of the Roman population. The equation works in both directions: except in the case of the Lombards, such facts as we have are more favorable to the view that the larger landlords in Gaul and Italy were carefully spared than that they alone should have borne the costs of the allotments. To paraphrase Ennodius, the barbarians were enriched and the Romans—those who mattered—felt no loss.[38] A governing authority that permanently ceded part of the tax rosters had good reason to retain as its own taxpayers the most solvent and economically secure proprietors. Such an arrangement benefited more than just the royal treasury. As rich men had served the imperial government for the sake of remunerative exemptions, so did they now have the same incentive for bringing their knowledge and local prestige to the assistance of the barbarian kings.[39] However distant, therefore, the Roman landed aristocracy may have felt from the endowed barbarians, both groups participated in a community of economic interests, a community they shared, incidentally, with the Church and the government itself. As claimants to revenue from lands that they could not personally supervise, they were basically absentees, dependent on the public discipline that is indispensable to such ownership. And when the time came for a barbarian *hospes* to retire from active warfare and to think rather of managing the resources he had than of acquiring plunder in the next campaign, there was hardly another model for

[37] Wallace-Hadrill, "Gothia," pp. 43-47; Stein, *Bas-Empire*, vol. 1, p. 383.

[38] See above, Chapter IV n. 19.

[39] Stroheker, *Senat. Adel*, pp. 90-105; also above, Chapter V n. 25 and below, Appendix D n. 16.

him to emulate than that of a Roman landed gentleman.[40] It is little wonder that the oppression ascribed to Goths by sixth-century hagiographers is almost identical to that which Salvian had ascribed to Roman *potentes*.

Where the barbarian kingdoms endured, the allotments ultimately assumed the form of private property in land, as illustrated in embryo by several Burgundian laws. Among the various ways this situation might have been reached, the most harmonious and least visible would have been for the Roman host to commute his annual payment to the guest for a capital grant, consisting of a mutually acceptable portion of his lands and cultivators. Although documentation of such transactions is lacking, the possibility of their occurrence may nevertheless be indirectly inferred from the effect they were bound to have, namely, that the lands that Roman owners retained turned necessarily into the same kind of exempt holding as the lands ceded to the barbarian *hospites* in commutation for annual (tax) payments. The barbarian was tax free by profession; the Roman ex-host became so by permanent acquittal of his tax liability. The term *sors* might apply henceforth to the lands of each one, regardless of nationality.[41] If something like two-thirds of the assessments of southern Gaul had been made available for allotments, a great mass of property must eventually have fallen into this category of lands free and quit of tax obligations. Long before, when the empire still flourished, these assets had been declared to the state and entered into the *censuales paginae* as security for tax payments. They had then passed out of these rec-

[40] The conspicuous, but probably atypical, example of such conduct is Theodoric's nephew, Theodahad: Thomas Hodgkin, *Italy and Her Invaders*, vol. 3, 2d ed. (Oxford, 1896), pp. 636-639.

[41] The title of *LVisig* 10. 2. 1 (= *CE* 277. 1) refers to "sortes Gotice vel Romane." Fustel de Coulanges, *L'alleu et le domaine rural*, 4th ed. (Paris, 1927), pp. 168-169, also cited evidence from Ravenna. In fact, however, *sors* was rarely used. Perhaps a more promising word to examine is *alodis*, the standard Western substitute for *patrimonium*.

ords, as a long series of extracts awarded to individual barbarians to document their claims upon Roman hosts. Now, with the debt acquitted by the commutation of payment for capital, the official documentation could simply be torn up and thrown away; its utility was at an end.[42] Roman proprietary transactions had long called for the due transfer of public liability from one owner to the next, sometimes with strict limits upon those to whom property might pass. By contrast, the sixth-century legal sources introduce us to a new era of simplification, in which many landowners, regardless of nationality, disposed of their property without concern for the state.[43] It was not as though the Frankish kings, or the rulers they displaced, had taken it into their heads to lift the burden of taxation; they did as best they could with as much of it as was left for them to exploit.[44] But the larger part of the old tax base was no longer there for them to touch; the conditions of settlement had placed it beyond their reach. For a certain stratum of the population, property was now so private that it entailed no public obligation at all.

There is no reason to concur in the recent judgment that the importance of "*hospitalitas* agreements" has been overrated.[45] The evidence about them that we have is unmatched in its time as an indicator of institutional developments in the western provinces. It permits us to see that

[42] For a parallel evolution, Goffart, "Three Notes," pp. 186-187.

[43] Transfer of public liability: *CTh* 11. 3. 5 (391), pursuant to a law of Constantine (*Fragmenta Vaticana* 35); *LRB* 40; *Edictum Theodorici* 52-53 (cf. *CTh* 8. 12. 8 [415]), a public procedure that, as *PItal* 10-11 shows, included the transfer of public liability; Cassiodorus *Variae* 4. 14 (quoted above, Chapter III n. 68). Strict limits: the well-known restrictions on the alienation of various categories of property, discussed by Levy, *Law of Property*, pp. 41-43, 118-119. Sixth-century conditions: the formulary for land sales in *PDipl* 114-116, 118, 120-123; the early Gallo-Frankish formularies, ed. K. Zeumer, MGH *Formulae*, pp. 6, 11-13, 89-90 (sales), 7, 91 (exchanges), 20, 24, 31, 4, 6 (gifts).

[44] Above, n. 34.

[45] Musset, quoted above, Chapter VI at n. 29.

the barbarians in Gaul and Italy were initially provided with stipends, rather than with land; that the state, rather than private proprietors, met the cost of their establishment; and that the scheme of allotments to alien soldiers was a major step in the devolution of Roman fiscality. Far from being an improvised extension of military billeting, the "hospitality" accorded to the Goths and Burgundians was a deliberate novelty, designed to minimize friction between all parties concerned, and apparently successful in achieving this result. If the fifth century is less memorable for invasions than for the incorporation of barbarian protectors into the fabric of the West, the conditions of their settlement and the institutional changes that the settlements occasioned have a justified claim to our attention.

APPENDIX A

How Many Vandals Invaded Africa?[1]

That Geiseric led 80,000 Vandals and associated peoples from Spain to Africa in 429 has been called the one piece of certain information we have about the size of barbarian groups in the age of the invasions.[2] The certainty arises from its being vouched for by apparently independent informants, one Latin, the other Greek: writing in about 484, Victor Vitensis specified that a head count was taken before embarkation from Spain and, some fifty years later, Procopius supplied the same figure for the period of Geiseric's rule in Africa.[3]

[1] This question arises in connection with the evidence documenting the office of *millenarius* among the Vandals and Visigoths (Chapter III n. 53).

[2] Marc Bloch, "Sur les grandes invasions," pp. 106-107. Cf. Schmidt, *Ostgermanen*, p. 111; Bury, *Later Roman Empire*, vol. 1, p. 105 ("Appendix on the Numbers of Barbarians"), with the comment that the Vandal figure had "particular claims on our attention" (following the reasoning of Schmidt, next note); J. C. Russell, "Late Ancient and Medieval Population," American Philosophical Society, *Transactions*, new ser. 48, pt. 3 (Philadelphia, 1958): 75, "a real number based upon an exact count"; Schwarz, *Zur germ. Stammesk.*, p. 303; Perry Anderson, *Passages from Antiquity to Feudalism* (London, 1974), p. 113 n. 1.

[3] Victor Vitensis *Historia persecutionis Vandalicae* 1. (1.) 2, MGH AA, vol. 3, p. 2; Procopius *Bell. Vandal.* 1. 5. 18 (not clear whether before or after landing in Africa); *Anecdota* 18. 6 (at time of Justinian's invasion). Jones, *LRE*, p. 195, referred only to Victor; cf. Ludwig Schmidt, "Zur Frage nach der Volkszahl der Wandalen," *Byzantinische Zeitschrift* 15 (1906): 620-621, who offered a reason for dismissing the testimony of Procopius. Schmidt's basic account of Vandal numbers (*Histoire des Vandales*, trans. Del Medico, p. 42) dismisses as absurd Victor's allegation about Geiseric's motive and substitutes a reason mentioned by neither Victor nor Procopius, namely, that Geiseric was obliged to count heads in order to deter-

Although in agreement over the basic number, the two authors differ over what it represents: according to Victor, every possible soul down to the newest-born infant; according to Procopius, only able-bodied warriors. Testing and pondering each version on the basis of common sense leads ordinarily to the conclusion that, on balance, the earlier informant, who offers the lower number of adult males, deserves to be believed.[4] By following this procedure, however, one may fail to observe that the very same discrepancy, over precisely the same sum, occurs in a pair of earlier histories. Jerome's *Chronicle* tells us that 80,000 Burgundians, more than ever before, came to the banks of the Rhine in 370. When repeating this incident right out of the *Chronicle*, Orosius adds the detail "of armed men."[5]

---

mine how many ships were needed to ferry the Vandals to Africa; cf. Delbrück, *Kriegskunst*, vol. 2, p. 315. Schmidt's guess is unobjectionable, but it is only that: even supposing that Vandal heads were counted in 429, we have no reason to think that anyone bothered to remember the tally, much less to record it, after the crossing was complete. The numbers in Victor and Procopius can only arbitrarily be detached from the specific motives and contexts that the authors provide.

[4] Thus Courtois, *Vandales*, pp. 215-217. Contrary to Musset, *Vagues germaniques*, p. 235, I do not find Courtois showing that the figure "avait pris valeur de cliché." Musset, in Folz, *De l'Antiquité au monde médiéval*, p. 58, stated "environ 80,000" as though factual.

[5] Jerome *Chron.* 2389, ed. Rudolf Helm, *Eusebius Werke*, vol. 7, Griechischen Christlichen Schriftsteller 47 (Berlin, 1956), p. 247. Orosius *Historia adversus paganos* 7. 32. 11 (Zangenmeister's edition, *CSEL* 5 [Vienna, 1882], p. 514, points out the addition). On the incident, Ammianus 28. 5. 8-11, from which it is apparent that *armati* is correct (though the number need not be); residents of the left bank were very frightened. One would not guess from Jerome or Orosius that Valentinian had asked the Burgundians to come. Jones, *LRE*, p. 195, thought Orosius's change was "a good example of the reckless way in which numbers were exaggerated by historians . . ."; but Norden, *Alt-Germanien*, p. 64 n. 1, pointed out that, even in Jerome, "die Zahl ist grotesk übertreiben," since Ammianus speaks of *catervae lectissimae*. Accordingly, Orosius's insertion "armati" is likely to be closer to the truth than the number he borrowed from Jerome.

Here, an interpolation is obvious, but what *had* Jerome meant? After all, Orosius and he were personally acquainted.[6]

A more intriguing matter is the number itself. We learn from Vegetius that, unlike the 6,000-man Roman legion, the Macedonian, Greek, and Dardanian (that is, Trojan) phalanx was composed of "armatorum VIII milia."[7] This base also occurs in the *Chronicle* of Sulpicius Severus and the *Historia Augusta*: when two tribes of Israel separated from the other ten, they were able to furnish 320,000 *armati*; the enormous barbarian horde annihilated by Claudius Gothicus numbered 320,000. Whether in multiples of forty or of ten, the ideal "phalanx" appears to underlie all these computations and to limit their value for modern demographers.[8]

Cf. Jordanes *Romana* 309, MGH *AA*, vol. 5, p. 39, where the 80,000 *armati* become a coalition of Saxons and *Burgutiones* on the Rhine against which Valentinian was about to move the army when he died (at Brigetio!).

[6] Orosius wrote his histories some time after spending about a year with Jerome in the East (415-416); but they had absorbing nonhistorical subjects to converse about: J. H. D. Kelly, *Jerome. His Life, Writings, and Controversies* (London, 1975), pp. 317-321.

[7] *Epitoma rei militaris* 2. 2.

[8] Sulpicius Severus *Chronicon* 2. 11. 5-6 (ed. C. Halm, *CSEL* 1 [Vienna, 1867]), based loosely on Nehemiah 7, but with Sulpicius's own reminiscence of *Chron.* 1. 41. 4, where the number is 300,000 (in our editions), changed from the 180,000 in 1 (3) Kings 12:21. *HA, Claudius*, 6. 5-6; these too were *armati*, about whom the author comments (in high spirits): imagine how enormous the total would be if slaves, *familiae*, and wagon trains were included. See also Dexippus, fragm. 6. 4 in K. Müller, *Fragmenta historicorum Graecorum*, vol. 3 (Paris, 1849), pp. 682-683: in the time of Aurelian, the Juthungi could field 40,000 cavalry and 80,000 infantry; Ammianus 31. 10. 5, cites a force of 40,000 Alamanni that, he claims, was inflated to 70,000 by adulators of the emperor Gratian. These instances, which are a mere sampling for late antiquity, might be multiplied by a search among the authors of earlier periods: e.g., Xerxes's cavalry numbered 80,000 (Herodotus *Histories* 7. 87); the Getae and Dacians could once field 200,000, now only 40,000 (Strabo *Geography* 7. 3.

To return to Victor Vitensis and Procopius, one disquieting point on which they concur tends to be overlooked by those who accept their testimony on the Vandal head count. The two agree that the number 80,000, however it should be interpreted, resulted from a trick perpetrated by Geiseric in order to deceive the Romans into believing that his forces were greater than they were. For this reason, Victor says, he counted every possible soul; for the same reason, according to Procopius, he appointed eighty leaders of 1,000 (chiliarchs), rather than the fifty that then sufficed.[9] Quite apart from any precise consideration of links between the two authors or of a common source, it is obvious that both of them had encountered a developed story exemplifying Geiseric's well-known cunning. That the two should report the same (poetic) number seems less significant than that they locate it in variant versions of the same anecdote. How many Vandals and other barbarians Geiseric led into Africa continues to be anybody's guess.

---

13). Is it merely coincidental that Ammianus and Procopius subtract the same sum when emending a figure that they believe to be exaggerated: 70,000 Alamanni cut down to 40,000, and 80,000 Vandals down to 50,000?

[9] Courtois, *Vandales*, p. 217, criticized Procopius for assuming that Vandal *millenarii* were officers commanding 1,000 warriors; on his reading of the other evidence for *millenarii*, they were simply officials set at the head of 1,000 people. The criticism of Procopius is perhaps better founded than the substituted definition of the office. Courtois believed in the primitive Germanic thousand and somehow managed to infer from Cassiodorus *Variae* 5. 27 that an Ostrogothic *millenarius* was a "fonctionnaire à compétence territoriale" (p. 217 n. 4). The Visigoth of *CE* 322. 2 does suit this description.

APPENDIX B

INTERPRETATIONS OF *CE* 276. 3-4

The surviving fragment of Euric's Code begins in the midst of chapter 276, with a sentence highly relevant to *hospitalitas* but almost impossible to interpret. The text is as follows:

[3] . . . habent Romani fuerint, tunc Gothi ingrediantur in loco hospitum et ducant terminum ⟨ubi⟩ fuerat ostensus. [4] Tunc iudex, quos certiores agnoverit, faciat eos sacramenta praebere quod terminum sine ulla fraude monstraverint. [5] Nullus novum terminum sine consorte partis alterius aut sine ⟨in⟩spectore constituat. [6 and 7 set down penalties for unilaterally moving boundaries.][1]

[3] . . . should be . . . the Romans have, then let the Goths enter into the place of the hosts and follow the boundary where it is shown. [4] Then let the judge cause those whom he knows to be well informed to give oaths that they have shown the boundary without any fraud. [5] Let no one establish a new boundary without the partner of the other share or without an inspector.

The principal gloss to this passage is supplied by Leovigild's modernized version in the *Codex revisus* (*LVisig* 10. 3. 5), in which the sentences missing in *CE* may be assumed to survive: If something was alienated from a farm (*fundus*) by any kind of transaction prior to the arrival of the Goths, the alienation may remain with the farm to which the Romans prove that it was anciently attached. When, however, the composition (*proprietas*) of a farm is not apparent from obvious signs and boundaries,

[1] Ed. d'Ors, p. 21.

235

the following procedure must be followed: the inspecting official will choose the persons whom the affected parties agree upon and he will cause those whom he recognizes to be more trustworthy or senior to take oaths that they will show the boundaries without any fraud. In any case, let no one establish new boundaries. . . .[2] The reviser eliminated the most interesting part of *CE* 276 for our purposes— namely, the entrance of the *Gothi in loco hospitum*. But, if he retained at least the substance of the older law, then the procedure of *CE* 276. 3-4 had something to do with establishing the primitive boundaries of an estate (and of a territory?) whose confines were not marked by evident *signa* and *limites*. *LVisig* 10. 3. 5, therefore, leads us to understand that *CE* 276 was a comprehensive law on boundaries in four sections: alienations from farms prior to the *adventus Gothorum* may not be challenged (276. 1-2); what to do if original property boundaries are in doubt (276. 3-4); how boundaries may be legally changed (276. 5); penalties for unilaterally moving boundaries (276. 6-7).

Zeumer's interpretation of *CE* 276. 3-4 is implicit in his conjectural emendation of the opening clause, which stands in the Monumenta edition: "[If the boundaries of the farms] should be [in the 'one-thirds' that] the Romans

---

[2] (*Antiqua*) "Ut, si aliqua pars de alio loco tempore Romanorum remota est, ita persistat. Si quodcumque ante adventum Gotorum de alicuius fundi iure remotum est et aliquam possessionem aut vinditionem aut donationem aut divisionem aut aliqua transactione translatum est, id in eius fundi, ad quem a Romanis antiquitus probatur adiunctum, iure consistat. Cum autem proprietas fundi nullis certissimis signis aut limitibus probatur, quid debeat observari, eligat inspectio iudicantium, quos partium consensus elegerit; ita ut iudex, quos certiores agnoverit vel seniores, faciat eos sacramenta prebere, quod terminos sine ulla fraude monstraverint, et tamen nullus novum terminum sine consortis presentia aut sine inspectore constituat." The same penalty clauses as in *CE* 276 follow. Note that although all trace of *CE* 276. 3 is gone, the connection with *CE* 276. 4 (and 5-7) is close.

have. . . ."[3] In other words, when a change of boundaries took place in the Roman *tertiae*, the Goths were entitled to supervise the operation. This is a puzzling and paradoxical idea, especially in the perspective of expropriation, and of *sortes* divided from *tertiae*, that Zeumer presumably had. For what interest might the Goths be thought to have had in boundaries lying outside their allotments? Changes *in tertiis* are precisely those where the Romans would have been left to themselves.

Jones did not discuss *CE* 276, but, perhaps following Zeumer, he had it document the assertion that the Goths had a right to consent to "the subsequent changes in the boundaries" of Roman farms.[4] It seems beyond question, however, that boundary changes are dealt with in *CE* 276. 5-7 (which provide for official, but not "Gothic" supervision), and that *CE* 276. 3-4 are concerned only with the discovery of obscure or forgotten ancient boundaries. The Goths of *CE* 276 were not giving consent; rather, they look as though they were being very formally shown where the old consecrated boundary ran, without being called upon to do anything other than to absorb the information.[5]

D'Ors, although admitting the obscurity of the text, proposed that the Goths were allowed to enter the estates of the Roman hosts in order to restore the boundaries of their allotments when there was a change in the ancient delimitation.[6] The main objection to this is that it goes very far beyond the surviving words. It also begs several questions;

[3] Surprisingly, d'Ors retained Zeumer's conjecture in his revised edition (as above, n. 1).

[4] *LRE*, p. 252. He set the rule in a context of division (as Lot and d'Ors did with *CE* 277, above, Chapter IV n. 26), but no basis for this connection is offered even by *LVisig* 10. 3. 5.

[5] Even the procedure of *corporalis introductio*, which perhaps most closely evokes what we see in the text (below, n. 10), has nothing to do with consenting to the acts of others.

[6] *Codigo*, p. 200.

for example, why need the ancient boundaries change and, if they do, why need their change overturn the allotment boundaries?

Beyerle proceeded on the assumption that *LVisig* 10. 3. 5 had nothing to do with *CE* 276. 3-4, since whatever the latter contained was obsolete by Leovigild's time. He understood the two sentences to be concerned with boundary disputes. *CE* presumably contained the same rule as *LBurg* 22 and 55, namely, that barbarians must not intrude into lawsuits between Romans. The exception to this rule, set down in *CE* 276. 3-4, was that Goths were allowed to intervene when the disputed boundaries touched on allotments. In line with this theory, Beyerle devised a substitute for Zeumer's conjectural opening clause (which he rejected) and heavily emended the wording of the legible lines (inter*grediantur, dicant, terminus*, eis *erat* [for *fuerat*]).[7] The interpretation is bold and interesting, but, to accept it, one would have to admit both Beyerle's extensive emendation and his decision that *LVisig* 10. 3. 5 is irrelevant. Even his pertinent observation that the procedure of *CE* 276. 3-4 resembles the one laid down in *Lex Alamannorum* 81 and *Lex Baiuuariorum* 12. 8 for initiating a lawsuit over boundaries adds little to the argument.[8] *CE* 276. 3-4 still look as though they were concerned with the clarification of old boundaries, rather than litigation over them.

[7] Franz Beyerle, "Zur Frühgeschichte der westgotischen Gesetzgebung. Volksrechtliche Studien V," *ZRG*, Germ. 67 (1950): 10-11. As regards the invocation of *LBurg* 55, it is worth recalling that, contrary to Beyerle's conjectured rule about the boundaries of Visigothic *sortes*, the Burgundian law lays down that Romans were to be left alone to litigate over boundaries even if *sortes* were affected (above, Chapter v n. 63).

[8] The Bavarian and Alamannic codes are in MGH *Leges*, vol. 5; they are known to have been influenced by *CE*. The procedure regarding boundaries is that the contenders shall indicate their counterclaims *in situ* before a judge; then, unless other proof than boundaries is found or an accommodation takes place, the case goes to trial by battle. The resemblance to *CE* 276. 3-4 is distant.

This sense continues to be embodied to a limited extent in *LVisig* 10. 3. 5.

CE 276. 3-4 lack too many words to be anything but an obscure text; one ought not to rest an argument on such testimony. Nevertheless, a moderate reading, guided by *LVisig* 10. 3. 5, is consistent with the form of Visigothic settlement outlined in Chapter IV. The passage appears to set out a procedure that took into account the interest of Visigoths in the property boundaries of their Roman hosts: when the need arose for the clarification of doubtful limits, the Goths had to be involved in the process. Such a law has a logical relation to the mode of allotment earlier described: two-thirds of taxable resources, that is, of all declared Roman property, in the area of the Visigothic kingdom was allocated to the Gothic troops, whereas one-third went to the king. Out of the larger slice, each entitled Visigoth was awarded an allotment composed of the *professio* (full or partial) of one or more Roman landowner-taxpayer(s) designated as his host(s).[9] It follows from such a scheme that Goths would be interested parties in all clarifications of Roman property boundaries except those affecting the one-third of assessed properties reserved for the king.[10]

[9] Above, Chapter IV.

[10] The procedure of *CE* 276. 3-4 has considerable affinities to the formalities of *traditio* with *corporalis introductio* in the presence of *vicini*, mentioned in *Edictum Theodorici* 53 as taking place whenever real property changed hands. These formalities were originally prescribed by Constantine's famous law on land sales (*Fragmenta Vaticana* 35, where in parag. 4 *proprietas* is used just as in *LVisig* 10. 3. 5) and are rather vividly illustrated in *PItal* 10-11 (489). In line with this parallel, one might conceivably argue that *CE* 276 prescribed what was to be done whenever Roman hosts handed over full ownership of a *locus* of theirs to Gothic guests. Such conveyances would hardly be surprising, but, if that is what *CE* 276. 3-4 are about, the law leaves us in the dark about the circumstances occasioning the transfer. We could not infer from these lines that a formal conveyance of full ownership was the procedure par excellence of barbarian land

In addition to the main rule, two details of *CE* 276. 3 deserve notice. A legal ritual is involved in the entrance of the Goths into the *locus hospitum*; it is not as though they made their homes on the property and were familiar with the grounds. This is to be expected in a situation where the *sors* was chiefly a revenue paid to the (absentee) Goth, rather than being an estate on which he resided. Then there is the word *locus* itself: it precisely anticipates the indefinite term used in *LBurg* 54 to designate where *hospitalitas* was assigned.

---

assignment: if it had been, the forms and terminology of hospitality would be difficult to explain.

APPENDIX C

1. Houses

Ulpian's model form for census declarations makes no reference to buildings or orchards (*Dig.* 50. 15. 4), which are likewise omitted from the surviving Asian census inscriptions;[1] a prefectoral ordinance of 512 (Justinian *Novel.* 168) specifies, "in censum seu descriptionem praedia solum referantur, non autem domus vel aliae res." Although another model for a *plena describtio* includes the entry "quis aedificiis ac possessionibus ornatus," this is with a view, not to a census declaration, but to incorporation with the imperial *res privata* (*CTh* 9. 42. 7 [369]; cf. *CTh* 10. 9. 2 [395]).

I can find nothing to suggest that the state set a value upon country houses. Imperial indulgence toward house property in cities is nicely illustrated in *CTh* 13. 6. 7. 1 (375), which insists that, in the contribution of houses to the navicularian *munus*, no account is to be taken of improvements and observes that houses have value for the adornment (*cultus*) of cities rather than for their revenues (*fructus*).[2] The levy of one year's rent imposed in 405 on all city buildings—from warehouses and stores to dwell-

---

[1] These inscriptions are generally ascribed to the fourth century; they are analyzed by Déléage, *Capitation*, pp. 164-194; Cérati, *Caract. annon.*, pp. 385-412; and Goffart, *Caput*, pp. 113-121.

[2] This *munus* is not precisely assimilable to a tax. A naviculary was tax exempt on the grounds that his entire property was obligated to the *munus*—an essential public service; when he alienated part of his property, the obligation devolved *pro rata* upon the acquirer even if he was not a naviculary. The law of 375 in question here limited the liability incurred by those who bought city dwellings from naviculaties.

ings—was altogether exceptional (*CTh* 11. 20. 3). See also *CTh* 15. 1. 41 (401). The lesson suggested by the privileges listed in Chapter II n. 12 is that the quartering of soldiers and officials was the unique "tax" regularly imposed upon city houses. This resource was exploited in earnest during the fifth century in the East (note particularly *NTheod II* 25 [444], in which quartering gives rise through exemption to a money revenue). Justinian *Novel.* 43 and 59 (536-537) attest that taxes and services were levied upon shops in Constantinople from at least the time of Anastasius, but there is no apparent connection between these dues and the general fourth-century scheme of taxation.

2. Woods and Wastes

The distinction made by *LBurg* between woods and wastes (*silvae, campi*) and "arable" (*terrae*) seems consistent with the general direction of assessment in the later empire. Although *prata, pascua,* and *silvae* (*caeduae*) were subject to census declaration according to Ulpian (*Dig.* 50. 15. 4),[3] they do not appear in so many words in the Asian census inscriptions. In the surviving late Roman scale for conversion into assessment units (*iuga*), a special procedure, eschewing tax units, is laid down for assessing mountain lands sown with wheat and barley and for imposing a low payment in money (to the *res privata*?) on mountain pastures.[4]

Almost all the evidence in the law codes is concerned with so-called "desert" land, rather than with the descriptive categories of *LBurg*. The two need not correspond,

[3] The qualification that the *silvae* to be declared are *caeduae*, i.e., under exploitation, strongly suggests that all three items were assumed to contribute actively to the declarant's wealth; they were not "waste."

[4] Syro-Roman Lawbook, *leges saeculares* 121, *FIRA* 2, p. 796; for the assessment of arable according to this schedule, Goffart, *Caput*, pp. 33-34. Gregory of Tours *Virtutes s. Iuliani* 17 affords a startling parallel to the tax on mountain pastures described in the Lawbook.

for the fiscal concept of "desertion" has no precise agrarian meaning (above, Chapter IV n. 18). Nevertheless, *LBurg* 72 uses *deserta* as the antonym for cultivated land. As shown by the taxpayer's right to indulgence for land that unavoidably went out of cultivation (*Dig.* 50. 15. 4. 1; *CTh* 13. 11. 15-17 [417]), the state recognized a distinction between productive and nonproductive land; simultaneously, it insisted that new owners must take bad land with good (for example, *CJ* 11. 62. 3, 59. 5, *CTh* 5. 18. 8, 14. 30, 33, 34, and many others) and that *conlationes* and *munera* were borne by *gleba inutilis* together with *terrulae fertiles* (*CTh* 11. 24. 62 [415]). These rules illustrate the coexistence of divergent viewpoints: on the one hand, that taxes were owed by the total unit of ownership, at rates varying with the productive value of the land (rather roughly graded); on the other hand, that taxes were owed exclusively by the lands effectively producing the obvious commodities—grain, oil, and wine. Although the latter is characteristically a taxpayer's viewpoint, the state's practice of converting *professiones* into uniform assessment units (*iuga, capita, millenae*, and so forth) ought logically to have encouraged everyone concerned to identify the units at which an estate was rated with its productive arable, to the exclusion of its less profitable parts, such as woods and wastes.[5] A similar effect would have resulted from the

[5] Cf. my remarks in *Caput*, pp. 95 (Theodoret's misunderstanding of *iuga*), 108-110. When the tax declaration of a large and complex farm, expressed in the ordinary, and very diverse, measurement units of land survey was sifted through the schedules that converted real measures into abstract units of fiscal assessment, the result was a homogeneous figure of, shall we say, eight and three-quarters *iuga*. (Note that a very large proprietor like Sidonius appears to have been rated at a small total for all his declared assets: something between fifteen and thirty fiscal units, *Caput*, p. 131 n. 26.) Even though, in origin, our abstract 8.75 was the conversion figure for every exploitable resource that the declared farm contained, anyone converting backward from tax units to real assets might easily reach the simplified conclusion that the *iuga*—a small number—referred only to the most obviously productive sector of the total farm.

tendency for tax liability to devolve from persons to land:[6] when a person is the unit of contribution, he is understood to assist the state on the basis of his total fortune, but when "land" is expected to "pay," its contributory potential is narrowly limited by fertility. It seems correct, therefore, to conclude that, by the fifth century, woods and wastes would not normally appear in the registers of *professiones* or be thought to be referred to by the standard units of assessment.

The state, however, never surrendered its interest in these lands. Fourth-century veterans had been promised lands *ex vacantis* (CTh 7. 20. 8 [364]), and they were invited to appropriate "loca absentium squalida et situ dissimulationis horrentia, de solida fructuum indemnitate securi," with the owners being denied any right to collect rent from them (*CTh* 7. 20. 11 [368]). It would have been consistent with such laws as these to complement an award of *terrae* to barbarian troops with regulations specifying the rights of the beneficiaries to lands classified otherwise than as taxpaying arable.

[6] I argue in *Caput* that this devolution took place; for a summary, see pp. 94-98.

APPENDIX D

SIDONIUS ON "HOSPITALITY"

Stevens has rightly observed that references to barbarian quartering are remarkably rare in the works of Sidonius Apollinaris;[1] it is even more surprising that they have little value for a discussion of the subject. Nevertheless, the three relevant passages deserve a few comments, if only as a contribution to the annotation of this important author.

1. *Carmen* 12 (probable date 461, or soon after).[2] Sidonius explains half-humorously why he cannot bring himself to write poetry: his house is full of repulsive seven-foot Burgundians. It seems that they numbered ten—a military "tentful" (*contubernium*)—and that they were not permanent residents.[3] Sidonius is generally supposed to be writing from his house in Lyons, rather than from a country estate. In any case, owing to the numbers involved, the poem implies an instance of ordinary military billeting, not entailing any cession of land or revenue. It is not even clear that the Burgundians were eating Sidonius's food.[4]

2. *Epistolae* 2. 1. 3 (470): "daily [Seronatus] fills the woods with fugitives, the *villae* with *hospites*, the churches with criminals, the prisons with clergymen."[5] The context

[1] C. E. Stevens, *Sidonius Apollinaris and His Age* (Oxford, 1933), p. 74 n. 9.

[2] Dates and other details are based on the annotation of André Loyen, in his edition of Sidonius.

[3] For the number, line 15. On the *contubernium*, Vegetius *Epitoma rei militaris* 2. 13.

[4] Sidonius complains (lines 13-15) of the smells of their cooking, but not that he is supplying their provisions.

[5] For very close parallels to this phraseology, *Epistolae* 5. 7: a very

245

is a venomous character sketch of Seronatus, a high Roman official, perhaps the *vicarius* of Aquitanica. All we know of Seronatus is what Sidonius tells us of him here and in another equally scathing letter.[6] Seronatus's activities called for him to maintain close contact with the Visigothic court, to which he traveled at least twice; we have no reason to believe that these journeys lacked official sanction. The fact that Seronatus was later put to death for treasonable collusion, at the behest of the *concilium Galliarum*, may or may not confirm Sidonius's portrait; it primarily establishes that Seronatus's political enemies, including Sidonius, eventually prevailed. One would give a good deal for the opportunity to hear Seronatus and others like him speak in their own defense.[7]

Stevens is certainly correct in taking the reference to *hospites* as signifying an extension of Gothic allotments, perhaps even outside the established area of Gothic rule. But this need not mean that, as a result of Seronatus's activities, Roman owners of estates "might suddenly find a Visigoth quartered on them."[8] The passage is not a factual enumeration of Seronatus's actions, but a highly rhetorical indictment of his character and administration, which should be interpreted accordingly. One phrase suggests that Seronatus was scrawny, whereas *Epistolae* 5. 13 indi-

---

highflown denunciation of *delatores*, illustrative of the bad taste Sidonius sometimes succumbs to; notably, in Dalton's words, "strings of illustrative instances and persons, sometimes eight or ten where two would have sufficed, till the tail is out of all proportion with the kite" (O. M. Dalton, trans., *The Letters of Sidonius* [Oxford, 1915], vol. 1, p. cxxx).

[6] *Epistolae* 5. 13.

[7] Cf. the contradictory information available about Dardanus: Matthews, *Aristocracy*, pp. 321-324; Stroheker, *Senat. Adel*, pp. 162-163, no. 99; and the case of Agrippinus, discussed by Martine in his edition of the *Vita patrum Iurensium*, pp. 444-445, cf. Courcelle, *Hist. litt.*, p. 173.

[8] Stevens, *Sidonius Apollinaris*, p. 113.

cates that he was grossly fat.[9] Dalton drew attention to the paronomasia in another line, in which Seronatus is charged with treading the laws of Theodosius underfoot while propounding those of (the Visigothic king) Theodoric.[10] As one more in this string of expressively stated misdeeds, the phrase "to fill *villae* with guests" is unlikely to be a literal description of the process of Gothic *hospitalitas*. If, instead

[9] *Epistolae* 2. 1. 2, "ab avaritia ieiunus," as against 5. 13. 2, "sic ira celer, quod piger mole."

[10] Dalton, *Letters of Sidonius*, vol. 1, p. cxxx (in a survey of Sidonius's lapses from taste). On this line, see also above, Chapter IV n. 21. Several important points in legal history have been based on its sole testimony. Franz Beyerle asserted: "Prior to Euric there already was a legal collection of Theodoric II somehow comparable to the Theodosian Code" ("Frühgesch. der westg. Gesetzgebung," p. 8, full reasoning on p. 5); he was followed by Claude, *Westgoten*, p. 39; the same conclusion apparently uninfluenced by Beyerle, Giulio Vismara, "El *Edictum Theodorici*," *Estudios Visigoticos*, vol. 1, Instituto Juridico Español, *Cuadernos* 5 (Rome-Madrid, 1956), pp. 80-81, who went on to ascribe to Theodoric II (or a Roman helper) the paternity of the *Edictum Theodorici*. Alvaro d'Ors, "La territorialidad del derecho de los visigodos," *Estudios Visigoticos*, vol. 1, pp. 110-112, although not fully endorsing Beyerle as regards codification, used Sidonius as evidence for the territorial, rather than personal, character of Theodoric II's legislation. These conclusions proceed from insensitivity to the literary character of Sidonius's phrase—a phrase that should on no account be literally interpreted. There is no doubt that Theodorid (Theodoric I) promulgated the *leges* ascribed to him in *CE* 277, 305, 327; and Theodoric II surely issued similarly binding commands. But Sidonius should not be inferred to say anything more startling than that "Seronatus sets the orders of a barbarian over the laws of the emperors." The pattern of his phrases hammers away at the idea that Seronatus always prefers the lower to the higher: Goths to Romans, prefectoral underlings to the prefects themselves, Theodoric's scattered laws to the majestic Theodosian corpus. Vismara alone paid attention to Sidonius's rhetoric (p. 81), but his reasoning —that Sidonius recognized the equivalently organic character of both sets of laws before implying the "neta superioridad" of the Theodosian —is contradicted by the preceding noun pairs, *Romani-Gothi, praefecti-numerarii*, which Sidonius could hardly have proposed as hierarchic equals.

of striving for effect, Sidonius had written simple administrative prose, he might conceivably have said that Seronatus "awards allotments to Goths."

Sidonius does enlighten us on two points. As late as 470, the task of supplying Visigoths with *sortes* still entailed the active cooperation of the Goths with Roman officials outside Gothic territory. This is an astonishing, and regrettably isolated, fact.[11] More predictable is Sidonius's hostility to allotment: for Seronatus to engage in this activity, even if sanctioned by his superiors, was as wicked as for him to fill the prisons with clergymen. What we cannot tell is whether Sidonius's disapproval was motivated by the conditions of allotment (for example, that it meant dispossessing Romans) or, as I prefer to believe, by the fact that it was taking place at all.

3. *Epistolae* 8. 9. 2 (476). Released from exile, Sidonius was at Bordeaux, seeking audience with King Euric. One of his objectives was to secure something from the inheritance of his mother-in-law, widow of the short-lived emperor Avitus. He wrote to his old friend Lampridius, contrasting the latter's good fortune to his own inability to have his cause heard at Euric's court: "For I have not yet obtained anything from the inheritance of my mother-in-law, not even the usufruct of one third at the cost of one half."[12]

Dalton pointed to the passage as one of the most difficult to explain in the Letters.[13] At present, the main issue among interpreters is not so much what Sidonius precisely means as what category of laws his statement presupposes: is he referring to Gothic allotments (which, on the usual reading of *CE* 277. 1, would leave him a *tertia* of the land bequeathed) or, rather, to altogether different legal rules?

[11] It might well have something to do with tax records.

[12] "Necdum enim quicquam de hereditate socruali vel in usum tertiae sub pretio medietatis obtinui."

[13] Dalton, *Letters of Sidonius*, vol. 2, p. 154 n. 2, on p. 247.

Schmidt and many predecessors favored the former idea, Mommsen, the latter.[14]

Stevens strongly endorsed Schmidt's interpretation, adding that Sidonius's comparison between Meliboeus (a figure from Virgil's first Eclogue) and himself in the accompanying poem "supports the view that there was a Visigoth billeted on his land."[15] Although attractive, this suggestion appears to be mistaken. Sidonius evoked Eclogue I because the basic conditions of Meliboeus and Tityrus paralleled those of Lampridius and himself: one was safe at home, the other a dispossessed exile. Sidonius confirms the comparison by saying that Lampridius had recovered his lands (*rura post recepta*).[16] Whether Sidonius's poem has anything to do with his mother-in-law's estate is doubtful; Sidonius had much more than this to expect from Euric; he sought the cessation of his exile with complete reinstatement in his former position and possessions. In this context, it seems farfetched to take Virgil's line about a barbarian occupying the totality of Meliboeus's land and to transpose it to a Visigoth detaining some fraction of the

[14] Schmidt's work, referred to by Stevens, *Sidonius Apollinaris*, p. 163, was unavailable to me; I cannot find a discussion of this incident in Schmidt's *Ostgermanen*. The original connection between the line and Visigothic settlement occurs in Gaupp, *Ansiedlungen*, p. 389. For Mommsen, below, n. 19.

[15] Stevens, *Sidonius Apollinaris*, p. 163 n. 2.

[16] For *rura post recepta, Epistolae* 8. 9. 5, poem line 12. Why Lampridius would have lost his *rura* is never explained. It seems an exaggeration to infer from so little that Lampridius had once been an active opponent of Gothic conquest, as does Schmidt, *Ostgermanen*, pp. 522, 528. Sidonius, after all, needed to establish his parallel with the Eclogue. The factual basis for his statement might possibly be, not that Lampridius's property had once been confiscated, but that he stood in such high favor with Euric as to have received full immunity (cf. the suggestion above Chapter IV n. 38). I am happy to observe that Gaupp, *Ansiedlungen*, pp. 395-396, envisaged something of this kind. For Sidonius's dispossession, *Epistolae* 9. 3. 3-4. The evidence is not absolutely clear, but most authors reasonably assume that Sidonius's exile was accompanied by sequestration of all his property (e.g., Schmidt, *Ostgermanen*, p. 495).

bequest of Sidonius's mother-in-law. Sidonius may have mentioned the inheritance only to emphasize that, if even this small matter eluded him, how much farther was he from obtaining his main petition for total rehabilitation. In short, the Virgilian comparison does not strengthen Schmidt's case.

Loyen's interpretation, also along these lines, is that the Gothic share was one-third and that Sidonius was trying to keep half his two-thirds share at the cost of the other half.[17] This would work rather well if it were not for CE 277, where the Roman share is stated to be one *tertia*, not two.[18]

The thrust, if not the specific terms, of Mommsen's interpretation merits renewed attention.[19] It is too often forgotten that the fraction one-third is anything but an automatic signpost of allotment; it occurs in many other legal

[17] Loyen editorial notes to Sidonius, vol. 3, pp. 199-200 (complementary n. 34). Loyen assumed that the lady's property was "evidently occupied by the Visigoths," and concluded that Sidonius's petition must refer to the terms of this "occupation"; but the deduction is hardly compelling. A Visigothic allotment, if applied to the property, should not normally have had any bearing on its inheritance status; the role of host would simply have descended to the heir, or legatee, along with title to the lands.

[18] My reading of CE 277 does not, of course, admit the notion of a division of estates (above, Chapter IV), but Loyen's argument is contradicted by the terms of CE 277 regardless of how interpreted.

[19] MGH AA, vol. 8, p. xlvii n. 1 (translated from Mommsen's Latin): "usufruct of one-third of the assets (*bona*) was left to Sidonius on condition that he should make half the inheritance his by giving a set (*certum*) price to the declared heirs; [Sidonius] had paid the price, but hitherto he had neither acquired possession of his purchase nor obtained the usufruct given to him." If I understand Mommsen correctly, he suggested that Sidonius was bequeathed the right to buy a life claim to one-third of the revenue of the inheritance by paying the heirs a predetermined (and, one hopes, highly advantageous) price for one-half its total value. The main problem of this interpretation is that, if Sidonius's difficulties were entirely with the heirs, there would have been little reason for him to complain of the matter in a letter concerned basically with his inability to approach Euric.

contexts, notably, in the law of inheritance.[20] Sidonius's reference to a usufruct also points toward inheritance law, rather than to allotments, in which usufruct has no place. We know too little about the lawsuit itself: who were the other claimants to the lady's estate?[21] Was Sidonius's suit with them or against Euric? Lampridius, himself in Bordeaux, was familiar with the circumstances; we are not. The usufruct suggests an accommodation between Sidonius and the nearer heirs. A close analogue to the technicalities he mentions occurs in *CE* 321, where the cession of a *medietas* and the retention of a *usufructuaria tertia* are devices in a ruling on inheritance.[22] Another, less evocative, analogue occurs in *LBurg* 14.[23] The likelihood is that Sidonius is referring to a transaction of this type and does not have a Gothic *sors* in mind.

[20] Above, Chapter VI n. 5.

[21] Sidonius, a son-in-law, was not a direct descendant. It would hardly be surprising if the bequest to him had been contested by closer kin. Perhaps he was acting on behalf of his children.

[22] *CE* 321: (3) on marriage, children at once obtain their due share of their late mother's property with the father retaining a *usufructuaria tertia*; (4) unmarried children obtain half their due *portio* of maternal property on turning twenty-one, with the father retaining the other *medietas* during his lifetime. *CE* 322 is about a widow's *usufructuaria portio* of her husband's estate.

[23] *LBurg* 14 (*de successionibus*): (6) a woman vowed to God who has only one brother "non medietatem [of the paternal estate], sed tertiam consequatur" and will, of course, enjoy only usufructuary tenure.

APPENDIX E

VEGETIUS, MILITARY RATIONS, AND A POSSIBLE CONNOTATION OF *fara*

In connection with the question how individual barbarians were chosen to receive an allotment, attention was drawn in Chapter VIII to a passage of Vegetius concerning the issue of rations to the troops. There is no way to establish that Vegetius's *Epitoma rei militaris*, or the ideas it embodies, had any effect on the procedures applied in barbarian settlement. Nevertheless, Vegetius's date—the reign of Valentinian III (425-455)—lends weight to his remarks.[1] They deserve a closer look.

The directly relevant text reads: "In difficult campaigns, the ancients used to distribute rations by heads of soldiers rather than by 'dignities,' on the understanding [however] that, after the emergency, [the rations] would be returned to [the 'dignities']" (3. 3). Vegetius's reference to "the ancients" should not mislead us into thinking that an antiquarian aside is being made; the sentence as a whole is a proposal for current application, which the invocation of revered antiquity is meant to enhance.

The word *dignitates* needs interpretation, for neither

[1] W. Goffart, "The Date and Purpose of Vegetius' *De re militari*," *Traditio* 33 (1977): 65-100. In a note "The Date of Vegetius," forthcoming in *Phoenix*, T. D. Barnes attempts to restore the treatise to the reign of Theodosius I. He seems unaware that his main argument has force only if the long accepted *stemma codicum* is overturned.

Although the present appendix also couples *fara* with Roman military matters, it has little in common with Gian Piero Bognetti, "L'influsso delle istituzioni militari romane sulle istituzioni longobardi del secolo VI e la natura della *fara*" (1953), in *L'età longobarda*, vol. 3 (Milan, 1967), pp. 1-46. Bognetti does offer a stimulating reassessment of the Lombard interregnum (pp. 9-12), based on Byzantine evidence.

Vegetius nor anyone else understands it as a precise technical term. Among the variety of ranks that Vegetius mentions, did he have in mind persons like the *praefectus legionis* "holding the dignity of first-class count" (2. 9)? The implication would be that rations were normally issued to the troops through "lofty" dignitaries dispensing large masses of food supplies. Little if anything else in the *Epitoma* suggests that this was the case.

A more promising avenue is opened by a pair of passages concerning a lesser category of *dignitates*. The first occurs in connection with the building of a camp: "But lest any sudden attack should fall upon the workers, all the cavalrymen and the part of the infantry that does not perform fatigues (*quae non operatur*) takes position beyond the ditch in armed array by privilege of dignity" (3. 8). In other words, the army (or legion or unit) appears to have contained a body of soldiers who, by permanent privilege, had a more dignified role in camp building than to do the dirty work. For the list of these soldier-dignitaries, one turns to the chapter of Book II that supplies the "names and ranks" of the *principales milites* "according to the present rolls." The chapter closes with the statement: "These are the *milites principales*, who are provided with privileges. The rest [of the soldiers] are called 'laboring' (*munifices*), because they are forced to perform fatigues (*munera*)" (2. 7). The distinction between *principales* and *munifices* is vividly illustrated by the passage on making camp.

Vegetius is hardly alone as a source about privileged soldiers, whose history reaches deep into the past of the Roman army.[2] The interest of his list for our purposes resides in the little that he says about rations. Most of the ranks listed in 2. 7 are merely named, sometimes with an

---

[2] G. R. Watson, *The Roman Soldier* (London, 1969), pp. 75-92. Nevertheless, the specific situation portrayed by Vegetius need not be very old, particularly as it relates to rations; he is basically a witness to fifth-century conditions.

indication of their functions. Toward the end, however, we reach several ranks without stated functions that are distinguished by the number of rations they are entitled to: *armaturae duplares* and *simplares*; *duplares*, *sesquiplares*; *candidati duplares*, *candidati simplares*. There is an apparent oddity here in the occurrence of *simplares*, recipients of *singulae annonae*: were not all ordinary soldiers issued "single rations" and entitled to be called *simplares*? Vegetius does not say so; on the contrary, his statement about *dignitates* in 3. 3 implies the reverse. Normally, the total ration issue was divided, by established right, among only the *dignitates*, alias *principales milites*, on whom, by implication, the *reliqui milites* or *munifices* depended for their daily bread.[3]

If the ration issue was divided in this fashion, it is easy to understand the desirability of suspending distribution *per dignitates* when a hard *expeditio* was in prospect and of instituting distribution *per capita* of soldiers instead. Such a change would not have been only a matter of morale. The obvious way for a peacetime soldier-dignitary

[3] Cf. the complaints of Zosimus *Historia nova* 2. 33. 4-5, who specifies that the "general and his apparitors" intercepted most of the soldiers' rations.

The rather astonishing possibility that the *dignitates* fed the *munifices* is comparable to the practice, apparently followed in the Carolingian *palatium*, that the "absque ministeriis expediti milites"—a fancy way, one might think, of saying "royal vassals without benefices"—should be nourished and otherwise maintained at court, not by the king, in whose exclusive service they were even if he employed them only intermittently, but by the great officers (*capitanei ministeriales*). The latter were also responsible for the upkeep of *pueri vel vassi* of their own, yet their emoluments were deemed sufficiently vast for the king to impose upon them, as a kind of tax on their benefices, the day-to-day maintenance of his armed retainers. See Hincmar of Reims *De ordine palatii* 27-28, MGH *Capitularia*, vol. 2, p. 526. (As regards the imposition on beneficed officials, cf. at a lower level, the quartering of the king's hunting dogs upon the officials of royal estates, to be fed at their expense: *Capitulare de villis* 58, MGH *Capitularia*, vol. 1, p. 88.)

to maximize his profits would have been to encourage shrinkage in the number of *munifices* depending upon him; the files behind the ranks would tend to evaporate, probably in order to earn their living by civilian occupations.[4] The first priority in case of emergency would therefore be to bring the unit back to its established strength, and the best device for doing so was to guarantee everyone a ration, even if it meant temporary loss to the *dignitates*. Egalitarian practices were hardly honored in the abstract, but, in the event of *arduae expeditiones*, they had their uses.[5]

Were ideas like these confined to Roman military circles? The Germanic terms *fara* and *faramannus* are a reason for asking the question.[6] *Fara* is cognate with modern German *Fahrt*, "a journey"; it can refer to a group of people—a detachment, large or small—who go somewhere or engage in something that, in Latin, would be called an *expeditio*. The word shifts in meaning after the destination is reached, on the pattern of "pioneer (or Mayflower) descendant" and "founding families." *Fara* is well attested, alone or in compounds, among the place names of France and Italy.[7]

---

[4] Many suggestive facts on the possibilities for civilian employment can be culled from Ramsay MacMullen, *Soldier and Civilian in the Later Roman Empire*, Harvard Historical Monographs 52 (Cambridge, Mass., 1963). For the shrinkage of units and other pertinent details, Jones, *LRE*, pp. 644-645, 648-649, 662-663.

[5] Cf. Claudian *De bello Gothico* lines 39-41: "iamque [i.e., after a dire emergency] potestates priscus discriminat ordo / iustitiae, quas ante pares effecerat una / nube timor." (The date is 402.) Vegetius's proposal is, in effect, that the *ordo iustitiae* should be suspended when *timor* imposed equality.

[6] Cf. above, Chapter v n. 6. I should repeat that my remarks are based in part on unpublished work on *fara* by my former student, Dr. Alexander Murray, to whom I am very grateful.

[7] Hartmann, *Geschichte*, vol. 2, pt. 1, pp. 52-53; Brunner, *DRG*, vol. 1, pp. 117-118; Marc Bloch, "Mise au point," p. 133; Musset, *Vagues germaniques*, pp. 237-238. The interpretation of *fara* argued in this Appendix would permit us to recognize these localities as being, in effect, "colonies"—places to which *Gefolgschaften* came to estab-

LBurg 54 presents us with the term *faramannus*, meaning not only "man of the journey [to Sapaudia]" but also, in view of its date and context, "descendant of an original receiver of a Burgundian allotment." A story told by Gregory of Tours contains a pun implying that *fara* might denote a king's "expeditionary force"; Marius of Avenches reports that Alboin and all the Lombards attacked Italy *in fara*; and the Edict of Rothari evokes a free man authorized by the Lombard king to relocate wherever he wishes in the kingdom together "with his *fara*."[8] The last of these passages, when combined with a misleading sentence of Paul the Deacon, has occasioned the modern belief that *fara* meant a lineage or extended family group;[9] but the notion that runs uniformly through the four texts is that of a *Gefolgschaft* or "following"—the collectivity that accompanies a leader, king or free man, on an *ardua expeditio*.

There also seems to be something more to the term. After sharing their leader's dangers, the Burgundian *faramanni* had been rewarded with hereditary property. *LBurg* 54 refers to them exclusively from the standpoint of that reward, which, as the law implies, had originally been equal for each one. Should we therefore understand that

---

lish permanent residence. Cf. the line of investigation indicated in Chapter viii n. 6.

[8] *LBurg* 54 is at the beginning of Chapter v; Gregory of Tours *Historiae* 2. 42 (King Ragnachar had a favorite named Farro and used to say, when given something, that it was adequate for him and his Farro [*sibi suoque Farroni*]; the soldiers he sent out to scout Clovis's army reported that it was "adequate *tibi tuoque Farroni*"— meaning either "for you and your expeditionary force to handle," or "to deal with you and your Farro"); Marius, see below, n. 10; *Edictum Rothari* 177, MGH *Leges* (*in folio*), vol. 4, p. 41.

[9] Paul *Historia Langobardorum* 2. 9, uses *fara* so exclusively in the sense of "founding family" as to suggest that any other meaning of the word had been forgotten in late eighth-century Italy. For the family interpretation, Hartmann, *Geschichte*, vol. 2, pt. 1, pp. 43-44; also Brunner and Bloch as above, n. 7; Musset, *Vagues germaniques*, pp. 237-238, observed that the familial sense of *fara* is no longer unchallenged.

some notion of equal treatment was embedded in the term *fara* itself? Marius's report occasions the question. He says: "Alboin, king of the Lombards, together with his whole army left and set ablaze Pannonia, their homeland. He fell upon Italy *in fara* with the women and all his people."[10] Marius uses only two Germanic words in the whole of his chronicle.[11] It is hard to believe that, in this instance, he intended to belabor the obvious by telling us that the Lombards were engaged "in a migration." On the other hand, the import of the passage would be genuinely enriched if the sense Marius meant to convey was that, for the Italian expedition and no earlier, Alboin's entire people turned into a "following" entitled to the equal treatment of such a body once the destination was reached.

Vegetius informs us of an egalitarian measure that Roman military authorities believed to be necessary and proper when "arduous expeditions" were in prospect: contrary to normal conditions, rations were issued per head of soldiers. In similar circumstances, barbarian leaders may have resorted to a similar expedient—a suspension of established privileges in order to maximize fighting forces for a difficult campaign. When the goal was attained, the unusually egalitarian order applied as well to the distribution of rewards.[12] *Fara* as we meet it in Marius and in the

[10] *Chron.* a. 569 (MGH *AA*, vol. 11, p. 238): "Hoc anno Alboenus rex Langobardorum cum omni exercitu relinquens atque incendens Pannoniam suam patriam cum mulieribus vel omni populo suo in fara Italiam occupavit. . . ."

[11] The second one occurs in the closing entry, a. 581 (p. 239), "in *marca* Childiberti regis . . . confugit." Gabriel Monod observed, with some justification, that "one would think, on reading [Marius], that the Empire had experienced no setback and that Gaul was still subject to its power" (*Études critiques sur les sources de l'histoire mérovingienne*, BEHE 2 [Paris, 1872], p. 155). Yet Marius's Romanity did not hinder him from using a pair of Germanic words as though they were ordinary Latin.

[12] Cf. the legend told by Paul the Deacon *Historia Langobardorum* 1. 13 about slaves being manumitted in order to swell the army. The legend itself seems designed to explain a ritual of manumission "by

compound *faramannus* might just possibly have had that connotation. In a sphere where hypotheses outnumber certainties, one more conjecture can do little harm.

---

arrow," but its basis may have been a distorted memory of how the Lombard army had formerly been afforced by drafted personal dependents. Schmidt's interpretation of the legend, *Ostgermanen*, pp. 576-577, is rather too literal.

INDEX TO MODERN AUTHORS

CITATIONS ARE BY CHAPTER AND NOTE, IN ROMAN AND ARABIC
NUMERALS RESPECTIVELY; APPENDICES BY CAPITAL LETTER AND
NOTE NUMBER.

INDEX

actuarius, see paymaster
Adrianople, battle of, 7, 11, 33
Aëtiùs, patrician, 36, 58, 65,
    106, 111, 151, 176, 212, 213
Africa, modern, 11, 22n; Roman
    and Vandal North, 17, 36,
    44n, 46, 67n, 68n, 201n,
    226n, 231, 232n, 234
ager (field), *cum mancipiis,*
    128, 131, 133, 149n, 152, 153,
    156, 157, 161, 185, 187;
    desertus, 112, 113, 147, 217,
    242-43; in Burgundian laws,
    133, 137, 159. *See also terra*
agriculture, 28, 29n, 51, 55, 80,
    81, 82, 104, 110, 113n, 132,
    191, 205, 218, 221, 223, 225
Agrippinus, 246n
Alamanni, 9, 14, 30, 34n, 233n.
    See also Juthungi, *Lex
    Alamannorum*
Alans, 31, 33, 67n; settlements
    of in Gaul, 36, 57, 111-14,
    217
Alaric, king of the Visigoths,
    5n, 6, 7, 66n, 67n, 68, 115n,
    174n
Alboin, king of the Lombards,
    179, 256, 257. *See also*
    Rosamund
aldius, see bondage
allotment (*sors*), 36, 38, 40, 51,
    53-55, 162, 164, 166, 171, 172,
    207, 208, 210, 220, 228, 239,
    244, 248; as package, 140-42,
    149; Burgundian, 103-18 *pas-
    sim,* 127-61 *passim,* 186, 256;
    chronology of, 36, 50n, 60,

100, 105, 108, 109, 123-24,
    130, 150, 152, 159-61, 166n,
    184-85, 187, 196-97, 207, 216;
    in Vandal Africa, 68n;
    Lombard, 176-205 *passim;*
    Ostrogothic, 58-102 *passim,*
    103, 114, 144n, 160, 164n;
    practical implications of, 220-
    26; qualifications for, 88,
    172-73, 218-20; to others than
    barbarians, 81-82, 88, 99,
    101, 225; Visigothic, 96, 97,
    103-26 *passim,* 160, 237, 246,
    250. *See also* division,
    hospitatica, houses, *tertia,*
    woods and waste
alodis, 228n
Anastasius, emperor, 242
annona, see rations, taxation
annonarius, see paymaster
Antiqua, see Visigothic laws
Antony, monk of Lerins, 164n
Aquitaine, 6, 8, 11, 36, 41, 103,
    104, 216
Aquitania II, province, 110
Aquitanica, civil diocese, 246
Arabs (Saracens), 183, 193
Arcadius, emperor, 68; law of
    on billeting (398), 43n, 44,
    49, 124, 145, 162, 163, 176,
    182
archaeology, evidence of, 6n,
    15n, 21, 25, 28, 29, 181n, 206.
    See also toponomy
Arechis, duke of Benevento,
    189, 191, 192, 194, 195, 199,
    202
Arianism, 157n; as religion of

267

Arianism (cont.)
Goths and Burgundians, 226.
See also church
Arles, 115, 215n. See also
Caesarius, praetorian prefect,
of Gaul
armed forces and men, barbarian, 33, 35, 36, 47-48, 53,
171-74, 206, 217, 221, 226-27,
233, 244, 256-57; Burgun-
dian, 117, 138, 146, 150-51,
211-12, 232; Lombard, 179,
185, 198 (exercitalis), 214,
256-57; Odoacer's, 50, 60, 67,
69-70, 73-74, 100, 214;
Ostrogothic, 59, 82-83, 87-88,
93, 102, 222n; Roman recruitment of, 5n, 7, 12, 33-35;
Vandal, 232, 234; Visigothic,
7, 117, 123-25, 211-12, 219n,
221. See also foederati
Armorica (Brittany), 32n
army, Roman, 8, 9, 12, 33, 34,
43n, 48n, 51, 84, 163n, 171n,
186, 214, 226, 252-55. See
also camp, hospitalitas, mess,
muster rolls
Aspar, general, 35n
assessment, tax, 38, 92, 100,
113, 123, 138, 210, 215, 216,
217, 239; assets not declared
for, 142-43, 146-48, 151, 241-
44; declarations of (professio
censualis), 51-55, 60, 73, 79,
80, 82, 88, 90, 95, 103, 116,
121, 124, 150, 151, 154n,
213-14, 218, 221, 223, 226,
241-44; inscriptions of from
Asia Minor, 241, 242; records
of (censuales paginae), 53,
54, 75n, 78, 79, 80, 82, 92n,
95n, 101, 111, 112, 136,
142, 174, 213-14, 217, 218,
223, 228-29, 244; revisions of,
146, 147n; with and without

bondsmen, 120, 136-37, 139,
188. See also polyptych, tax
liability, units
Athalaric, king of the Ostrogoths,
83, 84, 93, 94n
Athanaric, Gothic ruler, 7
Athaulf, king of the Visigoths,
34, 104n, 140n
Attila, king of the Huns, 10,
65, 67n, 214n
Augustus, emperor, 9, 11
Aurelian, emperor, 34n, 233n
Aurelius Victor, historian, 186
Authari, king of the Lombards,
177, 178, 180, 186
Avignon, 155
Avitus, emperor, 248

Bacaudae, 59
Balkans, 6, 7n, 11, 32, 171n.
See also Illyricum, Macedonia
Baltic sea, 14, 18, 19, 20
barbarian invasions, 3-32 passim,
65, 164n, 205, 230, 231.
See also migration of peoples
barbarian kingdoms, 5, 13, 28,
42, 56-57 (maps), 115, 127,
175, 188, 213, 221n, 228;
called sors, 173-74; expansion
of, 151
barbarian laws, 169n. See also
Burgundian laws, legal evidence, Lex Alamannorum,
Lex Bauuariorum, Lex Salica,
Rothari, Theodoric, Visigothic
laws
barbarian settlement, 35-38, 40-
41, 49-50, 51, 54, 58, 59, 67,
107n, 150, 160, 162, 174, 207,
209, 212, 215, 216, 218, 220,
229, 252, and passim
barbarians, cooperation of with
Romans, 9, 67-69; indigenous
in Roman Empire, 26n; non-
Germanic, 25, 26n, 30; num-

centenarius (hundredman), 82,
219n. *See also millenarius,
decanus*
centuria, see unit
Charlemagne, 191
chiliarch, *see millenarius*
Chilperic, king of the Franks,
137n. *See also* Hilperic
church, clergymen, Christian,
31, 92, 120, 167, 189, 213,
222, 227, 245, 248. *See also*
Arianism, Butila, hospitality,
Christian, monasticism
Cimbri and Teutones, 12, 27, 28
civil servants, *see* bureaucracy
civilitas, 87, 173n, 220
Claudian, poet, 16
Claudius Gothicus, emperor, 233
Cleph, king of the Lombards,
177, 178, 179, 182, 184
Clermont, 125
Clovis, king of the Franks, 33n,
155, 156n, 256n
Code of Euric, *see* Visigothic
laws
Codex Iustinianus, 141, 242
Codex revisus, see Visigothic
laws
Codex Theodosianus, 49, 110,
162, 210, 242, 247; title *de
metatis* of, 41, 163, 167, 170,
197
coemptio, 46n, 198
Coliseum, 76
colonica (tenancy), 133, 134n,
152, 159. *See also* bondage,
rent, tenant
colonus, see bondage
commutation, of payment for
land, 161, 203-204, 217, 228-
29; of rations for allotment,
51, 160; of tax-in-kind to
money, 51, 79n
conductor (principal lessee),
135n, 205n

conduma, see mess
confiscation, *see* expropriation
consors (partner), 106n, 110,
141n, 143n, 174, 220, 235,
236n. *See also hospes*
Constans II, emperor, 183-84
Constantine I, emperor, 10, 11n,
34, 239n
Constantine II, emperor, 12n
Constantinople, 8, 16, 34, 43n,
46n, 242
Constantius, landowner, 93, 99
Constantius, patrician, 58, 104,
151, 176, 212, 213
contubernium (group sharing a
tent), 219, 245
conviva regis, 140
count, Ostrogothic, 92n, 222n
Cunigast, Ostrogothic official, 93
curialis (city councillor), 89,
113n, 164n
Cyprian, bishop of Carthage,
213n
Cyprus, 193

Dacians, 233n
Dalton, O. M., 247, 248
Danegeld, 137n
Danube river, 6, 16, 32n, 63n
Dardanus, 246n
debt, 52, 72n, 89, 90n, 95, 112,
113, 118, 121n, 217, 225, 229;
acknowledgment of (*cautio*),
72n, 90n; political, 153, 158.
See also bondage
decanus (military rank), 219
Delbrück, H., 208
delegatio, 51-52, 89, 218, 220;
by *pittacium*, 89-91
delegator, 61, 89, 90n
delegatoria, 89
demesne, *see* seigneurie
demography, *see* barbarians,
numbers of

270

hospitality, Carolingian official,
48n; Christian, 167; civilian,
43n, 45n, 168-69, 220; Germanic, 43n, 169-70
hospitatica (allotment in Liburia),
189, 195-97, 201, 202, 204
hospitium, 42, 43n, 44n, 47n,
49n, 144n, 168, 169, 173-74
house, housing, allotment of, 50n,
70n, 102, 123, 124, 129, 130n,
131, 138, 140, 142-45, 150,
163, 182, 204, 240, 241-42;
division of, 144, 150
Huns, 4n, 7, 8, 10, 17, 21, 27,
31, 62n, 65, 66n

illatio tertiarum, 60, 70n, 72n,
73-80, 100, 101, 116n, 216n.
See also tertia
Illyricum, 115n, 174n. *See also*
Balkans
inheritance, 68n, 159, 163, 196,
212, 219, 220n, 248, 250-51,
256
inquilinus, see bondage
Italy, 7, 17, 27, 37, 40, 48, 57,
58-102 *passim*, 103, 104, 112,
113, 115, 126, 144, 160, 176-
205 *passim*, 210, 214, 215,
216, 220, 221, 223, 224, 227,
230, 257
iugum, see unit

Jerome, St., Chronicle of, 11n,
232, 233
Jones, A.H.M., 70, 71, 206, 237
Jordanes, historian, 8n, 16, 20-23,
27n, 31n
Justinian, emperor, 34, 48n,
120, 175, 213n. *See also*
Codex Iustinianus
Juthungi, 233n. *See also*
Alamanni

Lampridius, 248, 249, 251

Landnahme, 160, 161, 216, 217,
226
landowners (*possessores*), 36, 39,
41, 82, 120, 125, 143, 145-48,
151, 154, 160, 161, 166, 180,
187, 202, 204, 214n, 220, 226,
228, 229; absentee, 35, 204,
226, 227; African, 67n; as taxpayers, 50, 74, 76, 77, 81, 91,
93, 101, 111, 117, 174, 193,
197, 216; barbarians as, 41,
90n, 102, 216, 221, 224-25,
229; Burgundian, 149, 154,
155n, 156, 160-61; Hispano-
Roman, 66n; in the later Visigothic kingdom, 120n, 122-23;
major, 59, 96-99, 107n, 125,
136, 139-40, 156, 183, 206,
217, 227; medium and small,
93-100, 136, 139-40, 156, 217,
225; Ostrogothic, 90, 91-93,
160n; Visigothic, 96, 206.
See also expropriation, oppression, *nobiles*, "superior" ownership, *tertiator*
lands, Roman public, 53, 66, 91n,
193, 212, 213. *See also res*
privata, royal domain
Langres plateau, 151
legal evidence, limitations of,
37, 210-11, 226
legati (official envoys), 43, 48,
49n
Leo I, emperor, 35n
Leovigild, king of the Visigoths,
105, 121, 174, 235, 238
Lex Alamannorum, 238
Lex Baiuuariorum, 238
Lex Romana Burgundionum, 148
Lex Salica, 140n, 169n, 183
Liberius, patrician, 62, 70-72,
75n, 88, 100, 101
Liburia (Terra di Lavoro), 189-
204
Loire river, 151

273

Romans by barbarians, 94-98,
103, 153, 155, 157, 158n, 165,
178, 179, 184, 192n, 217, 220,
224-25, 228. *See also* expropriation, landowners
optio, see paymaster
Orestes, patrician, 63n, 214n
Orleans, 57
Orosius, historian, 232, 233
Ors, A. d', 237-38
Ostrogoths, 5, 8, 11, 17, 36, 58-
102 *passim*, 133n, 185, 225;
early history, 9-10

Pannonia, 10, 11, 257
Paul the Deacon, historian, 20n,
166, 175-90 *passim*, 195, 204,
256
Paulinus of Pella, poet, 104,
105n, 144
paymaster, military, 48n
(*annonarius, optio*), 90n
(*actuarius*), 160, 171-72, 215
Persia, king of, 65
Philostorgius, historian, 10n, 104
Picenum and Samnium, provinces, 83, 86, 87
pigs, fattening of, 141n, 198
pilgrims, 167, 168n. *See also*
hospitality
pittacium (warrant), 61, 72n,
89-91, 101
Pliny the Elder, 18, 19, 21
Poland, 14, 18
polyptych, 101n, 136n, 199n,
209n, 210n. *See also* assessment
possessio, see property
possessores, see landowners
praetorian prefect, 62, 73, 76n,
215n, 223n, 241; of Africa,
213n; of Gaul, 115, 139n, 212,
247n; of Italy, 47, 81, 88, 89,
214n

prescription (time limit for lawsuits), 118-22, 136
Procopius, historian, 20n, 37,
46n, 60, 61, 79, 84, 109, 214n,
215, 231, 232, 234; credibility of, 62-70, 100
professio censualis, see
assessment
property, private (*possessio*),
53, 54, 60, 61, 72, 82, 90,
114, 116, 119-23, 133n, 134,
149n, 151, 152, 154n, 156,
159, 174, 180, 205, 223-25,
229. *See also* landowners

quartering, *see hospitalitas*

Radagaisus, Gothic leader, 17
Ragnachar, Frankish chieftain,
256n
rations, military (*annona*),
46-52, 55, 83n, 90n, 102, 104,
160, 171, 212, 213n, 218, 219n,
220, 222n, 252-55, 257
Ravenna, 83, 106n, 186
Reccesvinth, king of the Visigoths, 105, 106n, 121n. *See
also* Visigothic laws
Rechiarius, king of the Sueves,
106n
recruit tax, 75n
rent, agrarian, 74n, 75, 95, 116,
117, 194n, 204, 222, 223, 241,
244
Republic, Roman, 41, 64n
res privata, 241, 242. *See also*
lands
responsaticum (tax), 194
Rhine river, 9, 17, 28, 32n, 107n,
232
Roman Empire, as Romania, 34;
earlier history, 10-11; fall of,
32n, 35; mentioned *passim*
Roman government, 9, 10, 35,
36, 49n, 54, 58, 60, 81, 98-99,

Library of Congress Cataloging in Publication Data

Goffart, Walter A
    Barbarians and Romans, A.D. 418-584.

    Includes indexes.
    1.   Rome—History—Germanic invasions, 3d-6th
centuries.   2.   Rome—Foreign population.
3.   Acculturation—Rome.   I.   Title.
DG319.G63   940.1'2   80-7522
ISBN 0-691-05303-0